Sexuality in Literature for Children and Young Adults

Expanding outward from previous scholarship on gender, queerness, and heteronormativity in children's literature, this book offers fresh insights into representations of sex and sexuality in texts for young people. In this collection, new and established scholars examine how fiction and non-fiction writing, picture books, film and television, and graphic novels position young people in relation to ideologies around sexuality, sexual identity, and embodiment. This book questions how such texts communicate a sense of what is possible, impossible, taboo, or encouraged in terms of being sexual and sexual being. Each chapter is motivated by a set of important questions: How are representations of sex and sexuality depicted in texts for young people? How do these representations affect and shape the kinds of sexualities offered as models to young readers? And to what extent is sexual diversity acknowledged and represented across different narrative and aesthetic modes? This work brings together a diverse range of conceptual and theoretical approaches that are framed by the idea of sexual becoming: the manner in which texts for young people invite their readers to assess and potentially adopt ways of thinking and being in terms of sex and sexuality.

Paul Venzo is a senior lecturer in the School of Communication and Creative Arts at Deakin University. Paul has published widely on literature for young people, with a particular focus on representations of identity and sexuality. His writing can be found in publications such as the *Journal of Homosexuality* and the *Journal of LGBT Youth*, including the recent article 'Mums, dads and the kids: representations of rainbow families in children's picture books' (2020).

Kristine Moruzi is a senior lecturer in the School of Communication and Creative Arts at Deakin University. She published *Constructing Girlhood Through the Periodical Press, 1850–1915* in 2012. Her second monograph, *From Colonial to Modern: Transnational Girlhood in Canadian, Australian, and New Zealand Children's Literature (1840–1940)*, with Michelle J Smith and Clare Bradford, was published in 2018.

Children's Literature and Culture
Jack Zipes, *Founding Series Editor*
Kenneth Kidd and Elizabeth Marshall, *Current Series Editors*

Sexuality in Literature for Children and Young Adults

Edited by
Paul Venzo and Kristine Moruzi

Routledge
Taylor & Francis Group

NEW YORK AND LONDON

First published 2021
by Routledge
605 Third Avenue, New York, NY 10158

and by Routledge
2 Park Square, Milton Park, Abingdon, Oxon OX14 4RN

Routledge is an imprint of the Taylor & Francis Group, an informa business

Library of Congress Cataloging-in-Publication Data
A catalog record for this title has been requested

ISBN: 978-0-367-67472-4 (hbk)
ISBN: 978-0-367-67474-8 (pbk)
ISBN: 978-1-003-13143-4 (ebk)

Typeset in Sabon
by Newgen Publishing UK

Contents

Contributors

Robert Bittner (PhD) is a sessional lecturer at Simon Fraser University. He recently completed a Postdoctoral Research Fellowship (funded by the Social Sciences and Humanities Research Council of Canada) at the University of British Columbia, working with LGBTQ literature for teens, as well as transgender and genderqueer teen reading habits, and specifically reactions to trans and queer representation. He has an MA in Children's Literature from UBC and a PhD in Gender, Sexuality, and Women's Studies from Simon Fraser University. Robert is currently the President of the BC and Yukon Book Prizes and sits on a number of committees for the American Library Association.

Debra Dudek is an Associate Professor in the English Program at Edith Cowan University. She has published internationally on visual and verbal texts for young people, including picture books, graphic novels, television, film, and novels. She is particularly interested in how texts for young people engage with social justice issues, and a focus on love and ethics informs her research more generally. Her research has been published in journals such as *Papers, Jeunesse, Children's Literature in Education, Ariel, Canadian Review of Comparative Literature,* and *Overland;* in books including *Keywords for Children's Literature* (NYU Press, 2011), *Seriality and Young People's Texts* (Palgrave, 2014), and *Affect, Emotion, and Children's Literature: Representation and Socialisation in Texts for Children and Young Adults* (Routledge, 2017); and in her single-authored monograph *The Beloved Does Not Bite: Moral Vampires and the Humans Who Love Them* (Routledge, 2017).

Lara Hedberg is a late-stage doctoral candidate at Deakin University and teaches in Children's Literature and Media and Communication. Her research focuses on queer girls in young adult speculative fiction and the intersection of children's literature and queer theory. She has published a chapter on bullying with Clare Bradford in *Cruel Children in Popular Texts and Cultures* (2018), the article 'Mums, dads and the kids: representations of rainbow families in children's picture books' within the *Journal of LGBT Youth* (2020) and, most recently, the co-authored chapter 'Goldie Vance: Queer Girl Detective' in *The LGBTQ Comics Studies Reader* (forthcoming 2021).

Rebecca Hutton (PhD) is a Teaching and Learning Officer in the Academic Support Office at the University of Melbourne. Her research focuses on children's and young adult texts, with a particular interest in representations of sexuality and gender across genres and forms. Her publications include articles in academic journals such as *Papers: Explorations into Children's Literature*, *Interjuli*, and *The Journal of Popular Culture*, as well as chapters in *The Middle Ages in Popular Culture: Medievalism and Genre* (with Clare Bradford), *The Routledge Companion to Media and Fairy-Tale Cultures* (with Emma Whatman), and *The LGBTQ Comics Studies Reader* (forthcoming, with Lara Hedberg).

Adam Kealley is undertaking his PhD as part of a collaboration between Curtin University, Western Australia and the University of Aberdeen, Scotland. His thesis explores the Australian Gothic and its potential for representing the impact of convictism on shaping homophobia in Australia, and its haunting effects on the contemporary queer young adult subject. His research interests span the Australian Gothic and queer young adult literature and was awarded the 2016 Children's Literature in Education Emerging Scholar Award.

Elizabeth Little is a PhD student at Deakin University and a secondary school teacher in northern Melbourne. She is passionate about literature, education, sexuality and gender, and the girls who read Young Adult literature. In 2018 she completed a Master of Arts in Writing and Literature, completing a research project on *A Court of Thorns and Roses* (Maas 2015) and *The Bone Season* (Shannon 2013). She plans to continue interrogating the presentation of female protagonists in YA fantasy.

Auba Llompart Pons has a PhD in English Philology (Universitat Autònoma de Barcelona, 2014) and she specialises in English Literature. Her main research interests include Children's Literature, Fairy Tale Studies, Fantasy, Gothic Studies, and Gender Studies. She currently teaches English language and culture at the Translation, Interpreting and Applied Languages Department at Universitat de Vic-Universitat Central de Catalunya.

Elizabeth Marshall is an Associate Professor in the Faculty of Education at Simon Fraser University. She is the co-editor of *Rethinking Popular Culture and Media* (2011; 2016), the author of *Graphic Girlhoods: Visualizing Education and Violence* (Routledge, 2018), and the co-author of *Witnessing Girlhood: Toward an Intersectional Tradition of Life Writing* (Fordham, 2019).

Amber Moore is a SSHRC-funded PhD candidate and Killam Laureate at the University of British Columbia studying language and literacy education with the Faculty of Education. Her previous experience as a high school English teacher informs her research interests, which include adolescent literacy, feminist pedagogies, teacher education, and trauma literature, particularly young adult sexual assault narratives. Her scholarship can be found in *English Education, English Journal, Journal of Adolescent & Adult Literacy, Jeunesse,* and *Qualitative Inquiry,* among others. She also enjoys writing poetry and creative nonfiction.

Kristine Moruzi is a senior lecturer in the School of Communication and Creative Arts at Deakin University. She published *Constructing Girlhood through the Periodical Press, 1850–1915* in 2012. Her second monograph, *From Colonial to Modern: Transnational Girlhood in Canadian, Australian, and New Zealand Children's Literature (1840–1940)*, with Michelle J Smith and Clare Bradford, was published in 2018 by the University of Toronto Press. She has also co-edited *Affect, Emotion, and Children's Literature: Representation and Socialisation in Texts for Children and Young Adults* (Routledge, 2017), *Girls' School Stories, 1749–1929* (Routledge, 2014), and *Colonial Girlhood in Literature, Culture and History, 1840–1950* (Springer, 2014).

Troy Potter is a lecturer in the Melbourne Graduate School of Education at the University of Melbourne. His research interests include the use of genre in adolescent literature to construct, engage with, and respond to contemporary concerns, particularly those relating to gender, sexuality, and disability. He is the author of *Books for Boys: Manipulating Genre in Contemporary Australian Young Adult Fiction* (WVT Trier, 2018).

Paul Venzo is a senior lecturer in the School of Communication and Creative Arts at Deakin University. Paul has published widely on literature for young people, with a particular focus on representations of identity and sexuality. His writing can be found in publications such as the *Journal of Homosexuality* and the *Journal of LGBT Youth*, including the recent article 'Mums, dads and the kids: representations of rainbow families in children's picture books' (2020). Paul has contributed to numerous edited collections on both child and adult literature, including his chapter 'The Season Before Death' in *Death and Garden Narratives in Literature, Art, and Film* (Lexington, 2020). Paul is also the co-author of a marine science education picture book, due for release in 2021.

Cathy Yue Wang is a lecturer in Department of Chinese Language and Literature, School of Humanities, Shanghai Normal University in China. She received her PhD from Macquarie University in Australia. Her doctoral dissertation focuses on the transformation and adaptation of traditional stories in contemporary Chinese fantasy narratives. She is particularly interested in applying feminist and queer perspectives into examinations of East Asian popular culture, transmedia story-telling, as well as subcultures and fandoms. Her recent publications appear in *Children's Literature in Education*, *Asian Studies Review*, and *Series: International Journal of TV Serial Narratives*.

Acknowledgements

We would like to pay tribute to our colleagues from around the world who were steadfast in their commitment to this project, despite the challenges faced by so many in the past year. In particular, we thank Kenneth B Kidd, Lydia Kokkola, Michelle Salyga and the team at Routledge for their generous feedback, support and enthusiasm. We would also like to acknowledge the comradery that has sustained us over the many months working on this edited collection together. It is a testament to the value of collaboration, good humour and standing up for what you believe is important to say.

1 Introduction

Kristine Moruzi and Paul Venzo

Sexuality in children's literature has a lengthy history, beginning with oral folktales designed to warn girls about straying from the path and the dangers of the big bad wolf. Yet much of this history has been characterised by a (Western) cultural reticence to openly discuss sexuality and sexual identities. At the same time, the didacticism of children's literature is often regarded as axiomatic. Literature for young people thus faces a curious paradox in which its focus on instructing its readers clashes with a reluctance to discuss themes like sexuality. Historically, this has meant that – in fiction in particular – sexuality has been depicted through a normative lens, where the ideology of heterosexuality remained implicit and unquestioned. Kenneth B Kidd makes the important point that sexuality in children's texts is 'both specific and diffuse, at once a physical reality and a polyvalent social form' that is, 'to a degree, an adult construction/ projection' (1999, p. v). Representations of sex and sexuality in these texts are caught in the interstices between young people's experiences and desires and how adult authors choose to imagine and present these phenomena.

Much of the scholarship on sexuality in texts for children and young people tends to focus on coming of age as a liminal moment between childhood and adulthood. Lydia Kokkola, for instance, examines adolescent carnal desire for 'the ways in which it is used to symbolize a boundary crossing' (2013, p. 7), one of which is the transition between childhood and adulthood. A broader orientation can enable a consideration of childhood as a period in which the child becomes sexual, in so far as they demonstrate an awareness and acknowledgement of sex and sexuality. Children's sexual becoming is based on their embodiment as young people with subjectivity. Rosi Braidotti explains that 'becoming woman' is to be 'understood as neither a biological nor a sociological category, but rather as a point of overlap between the physical, the symbolic and the material social conditions' (2003, p. 44). Although adults are similarly interested in defining the sexual child based on biological and sociological categories, the tension that results from depictions of sexuality in children's literature emerges from the competing interests that operate at the intersection of physical, symbolic, and material social conditions of childhood. While representations of sexual becoming are readily apparent in much young adult fiction, where a shift manifests from innocence to experience, from immature to mature, it also appears in texts aimed at a much wider variety of children and young adults.

Child and teen readers have long used texts to inform themselves about becoming sexual and diverse modes of sexuality. Examining sexual intimacy in fictional forms enables not only a depiction of the sexual encounter, 'but also…the emotional component of intimacy' (Pattee 2006, p. 34). Fictional texts (whether aimed at adults or young people) offer opportunities for young readers to imagine sexual intimacy and to consider the emotional consequences without having to live them in real life.

Depictions of sexuality in children's literature have remained opaque until recently, aside from heterosexual expectations that girls would eventually grow up, marry, and have children, while boys pursued homosocial adventures before possibly settling down. Yet, as Tison Pugh remarks, 'Children cannot retain their innocence while learning about normative sexuality' (2011, p. 8), which means that child readers are positioned uncomfortably to be sexually innocent while also acknowledging a presumed heterosexual futurity. This leads to the curious paradox identified by Steven Bruhm and Nat Hurley, where 'children are (and should stay) innocent of sexual desires and intentions' while they are also 'officially, tacitly assumed to be heterosexual' (2004, p. ix). Thus, when the narrator in *Peter Pan* explains that 'All children, except one, grow up' (Barrie 1911, p. 1), the implied child reader soon learns that 'growing up' involves traditionally gendered expectations about adulthood and sexuality.

Despite the assumed 'heterosexual matrix' (Mallan 2009, p. 5) that is produced in and reinforced by children's literature, children's texts have been consistently hesitant to include explicit depictions of sexuality and desire. Kimberley Reynolds describes the 'unwritten code of practice' (2007, p. 27) that limits children's texts in terms of language, vocabulary, and subject matter. Neither the physical realities of puberty nor the awakening of adolescent sexual desire are to be included in children's literature.

Teen readers in the nineteenth and twentieth centuries turned to adult literature to find stories about sexuality. Not only did adult literature include more explicit sexual content, but it also offered non-heterosexual examples before any similar texts were being published for queer young people. Writing by Truman Capote, James Baldwin, Christopher Isherwood, and Radclyffe Hall, for example, included homosexual characters and voices. Cart and Jenkins note that in the 1950s 'the appearance and subsequent popularity of adult lesbian pulp paperbacks were a boon to teen readers' (2006, p. 4). Coming-of-age stories, such as James Baldwin's *Go Tell It on the Mountain* (1952) and Rita Mae Brown's *Rubyfruit Jungle* (1973), were another means by which readers might find their own experiences reflected in 'adult' literature.

There is evidence of a consistent trope of intense homosocial bonds in writing that precedes the more obviously queer stories that emerge in the late 1960s and later. Kidd notes that the homosocial 'same-sex friendships and family bonds' that feature in some of the 'classics' of Anglophone literature (such as Tom Hughes' 1857 novel *Tom Brown's School Days*) may, in hindsight, be read as queer (1998, p. 114). Similarly, Eric L Tribunella argues that Edward Stevenson's novel *Left to Themselves*, published in 1891, features a love story between two boys: 'Stevenson identifies his writing for children as "homosexual in essence" and *Left to Themselves* in particular as a depiction of "Uranian adolescence"' (2012, p. 374). While homosexual desire is coded rather than explicit in such stories, and the very idea of a homosexual or gay identity was still in development in the course of the late nineteenth and early twentieth centuries, these historical texts indicate a trajectory of queerness in children's literature that informs more obvious depictions of homosexuality over the past seventy-five years.

Girls' literature over the past two centuries can likewise be read queerly. Michelle Ann Abate discusses the cultural history of tomboyism in children's texts like Susan Coolidge's *What Katy Did* (1872) and Louisa May Alcott's *Little Women* (1868), noting that girl figures are often omitted from literary histories of women's gender roles and sexual identities (2008, p. xi). Laura Robinson has argued that LM Montgomery's Anne of Green Gables books contain depictions of lesbian desire (2004). Like the boys' fiction of the nineteenth and early twentieth centuries, girls' fiction also includes numerous examples of homosocial bonding, especially in the girls' school stories that flourish from the 1890s. This 'world of girls' (Moruzi and Smith 2014, p. xvi) offered opportunities for freedom and transgression. To be clear, though, these representations of girlhood were remarkably asexual, as the girls maintained their virtue and purity.

Only in the last few decades have writers begun to challenge cultural norms to include sexual content for the young. This is owing, at least in part, to the correlation between the emergence of adolescence as a social category (Cart 2016, p. 4) and the publication of texts that depict desiring adolescents who can be understood as sexual subjects. Nonetheless, these more explicit depictions of sexuality have prompted widespread concern. Judy Blume's *Are You There God? It's Me, Margaret* was published in 1970, where pre-adolescent Margaret has her first period and obsesses over her physical development. Blume's *Forever* (1976) went even farther, depicting teen girl Katherine having intercourse with Michael. These texts were followed by a number of novels in which the teen protagonists are punished for having sexual relations by unplanned pregnancies and sexually transmitted diseases. This is because, as Roberta Trites explains, the preoccupation with sexuality in adolescent literature as 'an ideological tool used to curb teenagers' libido' (2000, p. 85). The tension between teenage sexual desire and adult didacticism emerges in the uncertainty with which sexuality is addressed in texts for young people.

While depictions of sexuality and sexual identities broke new ground in literature for children and young adults, they proved to be controversial. Both of the Blume books mentioned above were the target of frequent challenges. According to the American Library Association, they were both listed in the top 100 banned and challenged books from 1990 to 1999, with *Forever* also being listed in first decade of the twenty-first century. These attempts to censor the books available to young people reflect adult discomfort with certain topics for young readers, even as they reflect the realities of childhood. Since 2010, the nature of the types of books being challenged has shifted, with the majority of the top ten books being challenged each year for featuring 'LGBTQIA+ content' (ALA 2019, np).

Awards and prizes both laud significant contributions to children's literature and function as a form of gatekeeping and censorship. Studies of prizes and awards in children's literature focus on the way in which they tend, on the whole, to privilege a white, heterosexual, Western, male-centric view of things, with a tendency to sideline other voices, characters and experiences (Crisp et al. 2018, Kidd 2007, Kidd and Thomas 2017). Non-normative sexual identities, in particular, have been excluded. Thomas Crisp, Roberta Price Gardner, and Matheus Almeida observe that although

> award-winning nonfiction books provide an array of depictions of both 'ordinary' people and 'extraordinary' individuals living in the contemporary world and across history, the world according to Orbis Pictus Award books includes no one identified as LGBTQ; heterosexuality is the only form of desire made directly visible to the readers of these books.

> (2018, p. 252)

Similarly, Kidd notes that 'never has a book with lesbian/gay/bisexual content received Newbery recognition (not even Honor status), in spite of or perhaps thanks to the ALA's creation of the Stonewall Book Awards[1] in 1971' (Kidd 2007, p. 183).

The Lambda literary awards[2] for child and young adult literature are a response to the lack of recognition of sexual diversity in award-winning writing for young people, in so far as they 'provide images and representation of LGBT people' (Crisp 2011, p. 95). At the same time, these awards have been the catalyst for debate about whether or not they should conform to an 'own voices' approach that excludes authors who do not self-identify as queer but who nevertheless showcase LGBTIQA+ characters and storylines in their writing (Crisp 2011). In attempting to provide something of an antidote to the dominant tropes of prizes for children's literature, the Lambda awards bring into sharp relief the identity politics that still surround representations of sexuality in writing for young people.

Scholars have recognised the rich vein of queer readings that are possible when looking across the 'canon' of children's literature (Abate and Kidd 2011, Pugh 2011). However, there is also a recognisable history of queer literature for child and adolescent readers that emerges in the second half of the twentieth century. John Donovan's *I'll Get There. It Better Be Worth The Trip* (1969) is generally acknowledged as the first young adult novel to depict homosexuality (Jenkins 1998, p. 2, Wickens 2011, p. 148). The main protagonist, a teenage boy called Davey, engages in erotic frottage with his schoolmate Altshuler. They wrestle, share a kiss, and fall asleep in each other's arms. This book was published in the same year as the Stonewall riots, a watershed moment in the gay rights movement that ushered in a period of activism and the beginning of what we might now understand as gay communities. While the book did not have the obvious impact on homosexual law reform and community-building that is attributed to Stonewall, it is significant in so far as it heralded a new era in which representations of young queer people would eventually become a regular occurrence in child and adolescent literature.

Cart and Jenkins, in their study of LGBT+ texts for young people between 1969 and 2004, discuss the evolution of writing for and about young queer people in children's literature, with a specific focus on young adult literature (2006). They identify a number of phases in this branch of writing that mirrors – to an extent – the coming of age of rainbow communities and identities. One such phase included the tendency to present homosexuality in pejorative terms, in so far as gay and lesbian protagonists were often subject to poor narrative outcomes. For example, because homosexuality was viewed by many in the 1970s as a social problem, it 'exacerbated the tendency to regard literature with gay content as belonging in the "problem novel" category, which robbed homosexuals of individuality and perpetuated stereotypes' (Cart and Jenkins 2006, p. 30). These stereotypes included loneliness, danger, homosexuality being framed as a result of trauma, homosexuality being treated as a phase, and the suggestion that the future for gay and lesbian people was likely to be miserable. Just as texts of the 1970s and 1980s often presented the negative consequences of intercourse for heterosexual couples, the outcomes for young gay and lesbian people tended to be similarly bleak. This reflected the fact that, despite the gay rights and women's movements, many lesbian and gay people faced discrimination, rejection from their families, public harassment, legal inequality and – by the time of the HIV/AIDS crisis of the 1980s and 1990s – illness and death.

Across a twenty-year period, from the 1980s until the early 2000s, a new trope emerged in gay and lesbian young adult fiction: the coming-out story. Examples include Nancy Garden's *Annie On My Mind* (1982) and *Good Moon Rising* (1996), Stephen Chbovsky's *The Perks of Being a Wallflower* (1999) and later David Levithan's *Boy Meets Boy* (2003) and Brent Hartcher's *Geography Club* (2003). Coming-out stories imply, at least to some degree, that there is something to come out 'as' and 'to'. In the period during which these novels were published, being gay emerged as a culturally understood identity category, connected to communities of people rather than simply a descriptor of an individual's homosexual orientation. For young readers, these stories presented versions of sexual identity beyond the representations of heterosexuality in other forms of young adult literature.

The sexual identities on offer in these stories are not without their limitations, however. In her study of award-winning LGBT+ young adult literature, Laura M Jiménez argues that

> a study of the protagonists in Lambda- and Stonewall-winning YA novels from 2000–2013 reveals three findings: the dominance of White, gay, male characters contradicts the trend toward strong female protagonists in mainstream YA; stories about lesbians are primarily tragic; and there are no bisexual protagonists.
>
> (2015, p. 406)

While there is no recent, comprehensive study of representation of race and/or intersectionality in this branch of children's literature, research into intersectionality in LGBT literature generally supports the idea that representations of non-white and intersectional protagonists are still lacking (Sandy et al. 2017). Where research into sexual diversity is concerned there is still work to be done, particularly where the relationship between gender and sexuality is concerned. Lara Hedberg observes that 'there has been less focused engagement with queer girls specifically' (2020, p. 1), echoing June Cummins' comment that 'even in spaces dedicated to the edgy topic of sexuality and children, lesbians get less of a look' (2015, p. 401).

We have thus far concentrated our discussion on LGBT+ young adult literature, recognising that this kind of writing, pitched at teen readers reaching sexual maturity, is an important staging post for representations of sexuality. However, this is not to say that other text forms and genres do not address children and young people about queer sexualities – far from it. The socialisation of children into discourses around sexuality are not confined to prose offerings, in so far as fairy tales, picture books, television programmes and films may also shape ideas about sexuality, gender, family, bodies and so on. Picture books, in particular, continue to play an integral role in representing sex and sexuality for young people. This branch of children's literature has long been a venue for providing information about puberty, heterosexual sex, and reproduction, and in the 1990s and 2000s sex education picture books for children also began to include information about same-sex attraction and homosexuality.

In the 1980s a distinct sub-genre of picture books emerged that typically featured families with two mums or two dads and their children. This sub-genre began with Susanne Bösche's fictional photo-essay *Jenny*

Lives with Eric and Martin, first published in Danish in 1981 and then in English in 1983. The book depicts a day in the life of Jenny, her father Martin, and his partner Eric. Since that time, representations of queer families have become increasingly prevalent, in both anglophone and non-anglophone texts (Hedberg et al. 2019, Naidoo 2012).

Criticism has been levelled at the degree to which rainbow family picture books often lack diversity and tend to present queer families as 'just like' heteronormative ones (Esposito 2009, Lester 2014, Sapp 2010, Taylor 2012). For example, in *Jenny Lives with Eric and Martin* we see the trio cooking dinner, working the garden and doing laundry, as well as bickering over household chores. Picture books such as *Daddy's Roommate* (Wilhoite 1990), *Heather Has Two Mommies* (Newman 1999) and *Mommy, Mama and Me* (Newman 2009) follow a similar model, in which rainbow families are often depicted doing 'ordinary' things, such as going to school, preparing meals, and going on holiday. However, the adverse reaction to these titles, such as the attempts to ban titles such as *And Tango Makes Three* (Richardson et al. 2005) – the story of two male penguins who raise a chick together – suggests that the alternative to the traditional nuclear family that is embodied by rainbow families draws attention to the political and cultural impact of these picture books. As Esposito argues, despite attempts to normalise rainbow families, ultimately 'it does matter how many mommies or daddies you have' (2009, p. 62).

In addition to representations of rainbow families a small but increasing number of picture books now focus on trans identities, including works such as *10000 Dresses* (Ewert 2008), *My Princess Boy* (Kilodavis 2009), *I Am Jazz!* (Herthel 2014), *Introducing Teddy* (Walton 2016) and *Jack (not Jackie)* (Silverman 2018). The majority of these texts focus on male-to-female protagonists. However, more recently, they have begun to include gender diverse and female-to-male characters as well. While these texts are not concerned with sexuality per se, they fit within the broader context in which queer identities are represented in children's literature and pave the way for trans fiction and non-fiction texts that explore ideas about the relationship between gender and sexuality.

One of the aspirations for this collection was that it would respond to the ways in which sexuality is crafted and embodied in relation to movements in history and culture, capturing, at least to some extent, both established and emerging sexual identities as they are represented in writing for young people. Along these lines, an edited collection such as this could follow a 'checklist' model to try and account for a gamut of specific sexual identities (unkindly referred to as the 'alphabet soup'). However, this would require a very narrow historical and cultural window, and broad agreement on what those sexual identities *mean* in any given time or place. For example, a term such as 'gay' has been used in relation to law reform, HIV/AIDS, the education system, families, gender, queer theory, marriage equality, post-coloniality, the study of sexual geography, linguistics, and so on. What terms such as 'straight', 'gay' and so on mean depends on how, when, where, and by whom they are deployed.

In shifting away from the idea of a checklist of sexuality and sexual identities, the chapters chosen for inclusion in this collection are linked by the central notion of *sexual becoming*: the idea that children's literature does not merely promote or socialise children into specific identities, but that it has much to say about the relationship between sex, sexuality, and young people per se, particularly where that relationship points towards coming of age and the adoption of adult subjectivities. Such an approach allows our contributors to examine how implied child readers are positioned by the politics of sex and sexuality.

Any edited collection reflects the response to a call for papers, which means that there will always be gaps that remain to be filled. Just as we did not receive interest in more contemporary queer identities, nor did we receive contributions on object relations, cyborg, anthropomorphic, or animorphic sexualities. This presents an opportunity for future scholarship that involves the deep, archival work necessary for uncovering those texts for young people that represent these sexualities, identities, and experiences.

It is also notable that the chapters we received were focused primarily – though not exclusively – on anglophone texts, many of which are British or American. This demonstrates the dominant role of anglophone children's literature in the global context, and the pervasive ways books, television programmes, and films for young people produced in English contribute to a dominant view of children, childhood, and coming of age generally. The study of children's literature in languages and cultures beyond the English-speaking world may indeed provide new ways of thinking about the connection between young people and sexuality in culturally specific ways.

Many of the chapters chosen for this collection investigate intersections between gender and sexuality. Notions of boyhood and girlhood, as well as trans and non-binary subjectivities, are explored in the chapters included here. However, our decision to put this collection together stemmed from the realisation that much had already been written about gender, but far less had been said about sexuality. In this sense, those chapters that take up gender as a subject for analysis do so in relation to how it intersects, challenges, and complexifies representations of sexuality.

The collection is organised into three sections. In the first section, 'Shaping Sexual Subjectivities', the chapters focus on how, across different historical contexts and narrative forms, texts for young people shape information about sex and sexuality and model certain sexual behaviours and identities for their implied readers. The narrative forms of young adult fiction, memoir, and picture books are examined for how they articulate and shape sexual subjectivities. Auba Llompart Pons takes us into the fictional world of Philip Pullman's *His Dark Materials* series to investigate how these books shape ideas about preadolescent sexuality – at once concealing and revealing various models of sexual maturity on offer in the texts. Paul Venzo takes up the hitherto under-examined world of sex education picture books to show how these texts, despite promising a frank and open discussion of puberty, sex, and sexuality, tend to promote heteronormative ideas about gender, reproduction, and sexual desire – with only a narrow range of sexualities on offer. Robert Bittner and Troy Potter investigate two more areas that have, until recently, received little scholarly attention. Bittner examines trans memoir and its tendency to minimise discussions of sexuality in lieu of focusing on themes such as gender identity and transition. Bittner notes, however, that certain examples of young adult trans memoir do approach sexuality as part of the experience of being trans, with implications for the more traditional straight/gay binary that we might find in other LGBT+ texts. In his chapter, Troy Potter conducts a close analysis of a number of examples of young adult fiction that feature 'bromantic' relationship between boys and young men. Potter argues that these stories promote homo*sociality* over homosexuality by placing limits on gay identities and experiences.

In the second section on 'Rethinking Sexuality and Girlhood', we turn our attention to the way children's and young adult literature connects girlhood with discourses and ideologies about sex and sexuality. This section reflects recent scholarly activity in girlhood studies, seeking to identify how discourses around sex and sexuality operate in young adult texts to propose certain forms of sexual behaviour and identity for young women. Drawing on examples including television, fantasy and historical fiction, as well as graphic memoirs and fiction, these chapters reflect on the sexual potential of adolescent girls as a contemporary concern. Kristine Moruzi and Elizabeth Little study Sarah J Maas' two series *A Court of Thorns and Roses* (2015–2017) and *The Throne of Glass* (2012–2018). They put forward the argument that these texts paradoxically feature strong female protagonists while also encouraging traditional modes of femininity and sexuality. Power, violence, and sexuality intersect to create models of femininity that fail to interrogate the patriarchal structures that inform female experiences in the world. Meanwhile, Lara Hedberg and Rebecca Hutton take a different view of young female sexuality, suggesting that contemporary fantasy comics present fictive worlds in which queer sexuality is placed firmly in the spotlight, going against the conventions of the genre, which have traditionally sidelined or overlooked sexual diversity in relation to female protagonists. Finally, in this section, Debra Dudek's chapter on the *Chilling Adventures of Sabrina* suggests that Sabrina's witch-becoming is also a sexual-becoming, one that challenges the dominant heteronormative model of female sexuality.

In the final section, 'The Politics of Sexuality and Desire', attention is turned to three distinct but interconnected cultural contexts that frame adolescent sexual identity in relation to the politics of sex and sexuality, demonstrating the interconnectedness between adolescence, stories, and specific socio-political environments. Yue Wang's study of female doubles in Chinese young adult literature and film demonstrates the way that cultural politics shapes 'versions' of gender and sexuality that are effectively workshopped in texts for young people. In this case, Wang's chapter suggests that sexual freedom is ultimately made to conform to the dominant moral codes of the culture in which these texts are produced and consumed. Elizabeth Marshall and Amber Moore shift focus to young adult novels that feature sexual violence and drinking culture, in the age of the global #MeToo movement. They put forward the idea of the 'costliness of compulsory heterosexuality', drawing together a number of examples of young adult fiction in which drinking is used to excuse male violence and blame female victims. The final chapter in this collection addresses the recent political context of marriage equality. Adam Kealley's study of three Australian queer young adult novels suggests that the struggle to achieve marriage equality in several Western nations, including Australia, informs narratives in which young queer people are encouraged to eschew sexual promiscuity and set their sights on a homonormative model of long-term, committed monogamy.

Overall, this collection offers fresh insights into dominant representations of sexuality in writing for young people, as well as investigating a number of new and emerging ways in which such texts approach this topic. The common goal of this collection is to question whether diversity is addressed or elided, whether texts are challenging or reinscribing dominant tropes, and whether or not they are training children to model traditional modes of sexual identity or encouraging them to create new embodiments of sex and sexuality.

Notes

1 The Stonewall Book Awards includes the Mike Morgan and Larry Romans Children's and Young Adult Book Award for English language books related to gay, lesbian, bisexual, and/or transgender experiences. The award for children's literature was first introduced in 2010.
2 The Lamdba Literary Awards are named after the Lambda Rising bookstore of Washington DC, which produced a report on LGBT+ books in 1987 that gave rise to the literary awards that were first presented in 1989. There are now a number of award categories for books available in the United States that focus on LGBT+ children's/middle grade and young adult books.

References

Abate, MA 2008, *Tomboys: A Literary and Cultural History*, Temple University Press, Philadelphia, PN.
Abate, MA and Kidd, KB (eds.) 2011, *Over the Rainbow: Queer Children's and Young Adult Literature*, University of Michigan Press, Ann Arbor.
Alcott, LM 1868, *Little Women*, Roberts Brothers, Boston, MA.

American Library Association 2019 www.ala.org/advocacy/bbooks/frequently challengedbooks/top10.

Baldwin, J 1952, *Go Tell It on the Mountain*, Dell Laurel, New York.

Barrie, JM 1911, *Peter Pan (Peter and Wendy)*, Hodder and Staunton, London.

Blume, J 1970, *Are You There God? It's Me, Margaret*, Bradbury Press, New York.

Blume, J 1976, *Forever*, Gollancz, London.

Bösche, S 1981, *Jenny Lives with Eric and Martin*, Gay Men's Press, London.

Braidotti, R 2003, 'Becoming woman: or sexual difference revisited', *Theory, Culture & Society*, vol. 20, no 3, pp. 43–64.

Brown RM 1973, *Rubyfruit Jungle*, VT Daughters, United States.

Bruhm, S and N Hurley (eds.) 2004, *Curiouser: On the Queerness of Children*, University of Minnesota Press, Minneapolis.

Cart, M 2016 *Young Adult Literature: From Romance to Realism*, Third Edition, American Library Association, Chicago.

Cart, M and Jenkins, C 2006, *The Heart Has Its Reasons: Young Adult Literature with Gay/Lesbian/Queer Content, 1969–2004*, Scarecrow Press, Lanham, MD.

Cart, M and Jenkins, C 2018, *Representing the Rainbow in Young Adult Literature: LGBTQ+ Content Since 1969*, Rowman & Littlefield, Lanham, MD.

Chbovsky, S 1999, *The Perks of Being a Wallflower*, Pocket Books, New York.

Coolidge, S 1872, *What Katy Did*, Roberts Brothers, Boston, MA.

Crisp, T 2011, 'It's not the book, it's not the author, it's the award: the Lambda literary award and the case for strategic essentialism', *Children's Literature in Education*, vol. 42, pp. 91–104.

Crisp, T, Price Gardner, R and Almeida, M 2018, 'The all-heterosexual world of children's nonfiction: a critical content analysis of LGBTQ identities in Orbis Pictus Award Books, 1990–2017', *Children's Literature in Education*, vol. 49, pp. 246–263.

Cummins, J 2015, 'Foreword: from overlooked to looking over: lesbians in children's and young adult literature', *Journal of Lesbian Studies* vol. 19, no. 4, pp. 401–405.

Donovan, J 1969, *I'll Get There. It Better Be Worth The Trip*, Harper & Row, New York.

Esposito, J 2009, 'We're here, we're queer, we're just like heterosexuals', *Educational Foundations,* vol. 23, no.3–4, pp.61–78

Ewert M 2008, *10000 Dresses*, Seven Stories Press, New York.

Garden, N 1982, *Annie On My Mind*, Farrar, Strauss & Giroux, New York.

Garden, N 1996, *Good Moon Rising*, Farrar, Strauss & Giroux, New York.

Hartcher, B 2003, *Geography Club*, Harper Collins, New York.

Hedberg, L 2020, 'Queer girls, queer landscapes in texts for young people' [PhD thesis] Deakin University, Geelong.

Herthel J 2014, *I Am Jazz!*, Dial Books for Young Readers, New York.

Hughes, T 1857, *Tom Brown's School Days*, Macmillan, London.

Jenkins, C 1998 'From queer to gay and back again: young adult novels with gay/lesbian/queer content 1969-1997', Library Quarterly, vol. 68, no. 3, pp. 293–334.

Kidd, KB 1999 'Editor's Introduction', The Lion and the Unicorn, vol. 23, no. 3, pp. v–viii.

Kidd, KB 2007, 'Prizing children's literature: the case of Newbery gold', *Children's Literature*, vol. 35, pp. 166–190.

Kidd, KB and Thomas, JT (eds.) 2017, Prizing Children's Literature: The Cultural Politics of Children's Book Awards, Routledge, New York.

Kilodavis, C 2009, *My Princess Boy*, Aladdin, New York.

Kokkola, L 2013, *Fictions of Adolescent Carnality: Sexy Sinners and Delinquent Deviants*, John Benjamins, Amsterdam.

Lester, JZ 2014, 'Homonormativity in children's literature: an intersectional analysis of queer-themed picture books', *Journal of LGBT Youth*, vol. 11, no. 3, pp. 244–275.

Levithan, D 2003, *Boy Meets Boy*, Alfred A Knopf, New York.

Mallan, K (ed.) 2009, *'Introduction: rethinking gender', Gender Dilemmas in Children's Literature*, Palgrave Macmillan, New York.

Moruzi, K and Smith, MJ 2014, 'A great strange world: reading the girls' school story', *Girls' School Stories, 1749–1929*. Eds. K Moruzi and MJ Smith, Routledge, London, pp. xiii–xxxii.

Naidoo, JC 2012, *Rainbow Family Collections: Selecting and Using Children's Books with Lesbian, Gay, Bisexual, Transgender, and Queer Content*, Libraries Unlimited, Santa Barbara, California.

Newman, L 1999, *Heather Has Two Mommies*, Alsyon Books, Boston, MA.

Newman, L 2009, *Mommy, Momma and Me*, Tricycle Press, Berkeley, CA.

Pattee, A 2006, 'The secret source: sexually explicit young adult literature as an information source', *Young Adult Library Services*, vol. 4, no. 2, pp. 30–38.

Pugh, T 2011, *Innocence, Heterosexuality, and the Queerness of Children's Literature*, Routledge, New York.

Reynolds, K 2007, *Radical Children's Literature: Future Visions and Aesthetic Transformations in Juvenile Fiction*, Palgrave Macmillan, Houndsmills.

Richardson, J, Parnell, P and Cole, H 2005, *And Tango Makes Three* 1st edn, Simon & Schuster Books for Young Readers, New York.

Robinson, L 2004, 'Bosom friends: lesbian desire in L.M. Montgomery's Anne Books', *Canadian Literature,* vol. 180, pp. 12–28.

Sandy, HM, Brendler, BM and Kohn, K 2017, 'Intersectionality in LGBT fiction: a comparison of a traditional library vendor and a nontraditional eBook platform', *Journal of Documentation*, vol. 73, no. 4, pp. 432–450.

Sapp, J 2010, 'A review of gay and lesbian themed early childhood children's literature', *Australasian Journal of Early Childhood*, vol. 35, no. 1, pp. 32–41.

Silverman 2018, *Jack (not Jackie)*, Little Bee Books, New York.

Stevenson, E 1891, *Left to Themselves*, Hunt and Eaton, New York.

Taylor, N 2012, 'U.S. children's picture books and the homonormative subject', *Journal of LGBT Youth*, vol. 9, no. 2, pp. 136–152.

Tribunella, Eric L 2012, 'Between boys: Edward Stevenson's *Left to Themselves* (1891) and the birth of gay children's literature', *Children's Literature Association Quarterly*, vol. 37, no. 4, pp. 374–388.

Trites, R 2000, Disturbing the Universe: Power and Repression in Young Adult Literature, University of Iowa Press, Iowa.

Walton, J 2016, *Introducing Teddy*, Bloomsbury, London.

Wickens, CM 2011, 'Codes, silences, and homophobia: challenging normative assumptions about gender and sexuality in contemporary LGBTQ young adult literature', *Children's Literature in Education*, vol. 42, pp. 148–164.

Wilhoite, M 1990, *Daddy's Roommate*, Alyson Books, Boston, MA.

Shaping Sexual Subjectivities

2   'Just a Little Cut'

Censorship and Preadolescent Sexuality in Philip Pullman's *His Dark Materials*

Auba Llompart Pons

Children's literature has always been a space where adults have exercised their power over young people through fictional representations of child characters that set up normative models of what children should be like, portraying different ways in which they can become socially acceptable adults. As Jacqueline Rose reminds us in her seminal study *The Case of Peter Pan or the Impossibility of Children's Fiction*, 'If children's fiction builds an image of the child inside the book, it does so in order to secure the child who is outside the book, the one who does not come so easily within its grasp' (1994, p. 2). Along the same lines, Kristine Moruzi affirms that 'Adult writers for children, then, are part of a project to construct images of children that reinforce adult expectations of appropriate child behaviour' (2005, p. 64). This, of course, includes exercising control over the child's sexuality as well, a topic that is often repressed, censored, and tackled metaphorically or vaguely in literature for the young.

This chapter explores how British author Philip Pullman criticises and challenges adult conservative attitudes toward children's sexuality in his fantasy trilogy *His Dark Materials* (1995–2000), composed of the novels *Northern Lights* (1995),[1] *The Subtle Knife* (1997) and *The Amber Spyglass* (2000).[2] Pullman's works—and *His Dark Materials* in particular—have attracted plenty of scholarly attention and have been examined from multiple academic perspectives.[3] Critics of children's literature have identified a rich variety of themes in Pullman's novels, and his subversive treatment of preadolescent sexuality has not gone unnoticed. For example, Moruzi states that 'Evoking the Bible and Milton's *Paradise Lost*, Pullman reworks the fall of humanity into an ascent and suggests that ascent into adulthood through sexual experience is the desired goal for children' (2005, p. 55).[4] This subversive take on children's sexual desire is uncommon in books that are widely read by preadolescents and, as such, will be the focus of this chapter.

In order to analyse Pullman's treatment of preadolescent sexuality in *His Dark Materials*, I will concentrate on two major plot elements in the trilogy: first, the fictional concept of 'intercision', which is the metaphorical castration that some kidnapped children are subjected to by adults in *Northern Lights* (Book I); and second, the representation of child protagonists Lyra Belacqua and Will Parry's sexual awakening in *The Amber Spyglass* (Book III). I contend that parallels can be drawn between how children in Pullman's novels are prevented from discovering sexuality by means of intercision, and how in real life this knowledge is often hidden from child readers through the censorship that is imposed on the cultural products that are aimed at them, an issue that Pullman has been very critical of. Will and Lyra's sexual awakening will therefore be read as a reaction against the absence of sexuality in children's fiction, even though Pullman himself is sometimes unable to tackle this subject without resorting to metaphors and other censorial filters.

'Just a Little Cut'

According to Heather Montgomery, 'Children's sexuality is one of the great concerns of early 21st-century Western societies' (2009, p. 181), and yet, as Warner points out, 'As psychoanalytical understanding of children's sexuality has deepened, so have attempts to contain it' (1994, p. 45). In his 1905 essay on 'infantile sexuality', Sigmund Freud formulated the idea 'that germs of sexual impulses are already present in the new-born child and that these continue to develop for a time, but are then overtaken by a progressive process of suppression' (1991, p. 92). Today, this idea is still met with resistance, as Montgomery discusses:

> There is also still unease about whether children really are sexual beings from such a young age, or, if they do act in ways that adults might interpret as sexual, whether they are aware of this, or under-stand it as such.
>
> (2009, p. 186)

This adult attitude towards young people's sexuality is reflected in the literature that is produced for them.

Although sexuality is taboo in fiction that is targeted at children and preadolescents, authors still find ways of hinting at it in their narratives. As Maria Nikolajeva states, 'censorial filters may be imposed on the narrative' (2002, p. 29), but she adds, 'Many child characters do indeed meet either a friend or an opponent of the opposite sex who initiates a turning point in the protagonist's life' (Nikolajeva 2002, p. 29). We see this in classics like Catherine Storr's *Marianne Dreams* (1958), Philippa Pearce's *Tom's Midnight Garden* (1958) or Katherine Paterson's *Bridge to Terabithia* (1977), and also in more recent novels, such as Clive Barker's *The Thief of Always* (1992), Neil Gaiman's *The Graveyard Book* (2008) and, of course, Philip Pullman's *His Dark Materials*, just to mention a few. In all these works of children's literature—with the exception of Pullman's trilogy—interaction between girls and boys introduces the possibility that an eventual heterosexual romance might develop, but this is never brought to fruition. Another clear example of this absence of sexuality in novels that appeal to a preadolescent public can be found in JK Rowling's *Harry Potter* series (1997–2007). In the last book, Harry is seventeen, and yet he remains highly inexperienced about sexuality for a person of his age. As Perry Nodelman argues, children's literature is marked by

> its construction of childhood as asexual. In children's literature gender is at least theoretically divorced from sexuality, and boys must be boyish and girls must be girlish for reasons that have nothing to do with the underlying reasons that there are gender categories at all. The focus on gender implies a hidden awareness of children as at least potentially sexual beings and suggests the possibility that sexuality is at least part of the sublimated, hidden adult content of children's literature.
>
> (2008, p. 176)

When it comes to this relation between gender and sexuality, Pullman's trilogy differs from the other works mentioned. Although censorial filters are not completely elided, *His Dark Materials* explicitly deals with and celebrates the preadolescent child's sexual awakening and eliminates the negative connotations that are often associated with desire, and *sexual* desire in particular, in children's literature.

In accordance with Pullman's positive view of children's desire, what is demonised in *His Dark Materials* is the adults' attempt to contain it. Pullman denounces the repression of children's sexuality through his fictional concept of 'intercision'. In Lyra's universe, a person's imaginative sight is an external, animal-shaped entity named dæmon,[5] and intercision consists in separating children from their dæmons. The villainous Mrs Coulter describes 'intercision' to Lyra as 'a little cut, and then everything's peaceful. Forever!' (Pullman 2007a, p. 283). Intercision is also presented as an antidote to the ills of Dust, the name that Pullman gives to particles of consciousness, invisible to the human eye, which seem to be the cause of children's transition into adulthood. For Mrs Coulter, Dust is 'not something for children to worry about. ... Dust is something bad, something wrong, something evil and wicked' (Pullman 2007a, p. 281–282). Pullman's villainess uses common adult expressions to reassure children about undergoing intercision, such as 'the doctors do it for the children's own good, my love' and 'some of what's good has to hurt us a little' (Pullman 2007a, p. 282). Spoken by Mrs Coulter, however, these typically comforting words sound false, controlling and sinister, forcing the reader to rethink the language adults use with children and suggesting that what we think is good and soothing might be perceived differently by the child. Furthermore, at this point Lyra has already seen the effects of intercision after witnessing the ghostly existence and tragic death of a severed child, not to mention her own narrow escape from the silver blade, which clearly shows that Mrs Coulter's words are not to be trusted.

The brutality of intercision and its connection with death are further emphasised by describing the instrument to carry it out as 'a kind of guillotine' (Pullman 2007a, p. 272). This comparison already suggests that intercision is like a form of execution, the mutilation of an essential part of one's psyche. What is more, Lyra's uncle, Lord Asriel, openly compares it to castration, explaining to Lyra:

> There was a precedent. Something like it had happened before. Do you know what the word *castration* means? It means removing the sexual organs of a boy so that he never develops the characteristics of a man ... But the Church wouldn't flinch at the idea of a little *cut*, you see.
>
> (Pullman 2007a, p. 372, original emphasis)

Thus, the concept of intercision links sexual repression and emotional detachment to immaturity and incompleteness, comparing severed children to castrati who 'became fat spoiled half-men' (Pullman, 2007a, p. 372); incomplete people, in other words. It is clear at this point that, apart from symbolising children's imaginative sight, dæmons also symbolise their genitalia, and intercision can therefore be understood as both a physical and a spiritual mutilation that prevents children from becoming 'complete' adults.

The child who will never grow up is a recurrent motif in children's literature, and its representation tends to be ambivalent. Children's literature is torn between teaching and concealing, between letting the child character grow up and preserving some of its childlike qualities. Perpetual innocence in children's books is both desired and feared; it conveys nostalgia, but it also creates anxiety. On the one hand, perpetual innocence as a fantasy appeases adult anxieties about the child's potential, our fears 'that children will grow up to be even more like us than they already are' (Warner 1994 p. 48). Yet, on the other hand, innocence can also be threatening, as 'The child holds up an image of origin, but origins are compounded of good and evil together' (Warner 1994, p. 44). In other words, innocence is associated with purity and truth, but also with primitivism and irrationality.

In children's literature, most child characters reach intellectual and moral maturity, whereas they keep their innocence of other matters, such as sexuality. Thus, there is nostalgia for the qualities that we traditionally associate with children—the 'positive' aspects of innocence—such as imagination, the lack of prejudices, and the fascination of being 'in the making'. However, most novels eventually express a need to grow up and a recognition that eternal youth goes against the laws of nature and is therefore undesirable. Of course, it would not be possible to discuss this theme without referring to James Matthew Barrie's classic *Peter Pan* (1911). Peter is the embodiment of eternal childhood and, contrary to popular belief, influenced by the 1953 Disney version, he is probably one of the most disturbing—and disturbed—child characters that children's literature in English has ever produced. Peter's aversion to the world of adults leads him to create his own community of children in Neverland, and whenever the boys grow up, Peter 'thins them out' (Barrie 1995, p. 52). Although it is not specified what it is exactly that Peter does to the boys, the expression suggests some kind of mutilation or even murder, very much in line with intercision in Pullman's novels.

In *His Dark Materials*, the connection with *Peter Pan* is apparent in so much as the Church is trying to create a society of eternal children. As Mrs Coulter explains to Lyra:

> You see, your dæmon's a wonderful friend and companion when you're young, but at the age we call puberty, the age you're coming to very soon, darling, dæmons bring all sort of troublesome thoughts and feelings, and that's what lets Dust in.
>
> (Pullman 2007a, p. 283)

The whole idea of intercision consists, therefore, of keeping individuals in a prepubertal stage, unaffected by the worries and fears of adulthood, which is reminiscent of Barrie's Neverland. Significantly, the chapter in which Lyra finds the severed child is entitled 'The Lost Boy' (Pullman 2007a, p. 204), which seems to be an allusion to Peter Pan's 'lost boys', the neglected and abandoned children that Peter takes with him to Neverland (Barrie 1995, p. 31). Pullman's Neverland, however, is an oppressive system that stifles the child's potential to become a sexually and intellectually mature person, not for the child's own good, but for the adult's sake. Whereas many works of children's literature simultaneously celebrate and demonise desire, Pullman's trilogy takes a less ambivalent stance: villainy in *His Dark Materials* is not connected to desire per se but to adults' attempts to repress it in the child and in themselves.

Consequently, Pullman's ultimate preoccupation in *His Dark Materials* is not so much children, but grown-ups. According to Nodelman, 'adult writers wish to be free from and attack the conventions of other adults. It [children's literature] is a rebellion by some adults against other adults under the banner of something here identified as childhood' (2008, p. 182). Pullman's novels reflect anxieties about the way adults try to civilise children rather than about their failure to do so, a concern that has already been expressed by critics of children's culture such as Marina Warner and Jack Zipes. According to Warner:

> Grown ups want them [children] to stay like that for their sakes, not the children's, and they want children to be simple enough to believe in fairies, too, again, for humanity's sake on the whole, to prove something against the evidence.
>
> (Warner 1994, p. 42)

Along the same lines, Zipes claims that 'The more we invest in children, the more we destroy their future' (2001, p. ix). As Zipes further explains:

> We seek to improve our children's lives by getting rid of moral sewers and by constructing purification systems that confine them. We do not realize how much our purification systems actually produce the waste and turpitude that we complain about. ... We desperately want to save our children from the future that we have planned for them.
>
> (2001, p. xii)

Pullman's idea that children need true stories rather than protection from the ugly aspects of life also seems to respond to the same discontent that Zipes expresses. Thus, intercision may be read as a fictional representation of these 'purification systems' that Zipes criticises and to which children's books, films and other cultural products are contributors. Presented as an antidote to the ills of a fallen existence, Pullman uses the concept of intercision to represent how the attempt to do away with the preoccupations that come with sexual awakening eventually creates ghostly, zombie-like creatures who can only live a half-life. As a reaction to this censorship of sexuality in children's literature, what differentiates Lyra and Will's journey from that of other child protagonists is the fact that sexuality is also a part of it, and desire is neither sublimated nor demonised. Thus, Pullman's child heroes are allowed to mature, not only intellectually and morally, but also sexually.

Desiring Knowledge and Knowing Desire

Childhood in Pullman's trilogy is represented as a journey towards experience, maturity and a stable identity, and this is represented by the fantasy metaphor of the dæmon, which shapeshifts during childhood and acquires a fixed shape when the child becomes an adult. The possibility that some people may never achieve a stable identity and that their dæmon may never stop changing is not considered by Pullman. As I have already argued, however, child protagonists' journeys towards maturity do not typically include sexuality: child characters grow up, but only in certain aspects. What is interesting about the young heroes' journey in Pullman's novels is the fact that sexual desire is not excluded from it. As Tison Pugh affirms:

> Although children's literature often focuses thematically on a desire for stasis, on a child's innocent desire to remain a child and thereby to escape sexuality and adulthood, *His Dark Materials* emphasizes the necessity for sexuality to shatter reigning ideological paradigms.
>
> (2011, p. 62)

Accordingly, preadolescent sexual desire is dealt with naturally and openly. In fact, the reader can find hints of Lyra's latent sexuality early in the trilogy before her sexual awakening and her onset of puberty occur. At the beginning of the story, Lyra is a prepubescent girl, but Pullman provides clues that suggest that she is already a sexual being, even though she is not yet fully conscious of it: 'She had seen enough of society now to understand when men and women were flirting, and she watched the process with fascination' (Pullman 2007a, p. 89). This excerpt challenges common popular assumptions that sexuality is either beyond the child's understanding or unlikely to interest or trouble children. On the contrary, Lyra wants to know everything about those issues that adults reserve for themselves, and this includes sexuality. Another example of Lyra's perception of sexuality is her awkwardness when her friend Roger is taking a bath and she decides to sit and wait outside: 'They had swum naked together often enough, ... but this was different' (Pullman 2007a, p. 363). Although Lyra is not fully aware of what this means, it implies that she perceives their bodies as sexual. This passage, reminiscent of Adam and Eve feeling ashamed of their naked bodies after tasting the fruit of the Tree of Knowledge, also indicates that Lyra will soon become conscious of her sexuality, and this will bring about the second Fall feared by the Church in Lyra's world.[6]

Indeed, the young girl's journey culminates in her sexual awakening in *The Amber Spyglass*, triggered by her adult friend Mary Malone's story about her first romantic encounter with a man.[7] As Mary explains to Lyra and Will:

> [W]e kissed each other for the first time. It was in a garden, ... and I was *aching* – all my body was aching for him, and I could tell he felt the same – and we were both almost too shy to move. Almost. But one of us did and then without any interval between ... we were kissing each other and oh, it was ... paradise.
> (Pullman 2007c, pp. 445–6, original emphasis)

This is the moment when Mary plays the serpent and tempts Will and Lyra to taste the forbidden fruit by telling them a 'true' story. As this passage shows, Pullman deals with sexuality naturally and even poetically, dissociating it from shame or evil and presenting it, not as a curse, but as a turning point in Lyra's and Will's lives. While they listen to Mary's story:

> Lyra felt something strange happen to her body. She felt a stirring at the roots of her hair: she found herself breathing faster. ... The sensation continued, and deepened, and changed, as more parts of her body found themselves affected too.
> (Pullman 2007c, p. 445)

Pullman thus takes a bold step at representing how a female preadolescent character is emotionally and physically aroused. What is more, after listening to the story, Lyra wishes to experience what Mary has described.

Pullman tells us that she felt 'like a fragile vessel brim-full of new knowledge. … *Soon*, she thought, *soon I'll know. I'll know very soon*' (Pullman 2007c, p. 449, original emphasis). Thus, with this passage, in which Mary, Will and Lyra re-enact original sin, Pullman puts forth his own view of the Fall, his idea that tasting forbidden knowledge is not a disgrace, but 'the point where human beings decided to become fully themselves instead of being the pets or creatures of another power' (Pullman cited in Fried nd).

It must be noted, however, that despite Pullman's effort to deal with sexuality as something to be cherished rather than feared, there are certain aspects of this topic that are only vaguely hinted at or represented metaphorically in his novels, probably due to restrictions common to children's literature. For one thing, the trilogy focuses mostly on heterosexuality. Although homosexuality is not completely absent, as Zanichkowsky points out, 'Sexual nature, according to Pullman, is heteronormative', for 'The only gay couple in the story are Balthamos and Baruch, angels who have no flesh' (2017, pp. 188–189). Without a human body, these characters are deprived of carnal pleasures, unlike Will and Lyra. Homosexuality is also hinted at in other parts of the trilogy; for instance, there are characters whose dæmon is the same sex as themselves, which is a rarity in Pullman's universe, where most people's dæmons are the opposite sex of their owners. However, when asked in an interview if this indicated homosexuality, Pullman replied:

> I don't know. There are plenty of things about my worlds I don't know, and that's one of them. It might do! But it might not! Occasionally, no doubt, people do have a demon of the same sex; that might indicate homosexuality, or it might indicate some other sort of gift or quality, such as second sight. I do not know. But I don't have to know everything about what I write.
>
> (2000)

Thus, we cannot know if this reluctance to discuss homosexuality openly in his novels is due to the limitations that children's literature imposes or the author's lack of interest in the subject, or both. However, the fact that there *are* timid references to homosexuality, as in the case of Balthamos and Baruch, suggests that the former might be true: Pullman might have wanted to include homosexuality in his novels, but has had to resort to the metaphor of the angel to make it acceptable in a children's book.

There are still some aspects of life and human nature that can hardly be represented in a children's text without resorting to ambiguous language or metaphors, as Pullman does. Another example is how dæmons in Pullman's trilogy often symbolise people's sexual organs. The fact that 'it was the grossest breach of etiquette imaginable to touch another person's dæmon' (Pullman 2007a, p. 143) suggests a strong link between dæmons and genitals. As Pugh observes: 'This affective and spiritual register of daemons should not eclipse their allegorical symbolism as genitals .... Because Dust also symbolizes Original Sin, the nexus of Dust and daemons casts the latter as the physical incarnation of human sexuality' (2011, p. 76). The metaphor of the dæmon therefore allows Pullman to explore sexual taboos, as we have seen with the connection between intercision and castration. A passage in which two doctors grab Pantalaimon, Lyra's dæmon, also reinforces this reading: 'She [Lyra] *felt* those hands... It wasn't *allowed*... Not *supposed* to touch... *Wrong*...' (Pullman 2007a, p. 275, original emphasis). The emphasis on the words 'allowed', 'supposed' and 'wrong' indicates that Lyra is aware that something forbidden is being done to her and the scene has strong connotations of sexual abuse. Whereas children's literature often depicts several forms of child abuse—neglect, abandonment, bullying and physical violence, among others—sexual abuse is uncommon. In *His Dark Materials*, Pullman also breaks with this taboo, but he does so with caution. On the one hand, he omits the realistic psychological aspect: after this experience, Lyra has no trauma whatsoever and the incident is forgotten altogether. On the other hand, Pullman does not tackle this issue literally and realistically but metaphorically, with dæmons symbolising children's genitals.

Adult sexuality is also dealt with metaphorically. Scenes in which a child witnesses a romantic exchange between its parents are rare in children's fiction, even in books aimed at older children and adolescents. Pullman, however, pushes the limits of children's fiction and includes a passage in which Lyra sees Lord Asriel and Mrs Coulter, who turn out to be her biological parents, 'embracing so passionately' (Pullman 2007a, p. 392). The scene is not only romantic, but also clearly sexual: 'His [Asriel's] hands, still clasping her [Mrs Coulter's] head, tensed suddenly and drew her towards him in a passionate kiss. Lyra thought it seemed more like cruelty than love' (Pullman 2007a, p. 393). As the scene is focalised through Lyra, her sexual inexperience makes her fail to realise that what Lord Asriel is expressing may not be cruelty, but sexual passion. For this reason, when she sees her parents' dæmons, 'the snow leopard tense, crouching with her claws just pressing in the golden monkey's flesh, and the monkey relaxed, blissful', it is described as a 'strange sight' from her point of view (Pullman 2007a, p. 393). Metaphorically, this scene functions as if Lyra had caught her parents having intercourse and could not understand what they were doing. Again, her lack of sexual experience prevents her from understanding why the monkey is relaxed and blissful when it looks as if the leopard was attacking it—its tenseness potentially symbolising an erection.

Although we cannot know for sure whether Pullman's use of language and metaphors to describe and soften sexual scenes can be entirely ascribed to limitations of the genre, the author himself admitted in an interview that this had happened before to his juvenile fiction. Speaking about his novel *The White Mercedes* (1992), later republished as *The*

Butterfly Tattoo, Pullman stated that 'they [publishers] suggested I tone down the sex scene a bit in this country [Britain]. ... If they're called "teenage" books or "children's" books they have to be very much more fussy about it' (Anon 2000, p. 8). Although Pullman claims that 'I don't write for anyone, actually, except myself', he is also conscious that:

> Bookshops want to know who your audience is, and librarians want to know who your audience is, and parents like to know what sort of age it is, because they'll buy books for children without reading them themselves necessarily, and they want to know whether it's 'suitable' for a twelve-year-old or something.
>
> (Anon 2000, p. 8)

Thus, Pullman's experience and awareness of the limitations that the 'children's literature' label imposes might have inevitably influenced his writing, and his 'insistence on truth in storytelling' (Moruzi 2005, p. 56) cannot always be fulfilled.

The passages analysed above suggest that Pullman is forced to resort to fantasy metaphors, which conveniently represent what would otherwise be unacceptable in a children's book. Pullman thus portrays adults' and children's sexuality without crossing the boundaries of acceptability and good taste, typical of middle-class children's literature. As Cavallaro affirms, 'Children's tales that hinge on pitiable victims of merciless systems do not transcend the strictures of the adult world but rather articulate them in symbolic forms that enable some harsh truths to appear in a subtly mediated fashion' (2002, p. 83). In fact, Pullman himself has admitted that 'I have long felt that realism is a higher mode than fantasy; but when I try to write realistically, I move in boots of lead' (Pullman 2002, para. 19). Despite Pullman's preference for realism, *His Dark Materials* is actually an acknowledgement of how helpful fantasy can be to elude censorship and introduce taboo issues into children's fiction.

Although it is not always possible for Pullman to tackle the child's sexual experience openly, the author succeeds not only in breaking the silence that surrounds this topic in children's fiction, but also in presenting sexuality as connected to both desire *and* knowledge. Speaking about Lewis Carroll's *Alice* novels, Nodelman states that 'Alice does not oppose knowledge and desire so much as conflate them: far from undermining or denying the desirability of what one desires, knowledge is what one desires' (2008, p. 38). In this sense, Lyra—who sometimes calls herself 'Alice' when she does not want to be recognised (Pullman 2007a, p. 101)—shares many traits with Carroll's young heroine: in *His Dark Materials*, the object of the child's desire is knowledge as well, but also desire itself. As Will puts it, the two children eventually learn that the 'best part is the body .... Angels wish they had bodies. They told me that angels can't understand why we don't enjoy the world more. It would be sort of ecstasy for them to have our flesh and our senses' (Pullman 2007c,

p. 440). Thus, surprisingly for a work of children's fiction, Pullman's child characters learn that desire does not need to be subdued but cherished.

Nonetheless, Pullman's celebration of desire coexists with a very rational discourse on the importance of acquiring adult knowledge and leaving childhood behind. Like Alice's adventure culminating with the disappearance of Wonderland the moment she realises that a pack of cards cannot hurt her, Lyra's sexual awakening and entrance into adulthood make her lose the ability of reading the alethiometer by intuition.[8] She is told that from this moment onwards she will only be able to learn to read it again through hard work and study. This ending has led some critics to affirm that Pullman celebrates scholasticism and devalues other forms of knowledge (Zanichkowsky 2017, p. 190) and that 'Ultimately, Pullman suggests that the maturity of adulthood is more valuable to society than children and childhood' (Moruzi 2005, p. 56). What differentiates Pullman from other children's fiction authors, though, is that he defends growing up in every aspect and with everything that this entails: if his child characters are mature enough to save the world, they are also mature enough to experience sexuality.

Just Tell Them Stories

It is not a coincidence that the Fall in Pullman's trilogy is brought about by an adult telling a story to two children. Sexual awakening is represented as the result of the power of storytelling, an example of metalanguage that allows for a commentary on the genre of children's literature itself. By the end of *The Amber Spyglass*, the ghost of an old woman asks Mary Malone to

> Tell them [the children] stories. That's what we didn't know. All this time, and we never knew! But they need the truth. That's what nourishes them. You must tell them true stories, and everything will be well, everything. Just tell them stories.
> (Pullman 2007c, pp. 433–434)

The old woman means that children need to know about the so-called dangerous knowledge that adults have concealed from them in the name of protection. Shortly after, Mary tells Will and Lyra the story of her own sexual experience, thus triggering their own sexual awakening and saving Dust, which was quickly disappearing. This passage seems to encapsulate Pullman's ultimate plea that a genre that plays such an important part in educating human beings must not censor nor be censored; child readers need to know the whole truth about their existence and about growing up. This idea also reflects the views of certain children's literature scholars, like Zipes, who has also expressed his 'hope that childhood might be redeemed, not innocent childhood, but a childhood rich in adventure and opportunities for self-exploration and self-determination' (2001, p. x).

Pullman's inclusion of sexual content in a series of books aimed at preadolescents reflects his own view that children's stories should inform rather than conceal. As he has explained:

> High on any list of the storyteller's responsibilities must come a responsibility to the audience. Those of us whose books are read by children are not in danger of forgetting it, actually. Some commentators – not very well-informed ones, but they have loud voices – say that children's books shouldn't deal with matters such as sex and drugs, or violence, or homosexuality, or abortion, or child abuse … Against the keep-them-safe argument, I've heard it said that young readers should be able to find in a children's book anything they might realistically encounter in life. Children do know about these things; they talk about them, they ask questions about them, they meet some of them, sometimes, at home; shouldn't they be able to read about them in stories?
>
> (2002, para. 15)

As I have discussed, Pullman's representation of the child takes into account many aspects of childhood and growing up. Pullman does not exclude sexuality from Will and Lyra's journey, thus challenging one of the great taboos of children's fiction. However, other aspects of sexuality, such as non-heteronormative forms of desire, sexual abuse and adult sexual experience are not portrayed overtly and realistically in the novels. Instead, these topics are present, but mediated by the fantasy mode. Fantasy thus becomes a clever strategy to elude censorship *and* a form of censorship in itself at the same time. The metaphors of intercision, dæmons, angels and Dust, among others, allow Pullman to represent taboo issues in *His Dark Materials* that would otherwise be inappropriate in a children's book. Yet, at the same time, sexuality's taboo status is reinforced by the very notion that only through fantasy can this topic be discussed in children's fiction.

Notes

1 The first book was published in the United States with the title *The Golden Compass*, which also gave name to Chris Weitz's 2007 film adaptation.
2 The trilogy is currently being made into an HBO and BBC TV series (2019–), and Pullman has published two more books, *La Belle Sauvage* (2017) and *The Secret Commonwealth* (2019), which expand on the world and characters from *His Dark Materials* and constitute the first two volumes of his new series, *The Book of Dust*. This chapter focuses exclusively on the three original novels.
3 See, for example, the collection of essays *His Dark Materials Illuminated: Critical Essays on Philip Pullman's Trilogy* (2005), edited by Millicent Lenz and Carole Scott.
4 Pullman himself has confirmed that 'I set out to do Paradise Lost for teenagers in three volumes' (in Sharkey 1998).

5 Pullman has recently contradicted the widespread belief that dæmons are people's souls in a video by David Fickling Books, published on the author's Facebook page (2020). In his own words: 'It's a metaphor, of course, for a part of ourselves. I wouldn't call it "the soul" … It's an aspect of one's self that might be called, I suppose, "imaginative sight". The sight that's aware of things that the everyday person isn't aware of.'

6 The religious content of Pullman's trilogy is outside the scope of this chapter, but the novels contain numerous allusions to the Bible, and the connection between this scene and Adam and Eve is not coincidental. In fact, in *The Subtle Knife*, we learn about a prophecy that foreshadows that Lyra will be the second Eve. Mary Harris Russell (2005) has studied this subject in depth in her article '"Eve, Again! Mother Eve!": Pullman's Eve Variations'.

7 Mary Malone first appears in *The Subtle Knife*. She is a former nun and a physicist from Will's world—our world—who studies Dust at Oxford. With her help, Lyra learns that Dust is actually particles of conscience that are responsible for intelligent forms of life. Finally, in *The Amber Spyglass*, Mary plays the role of 'the serpent' from the Old Testament by telling Will and Lyra a personal story about her sexual awakening.

8 The alethiometer is a magical device resembling a golden compass that shows the truth to those who know how to read it. In *Northern Lights*, Lyra is given the alethiometer by the master of Jordan College, and the magical instrument will aid the young girl throughout her quest.

References

Anon 2000, 'Philip Pullman: storming heaven', interviewer unknown, *Locus*, vol. 45, no. 6, pp. 8–9.

Barrie, JM 1995, *Peter Pan*, Penguin Popular Classics, London.

Cavallaro, D 2002, *The Gothic Vision: Three Centuries of Horror, Terror and Fear*, Continuum, London & New York.

David Fickling Books 2020, 'Philip Pullman talks… Dæmons', Facebook, 7 October, retrieved 9 October 2020, www.facebook.com/watch/?v=341714267140005&external_log_id=a36547ff-fc71-4ae3-ab4b-d62fbe1fc3ca&q=philip%20pullman.

Freud, S 1991, *On Sexuality*, trans. J Strachey, Penguin, London.

Fried, K nd, 'Darkness Visible: an interview with Philip Pullman', Amazon.com, retrieved 22 May 2019, www.amazon.com.

Lenz, M and Scott, C (eds) 2005, *His Dark Materials Illuminated: Critical Essays on Philip Pullman's Trilogy*, Wayne State University Press, Detroit, MI.

Montgomery, H 2009, *An Introduction to Childhood: Anthropological Perspectives on Children's Lives*, Blackwell, West Sussex.

Moruzi, K 2005, 'Missed opportunities: the subordination of children in Pullman's *His Dark Materials*', *Children's Literature in Education*, vol. 36, pp. 55–68.

Nikolajeva, M 2002, *The Rhetoric of Character in Children's Literature*, Scarecrow, Lanham, MD.

Nodelman, P 2008, *The Hidden Adult: Defining Children's Literature*, The Johns Hopkins UP, Baltimore, MD.

Pugh, T 2011, *Innocence, Heterosexuality, and the Queerness of Children's Literature*, Routledge, New York & London.

Pullman, P 2002, 'Voluntary service', *The Guardian,* retrieved 22 May 2019, www.theguardian.com/books/2002/dec/28/society.philippullman.

Pullman, P 2007a, *Northern Lights,* Scholastic, London.

Pullman, P 2007b, *The Subtle Knife*, Scholastic, London.

Pullman, P 2007c, *The Amber Spyglass*, Scholastic, London.

Rose, J 1994, *The Case of Peter Pan or the Impossibility of Children's Fiction*, MacMillan, London.

Russell, MH 2005, '"Eve, Again! Mother Eve!": Pullman's Eve Variations', *His Dark Materials Illuminated: Critical Essays on Philip Pullman's Trilogy*, Eds. M Lenz and C Scott, Wayne State University Press, Detroit, IL, pp. 212–222.

Sharkey, A 1998, 'Heaven, Hell, and the hut at the bottom of the garden', *The Independent*, retrieved 4 April 2014, www.independent.co.uk/arts-entertainment/books-heaven-hell-and-the-hut-at-the-bottom-of-the-garden-1189628.html.

Warner, M 1994, *Managing Monsters: Six Myths of Our Times*, Vintage, London.

Zanichkowsky, E 2017, 'Paradise Contested: Sexuality and Sacrifice in Philip Pullman's *His Dark Materials*', *Gender(ed) Identities: Critical Readings of Gender in Children's and Young Adult Literature*, Eds. T Clasen and H Hassel, Routledge, New York & Abingdon, pp. 183–197.

Zipes, J 2001, *Sticks and Stones: The Troublesome Success of Children's Literature from Slovenly Peter to Harry Potter*, Routledge, New York.

3 That 'Tingly Feeling'

Sex and Sexuality in Children's Nonfiction Picture Books

Paul Venzo

Peter Mayle, author of the bestselling memoir *A Year in Provence* (1990), began his literary career with a sex education picture book for children. *Where Did I Come From? The Facts of Life Without Any Nonsense and With Illustrations* (1973) was the first of several books for children Mayle would write on the topic of sex, puberty, reproduction and adolescence. The title of Mayle's first foray into sex education suggests that, up until the publication of this picture book, the 'facts of life' for children had not been treated in a matter-of-fact way, and that such a text – with illustrations – would take a new approach. In fact, Mayle's picture book would set the tone for a new, frank and child-friendly way of learning about sex, initiating a sub-genre of picture books dealing with sex education for young people.

Nearly fifty years later, there are over a thousand nonfiction print titles in English dealing with themes of sex, reproduction, puberty and sexuality published for juvenile audiences.[1] This number represents a significant area of children's publishing beyond the confines of storytelling through fiction. By focusing on a range of examples from this corpus it is possible to identify the key themes, motifs and narrative and visual strategies that underpin this group of texts. More importantly, however, it is also possible to identify how these nonfiction picture books combine writing, illustration and image to shape dominant representations of sex and sexuality for the implied child reader.

The examples I have chosen include popular and widely available nonfiction picture books that have been published in the last fifty years, drawn from a survey of popular retailers, review websites and public library catalogues. Some of the most well-known titles include early works such as *What's Happening to Me?* (Mayle 1975), as well more contemporary titles such as *It's Perfectly Normal* (Harris 2014, originally published in 1994), and *Sex is a Funny Word* (Silverberg 2015). This methodology reflects my own position as a scholar working in a primarily anglophone context. While it is not within the scope of this chapter to discuss all the many sex education picture books for children in the international marketplace, the examples cited here feature dominant tropes and themes around reproduction, gender and sexuality that are hallmarks of this corpus that sits within children's literature more generally.

Texts in this subgenre have developed in the scope and manner in which sex education is discussed and implemented, and a small number of examples show a willingness to address contemporary ideas on this topic. However, on the whole, these books typically frame puberty, gender, sex, reproduction and sexuality in standardized, binary and heteronormative ways, and emphasize biological processes over more nuanced ways of imagining sexual relationships and identities. Different possibilities for imagining, performing and embodying sex and sexuality are often ignored, sidelined or avoided. While many texts acknowledge young people as emerging sexual subjects, rarely do they depict how this subjectivity might translate into sexuality, especially when it is beyond a set of common, biologically driven experiences.

Scholarship around Sex Sducation Picture Books

Despite the number of texts available in the marketplace, relatively little scholarly attention has been paid to nonfiction sex education picture books for children. While histories of sex education refer to curriculum (Giesbers 1970, Nelson and Martin 2004), classroom textbooks (Zimmerman 2015), and online resources (Blackman et al. 2010, Osterhoff et al. 2017), relatively little has been said in relation to the role nonfiction picture books play in teaching young people about sex and sexuality. Lissa Paul's article 'Sex and the children's book' (2005) is an exception, though its overall focus is on tertiary students' experiences of sex education, rather than sex education in nonfiction picture books. Paul's study begins with an overview of sex education in the West across the past century, before attention is turned to a case-study seminar in which the picture book *It's Perfectly Normal* (Harris 2014) is used as a springboard for university students to recount their own experiences of sex education. While the article links early forms of instructional children's literature to modern approaches in sex education generally, the growing corpus of nonfiction sex education picture that emerges from the 1970s onwards is not examined.

In both 'Where do I come from? Metaphors in sex education picture books for young children in China' (Liang, O'Halloran and Tan 2016) and 'Legitimating sex education through children's picture books in China' (Liang and Bowcher 2018) critical discourse analysis is used to identify key characteristics of a small number of sex education picture books in a specific cultural context. Though limited in scope, the results of both these studies suggest that the use of narrative and pictorial strategies to do with metaphor, personification and characterization may be used to carry ideological messages about sex and gender to child readers – ideas that are explored below.

In addition to the scholarship mentioned above, there is also a body of scholarship that focuses on fictional texts that explore sexual diversity and non-heterosexual sexual identities in child and young adult literature. Several large-scale surveys chart the development of such representations of sexual diversity in literature from the late 1960s to the present (Cart and Jenkins 2018, Lester 2014, Naidoo 2013). More recently, attention has been paid to the large number of picture books that portray rainbow families, in which representations of same-sex parents and their children feature (Hedberg et al. 2020). These studies focus primarily on fictional picture book texts, such as *Heather Has Two Mommies* (Newman 1989), *Daddy's Roommate* (Wilhoite 1990) and *And Tango Makes Three* (Richardson and Parnell 2005). While some of these texts – such as *Heather Has Two Mommies* – employ a relatively didactic tone, these works contribute to understandings of sex, sexuality and sexual identities obliquely, in comparison to the more direct, scientifically-informed approach that characterizes many of the nonfiction picture books discussed here.

The Purposes and Pleasures of Sex

The core aim of sexual education is multifaceted. On one hand, it may be said to convey 'the facts of life': that is, the scientific mechanics of puberty, sexual function, reproduction and childbirth. At the same time, 'sex' involves much more than that: whether that be in terms of gender and sexuality, customs and morals around sexual practice, or sexual desire and sexual pleasure. In this section I focus on this balance between the representation of biological processes and the messages around sexual pleasure that accompany them, in order to examine how nonfiction picture books navigate these twin aspects of human sexual experience. In so doing, my aim is to identify how these picture books construct parameters around sexual desire and pleasure and, in some instances, equate these things with danger.

The original publication of Peter Mayle's picture book *Where Did I Come From? The Facts of Life Without Any Nonsense and With Illustrations* coincided with a new openness about sex and sexuality in Western societies in the wake of the women's liberation and gay rights movements of the late 1960s and early 1970s. This provided a context for the book's frank descriptions of body hair, menstruation, wet dreams and so on. However, despite the relaxed and open approach adopted in this early example, the primary focus of *Where Did I Come From?* was on providing no-nonsense, fact-based information about puberty, heterosexual sex and reproduction.

The focus on heterosexual sex as a precursor to human reproduction is consistent across almost all of the texts discussed here. In *Where Did I Come From?* conception is depicted as a result of sexual intercourse between a man and a woman, while Babette Cole's *Mummy Laid an Egg*

(1993) and *Hair in Funny Places* (Cole 1999) culminate in the arrival of an infant into an established family unit. In *Hair in Funny Places* (Cole 1999) the initial description of experiences of puberty eventually transforms into a story about heterosexual sex and childbirth. It is only in the more contemporary works *The Amazing True Story of How Babies Are Made* (Kautauskas 2015) and *Let's Talk About Sex* (2014) that in-vitro fertilization is included as an alternative method of human reproduction.

Several examples acknowledge a connection between sex and pleasure, albeit in the context of procreation. In *Where Did I Come From?* a man and a woman are shown in bed, under the covers, smiling at each other. In *Mummy Laid an Egg*, the story of conception is taken up by the children, and they depict sex between their parents as an acrobatic source of great mirth. Meanwhile, in *The Amazing True Story of How Babies Are Made,* the text that accompanies an illustrated drawing of a man and a woman having intercourse reads: 'This is what we call having sex or making love.' Above a close-up of the man's erect penis ejaculating in the woman's vagina are the words: 'The man pushes his penis up and down inside the woman, which gives them both a tingly, excited, very loving feeling' (np). In these examples, sexual pleasure is simultaneously aligned with reproduction and love.

Masturbation is another area in which the potential for pubescent sexual pleasure is flagged. The messages about masturbation in *What's Happening to Me?* are rather complex, focused on communicating to young people that masturbation is acceptable, but only in certain circumstances. Across a double-page spread, a central illustration shows a teenage boy, in bed, wearing striped pyjamas. One hand is tucked into his lap. A big, yellow thunderbolt, running from right to left, is aimed at his head from above. The written text that accompanies this image explains masturbation as nature's 'solution' for 'sexual release without the full act of mating with a member of the opposite sex' (Mayle 1975, np). This notion is reiterated with the phrase 'This usually starts because you're thinking more and more about the opposite sex' (np). The illustration in this spread is accompanied by text in parentheses, which reads: '(Mating at too early an age is a mistake. You should first learn about birth control methods and how to use them. Also, about venereal disease and how to avoid it. Your doctor can give you good advice about both)' (np). In this case, masturbation is described as a kind of lead-in or substitute for heterosexual sex, framed by heterosexual desire. At the same time, the guilty look on the boy's face and the jagged thunderbolt acknowledge that masturbation is a taboo subject. Moreover, the image of the thunderbolt aimed at the child's head, and the warning against under-age sex and venereal disease, automatically connects sexual desire, feelings and activities with fear and danger.

Texts published in the early twenty-first century tend to refer to masturbation as a natural, normal activity for young people. While masturbation is not mentioned in *Secret Girls' Business* (Angelo et al. 2003), it is described as producing a 'warm, relaxed feeling' in the follow-up text *More Secret Girls' Business* (Anderson et al. 2008, np). Meanwhile, in *Secret Boys' Business* 'tingly, warm feelings' are associated with hormones that may spur a boy onto masturbation, which 'should be done in private' (Anderson et al. 2006, np). In *It's Perfectly Normal*, masturbation is discussed under the eponymous chapter title 'Perfectly Normal', in which sexual pleasure when masturbating is described as a 'good, tingly, excited feeling' (Harris 2014, p. 49). In *Sex is a Funny Word* two double-page spreads, including illustrations and text, are dedicated to the topic of 'touching yourself'. Employing language similar to the examples above, the texts reads: 'Masturbation is when we touch ourselves, usually our middle parts, to get that warm and tingly feeling' (Emberley and Smith 2015, np). To an extent then, in the past two decades these picture books have acknowledged the connection between masturbation and sexual pleasure to their implied readers.

However, this openness does not extend to forms of sexual behaviour beyond masturbation and heterosexual penis–vagina sex. *It's Perfectly Normal/Let's Talk About Sex*[2] is unique in so far as the written text refers to both oral and anal sex. This is arguably what has led to the US version *It's Perfectly Normal* being included on the 'Top Ten Most Challenged Books' list, according to the American Library Association (Flynn 2019). The short paragraph that covers this topic is included in a spread about reproduction and sexually transmitted diseases. While it seems odd to include information about oral and anal sex in a spread on reproduction, the reference to sexually transmitted diseases subtly links these activities with disease. In the contemporary era, it seems, sex and pleasure are connected, though this is often tempered by information about privacy, sexually transmitted infections, having sex 'too soon' and inappropriate touching.

Representations of Diversity

While gender identity is not the main focus of the examples under discussion, they do carry messages about how boys and girls are expected to embody gendered identities. Mayle's picture books, the oldest texts under discussion here, are clearly designed to reflect a heteronormative world and suggest clear divisions between sexual maturation in boys and girls. As the titles suggest, *Secret Girls' Business* (Angelo et al. 2003) and *Secret Boys' Business* (Anderson et al. 2006) and *Puberty Boy* (Price 2005) and *Puberty Girl* (Movsessian 2004) divide knowledge in a similar way. The use of blue and pink on the covers of these publications similarly denote a traditional gender binary. In the 2004 edition of *Let's Talk About Sex* a chapter is dedicated to gender, under the title 'Girl or Boy, Female or Male', although later editions include some limited information about trans identities, such as a brief definition of the term 'transgender'.

Meanwhile, in Katauskas' recent picture book *The Amazing True Story of How Babies Are Made* (2015) the moment after birth involves a baby being identified as either a boy or a girl – replicating the gender binary reinforced in earlier sex education picture books.

The versions of boyhood and girlhood on offer in these texts are also rather narrow in scope. For example. in *More Secret Girls' Business* a double-page spread is devoted to 'looking your best': with tips on 'posture', 'clothes', 'hair' and 'make-up' (Anderson et al. 2008, np). This suggests to pubescent girls that their successful transition into adulthood involves the importance of physical attractiveness. In contrast, the illustrations in *Puberty Boy* tend to depict adolescent males engaged in sport and outdoor activities, with less emphasis placed on how they look. In both cases, traditional interpretations of femininity and masculinity are on offer.

Where sexual diversity is concerned, more recent books acknowledge different sexual identities, although often in quite limited ways. While LGBTI+ identities are sometimes acknowledged, more often than not this is confined to brief discussion of same-sex attraction, rather than nuanced and holistic representations of the full spectrum of human sexualities. For example, both *Puberty Boy* and *Puberty Girl* discuss same-sex attraction. In *Puberty Girl* homosexuality is linked to a discussion of what it might be like to have gay or lesbian parents, reflecting changing attitudes towards gay families and the increasing prevalence of narrative picture books representing rainbow families, mentioned above. However, in both *Puberty Boy* and *Puberty Girl*, information pertaining to homosexuality comes in the form of written text. The lack of accompanying illustrations suggests that in these examples homosexuality remains a topic that can be written about but not visualized, acknowledged but not seen in any way.

Secret Boys' Business and *More Secret Girls' Business* both differentiate between same-sex crushes and being gay. This differentiation is reminiscent of the antiquated idea of homosexuality as a kind of phase that one might pass through on the way to achieving heterosexual maturity. Moreover, in both books, same-sex attraction is automatically linked to anxiety. For example, in *More Secret Girls' Business* the text reads: 'If a girl has a crush on another girl or woman this does not necessarily mean she is gay. However a few girls are naturally same sex attracted. This can be a confusing and worrying time for a while' (Anderson et al. 2008, np). In *Puberty Boy* same-sex attraction is also linked to issues around homophobia. The subtle inference is that while it is theoretically 'ok to be gay', young people who identify as LGBTIQ+ are likely to experience bullying and discrimination. While many young LGBTIQ+ people do experience this, connecting the two concepts reinforces the idea that coming out is likely to have negative consequences.

Several of the books discuss homosexuality and sexual diversity obliquely. *Let's Talk About Sex* frames homosexuality as part of an historical continuum of same-sex sexual desire, stretching back to ancient Greece. In *The Amazing True Story of How Babies Are Made* a double-page spread shows different family groups, two of which involve what appear to be same-sex couples. There is no written text to further unpack or explore same-sex parents/rainbow families, in ways that are now increasingly common in narrative fiction picture books (Hedberg et al. 2020). In *Sex is a Funny Word* the explanation of diverse sexual identities (under the headings of 'gay', 'lesbian', 'queer', 'asexual' and 'bisexual') is positioned within a section of the book looking at love and relationships, rather than in the sections dealing with sex and bodies, where representations of heterosexuality occur. In this instance, being gay is recognized as an identity category but is divorced from the idea of actually engaging in sexual activity.

Even when the possibility that pubescent teenagers may be gay or lesbian is acknowledged, the tendency in sex education picture books is to render homosexual identities as inherently 'other'. The most explicit representation of a gay teenager is found in *The Amazing True Story of How Babies Are Made*. A half-page spread shows three young, naked males showering. The first has red pubic hair, the second black and the third rainbow coloured. All the boys are depicted in identical poses, singing or whistling, and yet the 'rainbow' character has bright red lips: in contrast to the other two boys, this illustration appears to represent not merely that he is gay, but also stereotypically effeminate and camp. In this case, while there is an attempt to depict a young gay man, the image used is anachronistic at best, and stereotypical at worst: as if sexuality can be easily equated with how a person looks (or, indeed, the colour of their pubic hair).

The American publication *Sex is a Funny Word* (Emberley and Smyth 2015) represents other kinds of diversity. Colours not commonly associated with skin tones – such as purple, blue, green and orange – are used to denote differences between the characters featured in the book. Facial features, hair and dress indicate Afro-American, Latino, Asian and Indigenous people. Youngsters are pictured in wheelchairs and with walking aids, and of different sizes. In a double-page spread with the title 'Every body is different. Every body has beauty in it', the young characters who appear throughout the book are depicted among people of different ages and subcultures. In *Let's Talk About Sex*, the illustrations denote people of different ethnic/racial identities, though the majority of the figures appear to be Caucasian.

The only publications to deal explicitly and at length with disability and neuro-diversity in this sample are offshoots of the *Secret Girls'/Secret Boys'* business books, titled *Special Girls' Business* (Anderson et al. 2005), *Special Boys' Business* (Anderson et al. 2007) and *Puberty and Special Girls* (Anderson et al. 2009). While these texts represent isolated examples from a single publisher, they are unique in so far as they recognize that all young people, even those with learning difficulties or physical disabilities, are sexual subjects. At the same time, the fact that information about sex for people with special needs is corralled into publications separate to those of neuro-typical and able-bodied youngsters automatically positions them as different and 'other'.

Showing: The Role of Aesthetics

The dependency on drawn illustrations suggests that sex education in picture books for children requires careful mediation between reality and representation, at least in terms of visual imagery. In terms of aesthetics, all the books surveyed for this chapter employ the use of drawings to illustrate ideas about sex, sexual activity and sexuality. Avoiding highly naturalistic/realistic image-making techniques such as photography may allay the potential censorship of sexual content or nudity. In effect, the visual style and media adopted in these texts creates a certain kind of 'safe distance' between communicating ideas about sex and human bodies and other forms of representation that might be read as too explicit for children.

Drawn illustrations and even written narration are often presented in the style of cartoons and comic books rather than hyper-realistic artwork. A pertinent example of this is the layout and style used in *The Amazing True Story of How Babies Are Made*. Author, illustrator and political cartoonist Katauskas uses coloured markers and black outlines to create characters and scenes that have a sense of volume and space. Facial expressions are easily read and the illustrations are often accompanied by arrows pointing to hand-written text that underscores the ideas presented in the illustrations. Mini-storyscapes are included as 'interludes' in broader spreads, such as the small illustration of a caesarean section on a page about giving birth. *Sex is a Funny Word* also uses conventions of the graphic novel/comic strip: ideas are grouped into short chapters, to be read over 'weeks, months and years, rather than just a few sittings' (2015, np). These are presented through the use of both cells and speech bubbles as well as more traditional, picture-book spreads.

In the older texts, *Where Do I Come From?* and *What's Happening to Me?*, cartoonish drawings allow for a range of exaggerated characterizations (plump, skinny, short, tall, buxom, flat-chested, curly haired, straight haired, bald, spotty and so on). A good example of this trope is an illustration of a sperm in *What's Happening to Me?* The written text reads 'Sperm can't do very much except sit around until you get an erection' (1975, np). The accompanying illustration of the sperm takes up almost an entire page. It is rendered as flesh-coloured, rotund, with a waggling tail and masculine facial features, and is whistling a tune and twiddling its thumbs in anticipation of the aforementioned erection. In this case, using stylistic framework cartoon-drawing delivers a concept about human anatomy and biology in a humorous manner, a concept to which I return below.

While cartoons are often used as a device to tackle hitherto taboo subjects (sperm, wet dreams, horrendous acne), both *Where Do I Come*

From? and *What's Happening to me?* revert to realistic pencil drawings of naked human bodies to demonstrate physical maturation from childhood to adulthood. Detailed, grey-lead drawings of anatomy are presented as a kind of chart of human physical development. These illustrations, devoid of the colour and exaggeration found elsewhere in the text, underscore the idea that below the surface of this otherwise tongue-in-cheek discussion of sex and puberty lies an objective, scientific truthfulness. However, these images also reveal a standardization of the human form: the figures are slim, perfectly proportioned and muscularly defined archetypes. In this manner, the implied child reader is faced with two possibilities for identification with the human figures presented in these books: cartoon figures or impossibly perfect scientific models.

Babette Cole's *Mummy Laid an Egg* is unusual, in so far as the illustrations are at times detailed and at other points naïve and child-like. The opening double-page spread depicts a messy lounge room. Mum and Dad appear in the doorway, addressing two children lying on a couch, surrounded by a chaotic array of toys and animals, food-wrappers and other household debris. The various far-fetched explanations of sexual reproduction the parents offer are rejected by the children, who provide their own illustrations to explain to their parents how things *really* work. The children create rotund line-drawings in pink to depict the parents, their genitals rendered as little more than three lumps for penis and testes, and an oval for a vagina. In this example, anatomical accuracy is sacrificed to create the sense that the children are simultaneously better educated about sex than their parents realize and yet still possess a child-like way of depicting the world around them.

Though photography as a medium affords no inherent nor particular guarantee of displaying accuracy, objectivity or truthfulness, it is often associated with those qualities. These qualities – or at least the illusion of them – are also hallmarks of nonfiction literature (Kiefer and Wilson 2011). Despite this, photography is almost universally absent from the sex education picture books under discussion in this chapter. Mayle's *Will I Like It?* (1978) is an exception, though its text-heavy seventy-eight pages make it an outlier in this study of picture books. The general absence of photography within the popular examples referred to here means that any association between photographic images and the explicitness of pornography is avoided, as if to guarantee some distance between concept and 'real life'.

Though not designed as a sex education resource per se, another exception worth mentioning in this context is the picture book: *Jenny Lives with Eric and Martin* (Bösche and Hansen, first published in Danish in 1981 and then in English in 1983). Generally considered to be the first picture book to represent a rainbow family, the work of fiction is a photographic essay, depicting a few days in the life of a young girl, Jenny, her father Eric and his partner Martin. One spread within the book shows Eric and Martin in bed together, semi-naked. While the book received scant critical attention when released in Denmark, this image no doubt contributed to the reaction of conservative politicians in the United Kingdom, who passed legislation in 1988 to ban this book and others like it from state-run schools and libraries (Moran 2001).

The negative response to *Jenny Lives with Eric and Martin* intersected with a particular cultural moment in the HIV-AIDS era, in which homosexuality was targeted by conservative political forces within the United Kingdom. However, it could be argued that the realism of the photography in this picture book crossed an invisible red line that connected childhood with an awareness and acceptance of sexual diversity. In this light, the reliance on drawn imagery, cartoon-style illustrations and so forth in the examples discussed above may be understood as a more neutral or universally acceptable aesthetic mode for imaging/imagining sex education for young people.

Telling: Sex Education as Storytelling

The books under discussion in this chapter can be defined as nonfiction by the use of specialist language, of diagrammatic images, of rational explanation and, in one case, the use of a glossary. Some, such as *Where Did I Come from?*, *What's Happening to Me?* and *Let's Talk About Sex*, use a significant amount of written text to explain ideas. In *Let's Talk About Sex*, a long list of specialist consultants, such as doctors and psychologists, is also included in the final pages. Livingston et al. argue that 'Nonfiction has struggled to find its place as literature because children's literature is often considered to be synonymous with story' (2004, p. 582). Yet many of the nonfiction texts discussed in this chapter do in fact use storytelling to explain things, in combination with the other strategies for communication mentioned above.

This use of storytelling is perhaps unsurprising, given that the progression from puberty, to sexual maturity, to sexual intercourse, conception, pregnancy and birth lends itself to a rather familiar beginning, middle and end narrative structure. An example of this is *Hair in Funny Places* (Cole 1999). While its title indicates the book's topic of focus – puberty – the explanation of this facet of human development is framed as a conversation between a girl and her beloved teddy bear. The bear narrates the story of the girl's mother and father and their journeys through puberty, for which he was, seemingly, a witness. The narrative closure is framed by the coming together of the mother and father as a romantic couple who give birth to the narratee – the girl to whom the teddy bear has been explaining things.

The use of a talking toy or animal to assist in the telling of a coming-of-age story is a relatively common motif in children's literature. Despite this, Lynch-Brown and Tomlinson argue that in children's nonfiction '*Personification* – attributing human qualities to animals, material objects or natural forces – should be avoided because the implication is factually inaccurate' (2008, p. 193). In *Mummy Laid an Egg*, however, it is the information offered by the human characters – the parents in particular – that is untrustworthy. Meanwhile, in *Let's Talk About Sex*, cartoon characters in the form of a bird and a bee (wearing trainers) lead the reader through the book, pausing to add asides or to generate questions that the text then goes about answering. Lydia Kokkola suggests that animalism is a common motif in the representation of adolescent desires in children's literature: in effect, the expression of sexual interest renders young people 'bestial' and therefore 'not-child' (2013, p. 138). While children are not portrayed as animals or animalistic in these texts, the employment of anthropomorphic animal or object characters is a means to create a mediated distance between the implied child reader and the discussion of otherwise sensitive or traditionally censored ideas.

Characterization is also used to position the implied child reader as an 'insider' to the information on offer in these books. In *Mummy Laid an Egg*, the father's hand-knitted jumper features a Christmas pudding on the chest and his thinning hair is tied back in a stringy ponytail. The parents' clothing, hairstyles, and facial expressions help to underscore the idea that they are not very 'cool' and need their children to take the initiative when explaining sex. In this example, the children in the story are positioned as the holders of knowledge. This technique elevates the position of the implied child reader alongside the child protagonists, and effectively masks the fact that the information provided in the text is produced from an adult perspective.

With just a few exceptions, children's own voices are for the most part missing from these nonfiction texts. In *Sex is a Funny Word*, the four youngsters depicted on the front cover appear consistently throughout the book, a trait that was initially employed in *Where Did I Come From?* and *What's Happening to Me?* Children pose questions and occasionally intervene with commentary, but the vast majority of the books feature a disembodied third-person perspective. This narrative strategy allows for information about sex and sexuality to appear objective, despite the fact that it is a product of decision-making by adult authors and publishers.

One of the most obvious ways in which gatekeeping is apparent in these texts is through the use of euphemism, especially when describing objects and concepts that have traditionally been considered rude or taboo. For example, in *Sex is a Funny Word*, masturbation is referred to as 'touching': part of a longer section in the book about different forms of physical contact and consent. *The Amazing True Story of How Babies Are Made* uses terms such as 'penis and vagina', 'uterus and fallopian tube', but also reminds the reader that penis is sometimes referred to 'as a "willy", "doodle", "tackle", "dangly bits"' (2015, np).

Euphemism is often used in conjunction with humour, a strategy employed in all the books under discussion here. *Where Did I Come From?* and *What's Happening to Me?* represent the trend in the 1970s away from scientific, scholastic textbooks on biology towards more child-friendly educational resources. From picturing an acne-riddled teenage face as spouting oil geysers, to a boy on a diving board with an involuntary erection tenting his swim-shorts, to frogs looking quizzically at a diagram of a tadpole-like sperm, to the image of parents engaged in intercourse on a 'space hopper', comic relief is used regularly throughout these books as a means to describe various aspects of puberty and sexual function. The use of humour across these texts suggests that, on some level, sex education is associated with awkwardness and embarrassment, for both authors and implied readers alike.

The use of humour as a technique for imparting information about hitherto sensitive or taboo topics suggests that at the heart of this kind of literature lurks the assumption that while children must be provided with some form of instruction about puberty, reproduction, gender, sex and sexuality, they are also to be shielded from at least some of its complexity, its *realness*. In his oft-cited writing on assumptions about children and childhood that regularly feature in children's literature, Perry Nodelman critiques the idea that 'children have limited understanding', are 'inherently innocent' and that texts produced for them should attempt to limit realistic depictions that might lead to 'rudeness or immorality, that children might choose to imitate' (1996, p. 73). Paradoxically, for a group of texts that are almost universally pitched as frank and fearless in talking to and teaching young people about bodies and sex, the use of stand-in language and comic relief denotes an ongoing uneasiness about certain aspects of the 'secret business' of sex education.

Conclusion

On a basic level, nonfiction picture books are designed to teach child readers about aspects of human life. Lissa Paul refers to this kind of didacticism when she writes that 'there has been only one exception to the "instruct and delight" rule of children's literature: books on sex education. Sex education is not about delight ... Only instruction—and the more clinical the better' (2005, p. 22). Russell Freedman offers an alternative vision, however, when he argues that nonfiction texts are at their best when they involve and engage their readers beyond simple instruction:

> Certainly the basic purpose of nonfiction is to inform, to instruct, hopefully to enlighten. But that's not enough. An effective nonfiction book must animate its subject, infuse it with life. It must create a vivid and believable world that the reader will enter willingly and leave only with reluctance. A good nonfiction book should be a pleasure to read.
>
> (Freedman 1992, p. 3)

The wide range of written and visual narrative strategies observed in the nonfiction picture books discussed above certainly suggest that sex education in children's literature does 'animate' its subject matter in ways that go beyond dry and clinical information sharing.

At the same time, it is important to consider the degree to which these nonfiction children's picture books accurately reflect the ideas they seek to represent. On one hand, the development of ideas about natural and artificial conception show that knowledge changes over time, and the shifts in the way picture books handle this subject indicate the challenges faced by authors and publishers to keep up with the facts. On the other hand, this chapter indicates a number of ways in which more holistic representations of sex and sexuality continue to be avoided. For example, sexual pleasure – that 'tingly feeling' – is canvassed, but usually only in relation to masturbation or reproductive, heterosexual sex. Diverse sexual identities are sometimes flagged or alluded to, but not explored in any depth. Though heterosexual sex is depicted in the illustrations, sexual activity between same-sex people is never represented. Representation of other forms of diversity are similarly limited, especially in terms of race and ability. Gender diversity is another area where these texts fall behind their fictional peers: the notion of girls' business and boys' business as separate fields indicates the powerful way that the relationship between knowledge and gender are aligned and managed by adults.

Nonfiction picture books for children that deal with hitherto underrepresented or taboo topics such as sex, sexuality, puberty and reproduction face a dilemma: to what degree can accuracy be attained and preserved when what is known and what is said about these topics continues to change? While this is a question that eludes any clear answer, the key to a response may be in recognizing that these books do much more than simply present facts and information: they also carry values and beliefs about puberty, sex, sexuality and reproduction and shape what these concepts mean for young people growing up. The continued publication of these kinds of picture books indicates that adult authors believe that they hold the answers to children's questions, such as 'where did I come from?' and 'what's happening to me?'. However, even more complex questions about sex and sexuality, beyond the terrain of puberty, sexual health and reproduction, remain to be fully answered.

Notes

1 A search of the WorldCat database returned more than a thousand results for this category.
2 This book is published in the United Kingdom under the title *Let's Talk About Sex* and in the United States under the title *It's Perfectly Normal*.

References

Anderson, H, Angelo, F and Stewart, R 2005, *Special Girls' Business*, Secret Girls' Business Children's Book Publisher, North Balwyn.

Anderson, H, Angelo, F and Stewart, R 2006, *Secret Boy's Business*, Secret Girls' Business Children's Book Publisher, North Balwyn.

Anderson, H, Angelo, F and Stewart, R 2007, *Special Boys' Business*, Secret Girls' Business Children's Book Publisher, North Balwyn.

Anderson, H, Angelo, F and Stewart, R 2008, *More Secret Girls' Business*, The F.L. Angelo and H.A. Pritchard and R.M. Stewart Partnership, North Balwyn.

Anderson, H, Angelo, F and Stewart, R 2009, *Puberty and Special Girls*, Secret Girls' Business Children's Book Publisher, North Balwyn.

Angelo, F, Pritchard, H and Stewart, R 2003, *Secret Girls' Business*, The Authors, Mont Albert.

Blackman, L, Gahan, L, Hillier, L, Jones, T, Mitchell, A, Monagle, M and Overton, N 2010, *Writing Themselves In 3*, Australian Centre for Research in Sex, Health and Society, Latrobe University, Melbourne.

Bösche, S and Hansen, A 1983, *Jenny Lives with Eric and Martin*, Gay Men's Press, London.

Cart, M and Jenkins, C 2018, *Representing the Rainbow in Young Adult Literature: LGBTQ+ Content Since 1969*, Rowland and Littlefield, Maryland.

Cole, B 1993, *Mummy Laid an Egg*, Jonathon Cape, London.

Cole, B 1999, *Hair in Funny Places*, Random House Children's Books, London.

Flynn, K 2019, 'It's perfectly normal', *The Horn Book Magazine*, vol. 95, no. 5, pp. 21–23.

Freedman, R 1992, 'Fact or fiction', *Using Nonfiction Trade Books in the Elementary Classroom: From Ants to Zeppelins*. Eds. EB Freeman and DG Person, National Council of Teachers of English, Urbana, IL, pp. 2–110.

Giesbers, J 1970, *Cecil Reddie and Abbotsholme: A Forgotten Pioneer and His Creation*, Raboud University, Njimegen.

Harris, RH 2014, *Let's Talk About Sex: Growing Up, Changing Bodies*, Sex and Sexual Health, Walker Books (published in the US by Candlewick under the title *It's Perfectly Normal*), London.

Hedberg, L, Young, H and Venzo, P 2020, 'Mums, dads and the kids: representations of rainbow families in children's picture books', Journal of LGBT Youth, pp. 1–9, https://doi.org/10.1080/19361653.2020.1779164.

Katauskas, F 2015, *The Amazing True Story of How Babies Are Made*, ABC Books, Sydney.

Kiefer, B and Wilson, MI 2011, 'Nonfiction literature for children: old assumptions and new directions', *Handbook of Research on Children's and Young Adult Literature*. Eds. Shelby A Wolf et al., Routledge, New York, pp. 290–299.

Kokkola, L 2013, *Fictions of Adolescent Carnality: Sexy Sinners and Delinquent Deviants*, John Benjamins Publishing, Amsterdam.

Lester, JZ 2014, 'Homonormativity in children's literature: an intersectional analysis of queer-themed picture books', *Journal of LGBT Youth*, vol. 11, pp. 244–275.

Liang, JY and Bowcher, WL 2018, 'Legitimating sex education through children's picture books in China', *Sex Education*, vol. 9, no. 3, pp. 329–345.

Lian, JY, O'Halloran, K and Tan, S 2016, 'Where do I come from? Metaphors in Sex Education Picture Books for Young Children in China', Metaphor and Symbol, vol. 31, no. 3, pp. 179–193.

Livingston, N, Kurkjian, C, Pringle, L and Young, T 2004, 'Children's books – nonfiction as literature: an untapped goldmine', *The Reading Teacher*, vol. 57, no. 6, pp. 582–591.

Lynch-Brown, C and Tomlinson, CM 2008, *Essentials of Children's Literature*, Pearson, Boston, MA.

Mayle, P 1973, *Where Did I Come From? The Facts of Life Without Any Nonsense*, Carol Publishing, Seacacus, NJ.

Mayle, P 1975, *What's Happening to Me? The Answers to Some of the World's Most Embarrassing Questions*, Carol Publishing, Seacacus, NJ.

Mayle, P 1978, *Will I Like It? Your* First Sexual Experience: What *to* Expect, What *to* Avoid *and* How Both *of* You Can Get *the* Most Out *of* It, WH Allen, London.

Moran, J 2001, 'Childhood sexuality and education: the case of section 28', *Sexualities*, vol. 4, no. 1, pp. 73–90.

Movsessian, S 2004, *Puberty Girl*, Allen and Unwin, Crows Nest.

Naidoo, JC 2013, 'Over the rainbow and under the radar', *Children and Libraries: The Journal of the Libraries Association Library Service to Children*, vol. 11, no. 12, pp. 34–40.

Nelson, C and Martin, M 2004, *Sexual Pedagogies: Sex Education in Britain, Australia, and America, 1879–2000*, Palgrave Macmillan, New York.

Nodelman, P 1996, *The Pleasures of Children's Literature*, Addison Wesley Longman, New York.

Osterhoff, P, Müller, C and Shephard, K 2017, 'Introduction: sex education in the digital era', *IDS Bulletin – Institute of Development Studies*, vol. 48, no. 1, pp. 1–5.

Paul, L 2005, 'Sex and the children's book', *The Lion and the Unicorn*, vol. 29, no. 2, pp. 222–235.

Price, G 2005, *Puberty Boy*, Allen and Unwin, Crows Nest.

Richardson, J and Parnell, P 2005, *And Tango Makes Three*, Simon and Shuster Books for Young Readers, New York.

Silverberg, C 2015, *Sex is a Funny Word*, Seven Stories Press, New York.

Wilhoite, M 1990, *Daddy's Roommate*, Alyson Wonderland, Los Angeles.

Zimmerman, J 2015, *Too Hot to Handle: A Global History of Sex Education*, Princeton University Press, Princeton, NJ.

4 Trans and Nonbinary Teen Voices and Memoir

(Non-)traditional Mirrors of (Non-)traditional Lives

Robert Bittner

Trans memoirs and autobiography has traditionally been written by adults, with the majority reflecting on childhood, adolescence, and teenage years from a temporal distance. While these texts are useful and interesting in their own right, reminiscences of childhood are at times distanced to such an extent that there can be questions about accuracy and the influence of nostalgia in such recollections. Perry Nodelman, in his work on 'the other', notes that 'In the act of speaking for the other, providing it with a voice, we silence it. As long as we keep on speaking for it, we won't get to hear what it has to say for itself' (1992, p. 30). Young people are rarely the producers of content in traditional publishing, unless their personal stories are considered exceptional, as is often the case for transgender youth in the media spotlight – many young memoirists have started out as prominent YouTube personalities or, in the case of Jazz Jennings, a reality TV star.

Furthermore, trans youth memoirists are more immediately and linearly connected to their recollections, having experienced events in childhood and adolescence much more recently in relation to their published work. At the same time, as teens are not often seen by adults as reliable sources of knowledge – routinely being ignored until adulthood and its privileges come into effect – memoir gives them a voice and agency through which to affect change in their own communities and the larger social landscape. Memoir also allows young people to develop their individual identities through acts of recollection and confession.

Reliance on gender binaries and medicalization of trans lives affects the ways in which sex and sexuality are treated within texts and, more often than not, the authors focus on difficulties of sex in relation to gender dysphoria.[1] What is absent is exploration of sexual pleasure. At the same time, trans teen memoirs highlight the complexity and confusion around gender and sexuality, focusing on their respective journeys, from discovering new labels, to coming out multiple times, to jumping through the hoops of the medical establishment. This admission of confusion makes the trans teen memoir unique.

The current publishing industry emphasizes and privileges fiction *about* transgender young people, most often written *by* cisgender authors, leaving trans and nonbinary voices marginalized. Trans and nonbinary representation in young adult fiction, within North America at least, began with *Luna* (Peters 2004), although the representation was less than positive – the trans character is positioned as being a burden to their family, specifically their sister, the narrator. A number of fiction texts followed, including *Parrotfish* (Wittlinger 2007), *Almost Perfect* (Katcher 2009), *Beautiful Music for Ugly Children* (Cronn-Mills 2012), and *Freakboy* (Clark 2013), among others. In 2016 *If I Was Your Girl* (Russo) was published by Flatiron, marking the first young adult fiction text written by a transgender author and published by a major publishing house.[2]

When trans visibility became more mainstream – noted in Steinmetz's *Time* magazine article 'The transgender tipping point' (2014) – the young adult publishing industry took notice and books with transgender and nonbinary protagonists were published with greater frequency (Stoeve 2020). Yet these books continue to be authored most often by cisgender authors. This is one prominent reason for more frequent discussions on social media about trans and nonbinary representation in relation to #OwnVoices authorship. Within this context, the publication of two memoirs written by transgender teens (Andrews 2014; Hill 2014) and published by Simon & Schuster, highlighted new possibilities for centering transgender voices within the publishing landscape: memoir.

As of 2020, four memoirs by trans teens have now been published for youth readers in the US: *Rethinking Normal* (Hill 2014), *Some Assembly Required* (Andrews 2014), *Being Jazz* (Jennings 2016), and *Out! How to Be Your Authentic Self* (McKenna 2020),[3] along with *Finding Nevo* (Zisin 2017) in Australia and *TransMission* (Bertie 2019) in the UK (subsequently released in the US).[4] *Rethinking Normal* and *Some Assembly Required* chronicle the lives of Arin Andrews and Katie Rain Hill as they grow up, come out, start dating each other, break up, and try their best to navigate a less-than-accepting society. Hill and Andrews became the subjects of media coverage across the US, and even ended up the focus of an ad campaign for Barneys of New York. *Being Jazz* follows Jazz Jennings through her early years of transition and the harassment and rejection her family received throughout the process. *Finding Nevo* is a unique narrative in many respects, as it highlights the fluidity and confusion of identity development in ways that other narratives tend to avoid in favor of more linear and less chaotic trajectory. *TransMission* and *Out!* are unique in that they are not simply chronicles of lived experience but are also self-help guides to aid readers in understanding the basics of what it means to be transgender today.

The genre of memoir occupies a space between autobiography and fiction. Memoirs, while telling individual stories, conform to a much more literary narrative style. 'Memoir', as Kirby and Kirby (2010) note, 'is nonfiction but employs the techniques of fiction as well as those of exposition' (p. 24). Furthermore, these kinds of trans texts – like Leslie Feinberg's semi-autobiographical novel *Stone Butch Blues* (1993) and Kate Bornstein's *Gender Outlaw: On Men, Women, and the Rest of Us* (1994) – helped a new generation of transsexual individuals see and better understand themselves (Beemyn 2015, p. 3). Contemporary memoirs provide an 'honest unfolding of human struggles and triumphs from which important lessons are learned, significant family events are preserved, and generations of family members braid the cord of their lived experiences' (Kirby and Kirby 2010, p. 23). In this way, memoirs are able to build a sense of attachment or empathy, and a more universal approach to some aspects of lived trans experience.

Memoir and autobiography by trans individuals tend to focus on the physical body – dysphoria, surgery, transitioning – and/or the act of coming out, chronicling the social consequences and, in many cases, the road to a sort of fame or notoriety *because* of the non-traditional path to gender identity construction, both physically and mentally. Although both memoir and autobiography play a significant role in the history of trans storytelling, it can be difficult for some to differentiate between the two genres – and, in the case of trans teen memoir, the distinction is important. Rebecca Hussey, a professor of English Literature, notes: '[G]enerally speaking, autobiography aims to be comprehensive, while memoir does not' (2018, np). Hussey further explains:

> Memoirists will often choose *a particularly important or interesting part of their life* to write about and ignore or briefly summarize the rest .... Autobiography places greater emphasis on facts and how the writer fits into the historical record, while memoir emphasizes personal experience and interiority .... The facts matter in memoir, but it's understood that memoirists select and shape the facts of their lives to explore their chosen theme.
>
> (2018, np, emphasis added)

A chronological account of history – a series of facts and details – is in many ways abandoned in favor of truths examined through feeling, emotion, and the lens of a particular theme and, in the case of trans teen memoir, a moment of realization, a physical transition, or a series of interactions with family members or a given community. While physical transition is indeed a very influential component of trans lived experience, there is far less examination of sexual experiences, though this is to be expected when feelings of bodily disconnect and dysphoria come into play. For Zisin, for example, this feeling came early on when they started developing breasts:

> One day, our friend decided I was too old to swim without my shirt off, and my mum told me I would have to start wearing a shirt. I

was devastated. I didn't understand why I couldn't continue to be topless like my male friends, or brothers, or my dad. They were older than me but they were still allowed to expose their chests. My mum explained I was growing breasts, something I hadn't been aware of until that moment. I was suddenly acutely aware of my chest in a way I hadn't been before and felt the need to hide it. I felt embarrassed, ashamed and self-conscious.

(p. 13)

The sudden awareness of secondary sex characteristics, framed as something shameful, made Zisin acutely aware of that part of their body and the embarrassment they were supposed to feel based on social expectations around typically female bodies, and young bodies, for that matter. Any time there is even a possible implication of sexuality within childhood and early teen years, there is a societal undercurrent of panic.

Within accounts of childhood and adolescence, of particular focus is how trans youth adjust to a new and changing relationship to sex and sexuality. While many fictional representations of transgender teens fail to include sexual activity or pleasure, these memoirs at least allow for *some* frank discussion of sex without the hang-ups of adults trying to depict or interfere with teen sex lives. Physicality is one thing for those who feel at home in their own bodies, but for those who are not entirely at ease, sex can be incredibly complicated. Hill, for instance, notes that she first came out as gay because of her attraction to guys when she was younger, before she came out as trans. She recounts a time with her childhood friend, Brian, when they were wrestling: 'before I knew it, we weren't just wrestling anymore. We were rubbing into each other, moving our hips and breathing heavily' (p. 70). While sex is something integral to development in many young people's lives, it is not always a primary focus for youth who are first and foremost attempting to navigate their own gender identity.

Sex and intimacy as experienced by young people are often stigmatized, particularly in relation to queerness or whatever might be considered 'non-normative'. Steven Bruhm and Natasha Hurley, in their introduction to *Curiouser: On the Queerness of Children* (2004), write: 'People panic when ... sexuality takes on a life outside the sanctioned scripts of child's play [as in Hill's example, above]' (p. ix). They go on to explain: 'nowhere is this panic more explosive than in the field of the *queer* child, the child whose play confirms neither the comfortable stories of child (a)sexuality nor the supposedly blissful promises of adult heteronormativity' (p. ix). Trans youth memoir consciously disrupts these 'blissful promises' that many adults – parents, teachers, librarians, and so on – expect, even hope for. Sex and intimacy among transgender youth troubles expectations of 'normative' sex and sexuality.

Fame and Privacy

Fame and popularity are significant components for consideration when looking at viability and likelihood of finding a platform within publishing. What is notable among the trans teen memoirs currently on the market is that the authors are mostly white and, aside from one, adhere to fairly binary gender presentation. Andrews notes this explicitly in his memoir: 'I understood why the cameras liked us so much. We were *safe for the masses – white, telegenic, and heteronormative*' (Andrews 2014, p. 213; emphasis added). This overwhelming normativity must be considered when examining trans teen memoirs. What does it mean, for instance, for those who do not conform? What does it mean that even as trans youth voices are gaining prominence, those whose appearance or gender expression does not conform to social expectations are continuing to have their voices stifled?

Privacy is something that very few trans individuals are afforded in society these days and, while trans autobiography and memoir are in part written and published for the purpose of self-examination, they are also published for the purpose of revealing certain truths and experiences to a larger public audience. In essence this intrusive nature has created the trans autobiography: 'Many … early autobiographies were written by transsexual women whose gender identities had been revealed by the press' and were thus 'forced into the media spotlight' (Beemyn 2015, p. 1) This, of course, means that many earlier autobiographies 'served as a response to the stereotypes and misinformation circulated about their experiences' (Beemyn 2015, p. 1). Many of these autobiographies rely heavily on facts and thoroughly researched information to tell very specific stories and vignettes, and young adult memoir continues in this vein.

Much of the contemporary landscape of memoirs by and about young people has grown out of a tradition of online storytelling, particularly through sites such as YouTube, a space where many young trans individuals began to document their experiences of transition, since they lacked access to the realm of mainstream publishing. Arin Andrews, for instance, actually began documenting his transition quite early on – starting in 2011/2012 – and is one of the first to do so, laying bare his story and allowing others to participate in his transition through online videos. McKenna's popularity similarly came out of the tradition of chronicling his transition online.

It is interesting to consider the fact that so many of the prominent voices in this genre came from a tradition of online fame and visibility, an element that shows up repeatedly in most trans teen memoir. But, as Andrews notes in his memoir, now that he has been out for a while, he is more comfortable discussing his body in ways related to genitals, sex, and intimacy: 'In the right forum and context, I'm okay now with discussing sex and my own genital dysphoria, but it's *really* important to understand that many trans people aren't. And it sucks when that's the first thing a stranger asks about' (p. 216). Due to the preoccupation with dysphoria, transition, and coming out, many early online transition stories do not engage with topics of romance or relationships, especially due to family expectations, transphobia, and general discomfort with being in the public.

Physical Bodies, Dysphoria, and Sexual intimacy

Trans young adult memoir can be a way of understanding and discussing physicality, genitalia, sexual activity, and the challenges inherent within trans experiences for young people, but without the invasive questioning of those who do not wish to be under public scrutiny. Sex/sexuality is still most often referred to in relation to *wrongness* or a feeling of disconnection with the physical body one was born with. Andrews explains:

> I'm okay now with discussing sex and my own genital dysphoria, but it's really important to understand that many trans people aren't. And it sucks when that's the first thing a stranger asks about. Any topic relating to bodies, sex, and sexuality is going to different for everyone, and privacy should be respected.
>
> (2014, p. 216)

In *Rethinking Normal*, Hill writes that during an interview she felt that all that the adults were focused on was their genitals and what they did with them:

> There was a three-minute clip of Arin saying he hadn't had bottom surgery and me saying we don't have sex. It felt like the message we were trying to get across was lost. As if all cisgender people cared about was, 'Does your vagina work and does he have a penis?'
>
> (2014, p. 232)

In both these memoirs, sex is something that outsiders are fascinated with, but which Hill and Andrews are less than thrilled to talk about. When Hill starts dating Andrews, the couple became a media sensation because of their intelligibility – people see them as a straight couple, a boy and a girl. People began to ask questions about their ability to have sex and how they experienced physical intimacy, which is one of the reasons why trans youth consistently address the subjects of sex and their connections with their own physical bodies within their work.

Alex Bertie's text is a combination of memoir and guidebook, which chronicles his experiences while trying to also address common misconceptions and questions for young readers. Bertie notes:

> [S]ex and intimacy for trans people can be as simple or as complicated as it needs to be. Communication is always key for all parties involved, but the main thing to remember is that sex can be great, even if you're trans.
>
> (2019, p. 233)

Bertie's focus in *TransMission* is exploring gender, but he still acknowledges the connections between gender and sexuality, attraction, and intimacy:

> Before and during coming out, I had difficulties sustaining relationships .... But in particular, I found it incredibly hard to make things work when the other person initiated intimate contact. I'm not even talking about anything sexual – even just cuddling would make me feel insecure because I was so ashamed of my body.
>
> (p. 223)

Similarly, considering her own feelings of dysphoria and her relationship with Arin Andrews, Hill writes:

> Arin and I had tried having intercourse – as in penis-in-vagina sex – which had been a little weird, since in our case the penis was on a female and the vagina belonged to a boy. It had been a kind of virginity loss for both of us, and while it may not have been totally enjoyable, it had certainly brought us closer.
>
> (2014, p. 187)

But even as trans youth bodies are under scrutiny, and sexual intimacy is a prominent source of both concern and celebration in the experiences of trans teens going through puberty and discovering their physical desires and attractions, this does not mean that there is an abundance of sexually explicit scenes or discussion within existing trans teen memoir. As noted above, there are a few reasons that teen authors are more reticent to discuss their sex lives in public, but dysphoria and a disconnect from genitalia and secondary sex characteristics is a prominent component.

Alex Bertie (2019) notes:

> The center of all my problems as a trans person is body dysphoria. It's the whole reason I needed to transition. Dysphoria is the feeling that the body I was born with does not match the gender identity in my head.
>
> (p. 9)

This is a very commonly used way of describing what it means to be transgender, for a non-transgender audience.[5] This dysphoria – or disconnect between mind and body in relation to gender – often leads to questions about sex, intimacy, and what it means to experience physical intimacy with another person, whether their partner is transgender or cisgender.

Self-confidence is an important factor in the level of (dis)comfort experienced by trans youth during moments of sexual intimacy in these memoirs. Regarding her development and early dating experience, in *Being Jazz* (2016) Jennings writes that the feeling of assertiveness 'along with the safety of knowing that male puberty wasn't going to hit because of my new hormone blockers, really helped build up my dating confidence' (p. 103). The use of hormone blockers allowed Jennings to feel confident in her body, to feel as though her body would not betray her in a moment of intimacy. For Zisin, the feeling of dysphoria was compounded by weight issues:

> Whenever I was in a situation when I couldn't exercise for a while, I would feel immense self-hatred and disconnection from my body. Often the disassociation I had with my body due to gender issues was masked under this deep insecurity about my weight.
>
> (2017, p. 41)

Almost all existing trans young adult memoirs noted here adhere to a common series of events that can, in the absence of further research and education, give the appearance of a single story, namely that the physical body is most often a hinderance to sexual gratification. Andrews, for instance, notes that he seemed to feel whole only in dreams:

> I'd recently started having dreams that I was screwing girls with my very own dick .... The dreams were sort of like the ones you have when you remember that you can fly, and it's always this wonderful surprise. *Oh, right,* you think. *How could I have forgotten that I have this ability?*
>
> (2014, p. 81)

In this dream, Andrews feels complete not only by having a penis, but by using it to have sex with girls, giving the impression that heterosexuality is the ultimate goal of his physical transition: 'I felt more strongly than ever the absence of something between my legs. Thanks to the [sex] dreams, I knew what I was missing out on, how this was *supposed* to feel' (p. 81). But physical sensation alone does not equate to sexuality. One can feel sexual urges and sensations without another person. Andrews is initially making assumptions about who he wants to have sex with, but this is complicated when he ends up dating Hill, and they end up discovering much more about the fluidity of sexuality when gender and physical bodies are also in a state of flux. For Andrews, things become even more complicated when – after he and Hill break up – he meets Austin. When they go on a date, Austin asks if Andrews is gay, at which point Andrews is forced to confront a few of his older assumptions about sexuality, such as originally coming out as gay, then dating Hill and being seen as straight:

> The question sort of startled me. No one had asked me that in forever., and I wasn't even sure how to answer. I was attracted to him, but that was the point—I was attracted to *him*. Not guys in general, or girls in general. I think what I feel now is something separate from even bisexual.
>
> 'I don't really think in terms like that anymore,' I said. 'I mean, I definitely thought you were cute when I first saw a picture of you, but now I understand that I'm attracted to a person's spirit first, then their body. And by that time it doesn't matter what that body is.'
>
> (2014, p. 229)

For Andrews, his physical transition and his shifting, fluid sexuality, were linked in many ways. It was not until he was comfortable with his body that he could be comfortable with his more fluid sexuality, and therefore was able to experience sex and relationships more comfortably: 'My body dysphoria disappeared when I was with him. What we felt for each other transcended physicality and made me as comfortable as I'd been in the beginning with Katie' (p. 236). Zisin similarly did not see sexuality as singular and stable: 'I wasn't sure I was a lesbian. I wasn't certain I would never fall in love with a man, or someone who wasn't a woman' (2017, p. 59). Their identification as nonbinary was a factor in the fluidity of their later understanding of sexuality and attraction.

Since the teenage years are so often marked with disconcerting physical changes, development, and explorations of intimacy, it is necessary to consider the many ways in which teens experience adolescence within a non-cisgender context. Consider, for example, the beginnings of physical intimacy in the lives of Hill and Andrews. While their desires are quite normal in a sense, the exact ways in which they experience sexual fulfillment are unique:

> I kept my shirt and binder on, but when we finally made love, it didn't occur to me for even on second that my girlfriend was putting her penis inside me. I was still a man, and she was still a woman, and this was simply a way for us to be as physically close to each other as humanly possible.
>
> (Andrews 2014, p. 168)

The importance of physicality and intimacy in this moment, renders the body parts involved immaterial. It appears, in contrast to the other sexually intimate pairings discussed throughout each of the memoirs, that this particular situation is made more comfortable and enjoyable because both people involved are trans and have therefore experienced similar dysphoric feelings around their bodies:

> As uncomfortable as I was with my vagina, I wanted to [have sex] as well. I'm a man stuck in a female body, but the parts I was born with still have the ability to feel good. And since Katie had the same dysphoria about her own genitals, I felt safer about making myself that vulnerable.
>
> (p. 167)

Here, readers can see that physical pleasure is still possible even when gender dysphoria is a dominant feeling for both individuals. But this does not mean that the preoccupation with the physical body, with gender dysphoria, goes away in other moments or with cisgender sexual partners. Although Andrews, Bertie, Hill, Jennings, and Zisin each note that they are not comfortable discussing genitals in most contexts, they each take the time to note the degrees of importance that genitals and other physical aspects of their bodies mean to them at different times, particularly before and after medical procedures that aid in physical transitions. In Hill's memoir, *Rethinking Normal*, she discusses bodily changes a number of times, often referencing surgeries and genitals, answering questions that are often asked without thinking when cis people are confused about non-cisnormative physicality:

> Four months before I'd started college, I'd had GRS (gender reassignment surgery) in which my penis had been turned surgically into a vagina. After years of experiencing shame and hatred of my body, it was an amazing feeling to finally have the right part down there. Not to mention, I could now flirt with guys and know that if something ever happened between us, I wouldn't have to awkwardly explain why I had a penis between my legs.
>
> (2014, p. 6)

While part of the excitement that Hill feels is related to her own physical body and satisfaction that it now matches her conceptualization of gender, another part of this excitement appears to be related to sexuality, or at least the idea of scaring off potential heterosexual partners who may be unwilling to be with a girl who has a penis. Transphobia is the cause of much stress for trans youth, and part of that comes from the fear of being seen as 'lying' for not immediately disclosing that part of oneself. Hill, then, is not only excited because of her new body, but because the anxiety and fear associated with being a girl whose body does not conform to expectations could have potentially put her into a dangerous situation. This is especially prescient in light of the number of murders of trans people around the world, and the defenses that perpetrators of violence use to put the blame on their victims.[6]

Andrews, in *Some Assembly Required*, explains his process of transition and its effects on his overall mental and physical health, particularly in terms of the need to conform to the idea that he is mentally ill – suffering from gender dysphoria – in order to rely on the medical establishment for approval:

> I would need to live publicly as a guy for one full year before I would be allowed to get any sort of surgery, and I'd have that period documented by a gender therapist. ... If he agreed in his professional opinion that I was indeed transgender, he could write a recommendation to a doctor for me to start hormone replacement therapy in the form of regular testosterone injections, which would deepen my voice, stop my periods, increase muscle definition, and help me grow facial hair .... After my year was up, I could start reviewing surgery options with my Mom.
>
> (2014, p. 121)

In *TransMission*, Alex Bertie lays out his memoir with a table of contents and specific topics throughout, including 'Hormone Treatment', 'Top Surgery', and 'Bottom Surgery'. In the chapter 'Starting My Physical Transition', Bertie spends a significant amount of time detailing the frustrating and obstacle-laden process of navigating the National Health Service in the UK: "Just getting a referral to a gender identity clinic was a struggle, due to a lot of local general practitioners having no experience with trans patients. The first time I opened up to a doctor was a disaster" (p. 153). Uncomfortable experiences with the medical profession are an all too common part of trans life.

Continuing in this vein, Jennings – who is the youngest of the four trans authors (age fifteen at the time of publication), and the one who began physical transitioning the earliest – writes about a number of experiences related to medical care, psychological care, and the process of transition: 'Mom has a master's degree in clinical counseling', she explains, 'so she decided to start doing some research in her copy of the *Diagnostics and Statistics Manual of Mental Disorders* about what I was experiencing' (p. 9). She goes on later to discuss her very early experiences with a psychologist – 'I was three when we went in for the appointment' (p. 11) – and her future insights into hormone blockers and medical interventions.

It should be noted that even with all the discussion of fluidity and physical changes and medical procedures, gender binaries are still dominant within published work by trans teens. All of the memoirs discussed in this chapter end up adhering to a gender binary when it comes to each of the authors' decisions around gender expression, pronouns, and self-identification. Bertie, for example, explains:

> [I]f you look around today's society, people are breaking out of these stereotypes all the time. In recent years, people have begun to think

of gender as more of a spectrum with people not just falling on the 'male' or 'female' ends, but everywhere in between—and sometimes, nowhere on the spectrum at all.

(2019, p. 15)

Those who identify outside of a gender binary are often left out of traditional publishing and relegated to the less formal, yet more accessible, space of online media and social media platforms, with the exception of the author of *Finding Nevo*.

Zisin reveals the complicated understanding of sexuality in relation to gender when their classmates try to dictate what constitutes 'real' sex:

> Boys in my year level tried to argue with me that lesbian sex isn't real sex, showing me the definition of sexual intercourse in the dictionary as evidence against my identity, despite many of them having a rather large collection of lesbian porn on their computers.
>
> (2017, p. 60)

Zisin complicates this understanding further when discussing fluid sexual identity: 'The fear of uncertainty around my sexuality dissipated as I began to recognize there is no true certainty in something that is destined to be fluid' (p. 63). Furthermore, as Zisin grew older, they came to understand gender as even more complex outside of a binary definition:

> The more I thought about my gender and the more I was passing as male, the more I realised I wasn't a man. There was always a hesitation I felt when saying I was a man, as if I knew it wasn't the entire truth. I felt I would only be taken seriously if I was transitioning from one to the other.
>
> (p. 178)

The majority of mainstream instances of trans representation, including the body of work that is trans youth memoir, relies on a binary male-to-female or female-to-male transition. This is a very specific type of transgender existence that is easier for non-transgender audiences to understand. The fact that Zisin is not conforming to this conceptualization of transness disrupts the more commonly represented transition narrative: as they are seen as male, they realize that male is not how they identify, thus breaking down the binary that so often exists even within trans representation in mainstream media. As such, Zisin is not taken seriously as a transgender subject unless they conform to the notion of transitioning from one gender to 'the other'. This is similar, in a way, to the way Andrews complicates a gay/straight sexuality binary by noting how attraction works for him, not relying specifically on gender.

The existence of nonbinary and genderqueer youth disrupts a male/female binary in ways that help to ensure people are confronted with a reality that disrupts their assumptions and troubles their ideas of gender and sexuality. This is of particular interest as it relates to intimacy and how people with nonconforming physical bodies engage in and negotiate sex, as in the situation of Hill and Andrews being intimate with each other in ways that differ from how they are intimate with cisgender individuals. *Finding Nevo: How I Confused Everyone*, then, helps to disrupt gender binaries and the idea that gender is inherently connected to certain physical characteristics, such as genitalia.

Conclusions

Trans youth are both the same and incredibly different from their cisgender peers. Trans youth are human beings who want intimacy and connection, and privacy, just as so many others are afforded because they are cisgender or straight – in other words, seen as 'normal'. Publication of memoirs written by trans teens is both an important step forward, and also a difficult and complicated way for the authors to become public figures, open to interrogation from those who may be respectfully interested and also those who may be overly inquisitive. Sex and sexuality are important components of adolescent development[7] and, within these memoirs, sex is certainly not erased, but at the same time it is the entire life that is important, not simply the actions that a physical body can engage in. There is a tension within the genre of memoir that must be considered in light of these educational components.

Andrews, Bertie, Hill, Jennings, and Zisin provide readers with a window into their own personal experiences, while also providing a possible mirror for other teens, giving readers a safe space to question and explore. Their knowledge of certain elements of transitioning and sexuality provides readers with a source of information, whether for the purposes of educating cisgender readers or reflecting for trans and nonbinary readers a similar experience. In an article on trans YouTube star Miles McKenna, a number of fans pointed out that it is important and necessary for them to have positive examples to guide their own development:

> 'When you're a closeted transgender teen it's really important to have people to look up to,' says Leo, a 16-year-old in the Pacific Northwest. 'Miles has created this support for people who maybe don't know who they are or aren't totally sure.'
>
> (Lorenz, 2018, np)

As young celebrities, these teen memoirists, who sometimes start out as YouTube personalities and reality stars, provide a positive example for young readers, regardless of the reader's gender and/or sexuality.

In the same way that early autobiographies by trans adults were a way of explaining personal history, decisions and actions, the memoirs discussed here are also a form of explanation, but for a younger audience and with a different political and social goal in mind. In the end, trans teen memoirs are not only a vital space for young trans people to safely explore their own identity and development, but they can be a powerful tool to build understanding, empathy, and a greater knowledge of genders and sexualities outside of cisnormative curricula and media representations.

Notes

1 'Gender identity disorder' was the original term for 'gender dysphoria' in the *Diagnostics and Statistics Manual of Mental Disorders*, but was dropped in 2013 in an effort to reduce stigma around transgender individuals (Russo, 2017). But even so, gender dysphoria is a polarizing term, seen by activists as pathologizing trans people, but also seen as necessary by medical professionals to label a person's distress and guide their treatment (Russo, 2016). Although the term is still being debated, the majority of trans youth memoirs continue to use the term as a way of describing feelings of dissociation from the body they were born with and the gender they were assigned at birth.
2 The 'Big Five' publishers are HarperCollins, Penguin Random House, Macmillan, Simon & Schuster, and Hachette. Prior to *If I Was Your Girl*, a few other novels had been self-published or released by smaller publishing houses with a more limited reach than the Big Five (Stoeve 2020).
3 Although this book is a trans memoir and guide for trans youth, the content does not include anything with regard to sex and intimacy and will therefore not be discussed in much detail throughout the chapter.
4 This is not a comprehensive list, although it is representative of the current landscape of traditionally published trans teen memoir.
5 The 'wrong body narrative', a way of describing the feeling of disconnect that some trans people feel between their body and their gender, is useful in its simplicity, but it is also important to note that it is not a universal experience, even though it is commonly used within literature for youth, whether fiction or memoir. Transgender youth, like all youth, experience the world in many different ways and, as such, it is important to remember that even though it is a commonly used narrative trope, the 'wrong body narrative' is not how all youth understand or experience being transgender.
6 According to *Forbes*, '331 trans and gender diverse people have been killed this year [2019]' (Wareham 2019, np). Since the annual reports from Transrespect versus Transphobia Worldwide began in 2008, 'they have recorded 3314 deaths' (np).
7 Sex and sexuality are often seen as an inherent part of growing up in general, and although the memoirs discussed in this chapter all include youth who desire sexual intimacy with others, some trans youth are asexual and/or aromantic, and though they are not prominently represented or discussed, their existence needs to be acknowledged and affirmed.

References

Andrews, A 2014, *Some Assembly Required: The Not-So-Secret Life of a Transgender Teen*, Simon & Schuster, New York.
Beemyn, BG 2015, 'Autobiography, transsexual', in *glbtq Encyclopedia*, retrieved 3 March 2019, www.glbtqarchive.com/literature/autobio_transsexual_L.pdf.

Bertie, A 2019, *Transmission: My Quest to a Beard*, LBYR, New York.

Bornstein, K 1994, *Gender Outlaw: On Men, Women, and the Rest of Us*, Routledge, New York.

Bruhm, S and Hurley, N 2004, *Curiouser: On the Queerness of Children*, U of Minnesota Press, Minneapolis.

Clark, KE 2013, *Freakboy*, FSG, New York.

Cronn-Mills, K 2012, *Beautiful Music for Ugly Children*, Flux, New York.

Feinberg, L 1993, *Stone Butch Blues*, Firebrand, Ithaca, NY.

Hill, KR 2014, *Rethinking Normal: A Memoir in Transition*, Simon & Schuster, New York.

Hussey, R 2018, 'What are the major differences between memoir and autobiography?', *BookRiot*, retrieved 3 March 2019, https://bookriot.com/2018/11/27/difference-between-memoir-and-autobiography/.

Jennings, J 2016, *Being Jazz: My Life as a (Transgender) Teen*, Crown, New York.

Katcher, B 2009, *Almost Perfect*, Delacorte, New York.

Kirby, DL and Kirby, D 2010, 'Contemporary memoir: a 21st-century genre ideal for teens', *English Journal*, vol. 99, no. 4 pp. 22–29.

Kuklin, S (ed.) 2014, *Beyond Magenta: Transgender Teens Speak Out*, Candlewick, Somerville, MA.

Lorenz, T 2018, 'Transitioning on YouTube', *The Atlantic*, retrieved 12 February 2020, www.theatlantic.com/technology/archive/2018/06/how-youtube-star-miles-mckenna-is-helping-a-generation-of-fans-navigate-their-identity/563510/.

McKenna, M 2020, *Out! How to Be Your Authentic Self*, Amulet, New York.

Nodelman, P 1992, 'The other: orientalism, colonialism, and children's literature', *Children's Literature Association Quarterly*, vol. 17, no. 1, pp. 29–35.

Peters, JA 2004, *Luna*, Little Brown, New York.

Steinmetz, K 2014, 'The transgender tipping point', *Time*, retrieved December 2019, https://time.com/135480/transgender-tipping-point/.

Stoeve, R 2020, 'The YA/MG trans & nonbinary voices masterlist', *Ray Stoeve*, retrieved 6 February 2020, https://raystoeve.com/the-ya-trans-ownvoices-masterlist/.

Wareham, J 2019, 'Murdered, hanged and lynched: 331 trans people killed this year', *Forbes*, retrieved August 2020, www.forbes.com/sites/jamiewareham/2019/11/18/murdered-hanged-and-lynched-331-trans-people-killed-this-year/#2d5873882d48.

Wittlinger, E 2007, *Parrotfish*, Simon & Schuster, New York.

Zisin, N 2017, *Finding Nevo: How I Confused Everyone*, Black Dog Books, Newtown.

5 'Can Gay Boys Have Bromances?'

Regulating Masculinity and Sexuality in Gay Young Adult Novels

Troy Potter

In Bill Konigsberg's award-winning *Openly Straight* (2013), the gay male protagonist Rafe leaves Boulder, Colorado, to enrol in an all-boys boarding school in Boston, New England.[1] Feeling that he is defined only by his sexuality in his hometown, Rafe believes he can re-invent himself at his new school by re-entering the closet. Rafe's retreat to the andro-centric microcosm of the all-boys school enables Konigsberg to explore the tensions that exist between male homosociality and homosexuality, in part because Rafe begins to feel conflicted as he forges new friendships while hiding a part of himself. When he explains his reasoning to a friend back in Boulder, he is confronted with the question: 'Can gay boys have bromances?' (Konigsberg 2013, p. 206). This question is also addressed to varying degrees by the two other novels discussed below: Tim Federle's *The Great American Whatever* (2016) and Will Walton's *Anything Could Happen* (2015). All three novels depict friendships between a gay male protagonist and his straight male friend and are representative of sev-eral contemporary gay young adult (YA) novels that explore friendships between gay and straight boys.[2]

In this chapter, I propose a new subgenre of lesbian, gay, bisexual, transgender, intersex and queer (LGBTIQ) YA literature has emerged: the gay bromance novel. I define a 'gay bromance' as an intimate non-sexual friendship between a gay male and his straight male best friend. The gay bromance subgenre responds to both a revisioning of acceptable mascu-line characteristics and an increase in societal acceptance of homosexu-ality. Focusing as it does on male friendships, rather than exclusively on sexuality, the implied reader is one who identifies as male, not necessarily gay or queer. That said, the gay male protagonist's sexuality is perceived as a potential threat to the boys' platonic relationship, and thus sexu-ality and sex are implicated in the boys' enactment of acceptable mas-culinities and male friendships. In responding to and shaping norms and conventions about male intimacy and sexuality, the gay bromance sub-genre of LGBTIQ YA has implications for the construction and enactment of both straight and gay masculinities. In demonstrating that gay boys can have bromances, these novels expand our understanding of masculinity and the kinds of male friendships that are possible. However, limitations are placed on the expression of the gay friend's homosexuality, which ultimately maintains the subordination of homosexual subjectivities.

Like all literature, YA fiction responds to and shapes social concerns, including those relating to the gendered practices of the implied reader (Mallan 2009; Potter 2018). For YA literature that represents LGBTIQ characters, this ideological function specifically relates to the normalization of variant sexualities in an attempt to show the implied reader that she/he/they are not alone. The three novels under analysis in this chapter are also indicative of a more general marked increase in the number of YA novels that depict LGBTIQ characters, as noted by Christine A Jenkins and Michael Cart in *Representing the Rainbow in Young Adult Literature: LGBTQ+ Content Since 1969* (2018). Since 2004, the list of titles that engage with LGBTIQ issues has continued to grow, and several awards and honours categories now exist for LGBTIQ children's and YA fiction.[3]

Despite this increase in literary representation of variant sexualities (or because of it), there is a need to examine such literature to identify deep-seated cultural habits and practices that preserve, rather than redress, exclusionary processes related to sexuality and gender. As Thomas Crisp demonstrates through his reading of homophobia in contemporary YA novels, when novels depict homosexual characters through heteronormative frameworks, they 'often actually work to continue the invisibility of gay males by filtering queer existence and distancing readers' (2009, p. 345). In other words, when the representation of gay characters is filtered through a heteronormative lens, homosexuality and homosexual experiences are rendered 'safe' because they are constrained and sanitized. While superficially appearing to be inclusive, expansive or progressive, such novels ultimately reinscribe the very ideologies and intolerances they seek to redress. Similarly, I argue that the gay bromance novel places limitations on the gay characters' enactment of their masculinity, and that sexuality is regulated by the homosocial expectations of the bromance.

In part, the emergence of the gay bromance subgenre is in response to changing social attitudes, beliefs and opinions about masculinity and homosexuality. This is true of LGBTIQ YA fiction more generally and is reflected in the taxonomy of LGBTIQ YA fiction that Jenkins and Cart have developed based on the ideological agenda of individual novels. They identify three categories: 'homosexual visibility', 'gay assimilation' and 'queer consciousness/community' (2018, pp. xiv–xv). These categories of LGBTIQ fiction can be placed along a continuum that demonstrates increasing levels of societal acceptance of non-heterosexual identities and the potential revisioning of heteronormative discourses. Novels of homosocial visibility are predominantly about a coming out experience but still position the LGBTIQ character outside of a heteronormative paradigm.

Gay assimilation novels are defined as those that include characters who 'just happen to be gay' (Jenkins and Cart 2018, p. xv); homosexuality is just one of many forms of sexuality, all of which are seemingly accepted. In novels of queer consciousness, LGBTIQ characters are represented in a culturally accurate manner, demonstrating how LGBTIQ characters view themselves, and thus arguably position readers of any sexual orientation to feel empathy for them.

The categories Jenkins and Cart identify can be thought of as subgenres of LGBTIQ YA literature in several ways. First, they stress that an individual text may contain elements of more than one of these categories, which resonates with Charles L Briggs and Richard Bauman's claim that 'genre is quintessentially intertextual' (1992, p. 147). The novels discussed in this chapter contain elements of all three categories that Jenkins and Cart identify: the male protagonists who 'just happen to be gay' nevertheless have to come out at some stage, and the reader is positioned to empathize with them as they overcome their challenges, which is facilitated by the first-person narration. The ideological function of LGBTIQ YA fiction further establishes the generic conventions of this body of literature. As Amy Devitt proposes, genre is 'a reciprocal dynamic within which individuals' actions construct and are constructed by recurring context of situation, context of culture, and context of genres' (2004, p. 31). Thought of in this way, the various subgenres characteristic of LGBTIQ YA fiction function as a nexus between implied readers and contemporary concerns about sexuality and gender. Each subgenre reflects, shapes and responds to changing public opinions, attitudes and beliefs about homosexuality and associated issues.[4]

The emergence of the gay bromance subgenre is illustrative of the tensions created by the wider acceptance and visibility of homosexuality on the one hand and the expansion and increase in permissible male homosocial intimacy on the other. As I demonstrate below through my reading of three YA novels, the success of the represented gay bromances is made possible by a revisioning of acceptable straight masculine behaviours and is simultaneously contingent on the regulation of gay masculinity. In this chapter, I take up Michael DeAngelis' proposition to read the bromance as 'a litmus test for discerning not only the extent to which homosexuality has been assimilated into contemporary culture but also the degree of comfort (or discomfort) that this culture actually experiences with such assimilated homosexuality' (2014, pp. 14–15). I first offer a framework with which to read the gay bromance subgenre. I then apply elements of this framework to consider how masculinity and homosexuality are constructed within each of the three YA novels. My interest is not only in how gay bromances respond to and reconfigure contemporary masculinities, but also in the impact they have on the positioning of gay and straight masculinities. Put another way, how does the advent of the gay bromance in YA literature regulate male sexuality?

Reading the Gay Bromance

The neologism 'bromance' derives from brother and romance and was arguably popularized around 2005 when there was a sharp increase in the amount of on-screen male–male friendships in popular film and television (DeAngelis 2014). Bromance refers to an intimate and supportive asexual relationship between two straight men. Whereas simple romance—if there is such a thing—is often oriented towards sex, the 'bro' in bromance regulates the sexual aspect of the male relationship, emphasizing both heteronormativity and homophobia to allow love and intimacy to be expressed between two straight men (Chen 2012). Thus, the rise of the bromance has necessarily resulted in shifts in our understanding of what is considered to be acceptable male behaviour, reconfiguring the traditional boundaries of masculinity and male sexuality. Consequently, bromances can be a starting point to deconstruct the supposedly fixed boundaries of masculinity and male sexuality, and to analyze both the expansive and repressive aspects of the bromance within a climate of increasing acceptance of homosexuality.

David McRuer's (2006) theorization of 'flexible bodies' in contemporary popular culture provides some insight into how bromances impact on various masculine subjectivities. In his queering of disability studies, McRuer emphasizes the flexibility of individual subjectivities—or bodies—to propose that the flexible body is one that is both tolerated more, and more tolerant within, an environment of change. For McRuer, flexible bodies are able to manage moments of uncertainty because 'he or she can perform wholeness through each recurring crisis […]; ultimately, they adapt and perform as if the crisis had never happened' (McRuer 2006, p. 17). Although intimacy between men may introduce a moment of homosexual crisis within a bromance, as mentioned above, the 'bro' forecloses homosexual intimacy, thus enabling straight men to experience and express affection for one another, characteristics that have been traditionally excluded from the enactment of straight masculinity. Bromances thus expand our understanding of male heterosexuality and revise masculine dynamics. In doing so, they also provide social and emotional benefits for straight men, including offering them a new social space for emotional disclosure, social fulfilment, and better conflict resolution (Robinson et al. 2017).

However, the ability of flexible subjects to adapt and maintain the appearance of wholeness can negatively impact on other subject positions. According to McRuer, 'the heterosexual, able-bodied subject, as well as the postmodern culture that produced him or her, can easily disavow how much the subjective contraction and expansion of able-bodied heterosexuality […] are actually contingent on compliant queer, disabled bodies' (2006, pp. 18–19). In other words, when dominant forms of masculinity appropriate characteristics and behaviours of subordinated masculinities (or femininities), these subject positions are simultaneously restructured.

Thus, while bromances offer some men the opportunity to experience intimate friendships and emotional connection, they also exclude those who fall outside of the regulatory framework, and thus repress elements of alternative masculinities. As Chen (2012) argues, bromances maintain heteronormative hierarchies: they encourage men to stay within rigid boundaries of sexuality norms, restrain the pool of intimate friends men can have, and reinforce passive homophobia and the subordination of gay men in our culture. Gay men thus may experience bromances as a source of subordination because their homosexuality is perceived to threaten the asexuality that is integral to the intimate male friendship. For a gay man to be included in a bromance, he must curb his homosexuality to ensure the platonic nature of the relationship. This pattern of expansion and contraction of masculine subjectivities characteristic of bromances establishes a tension within the ideological function of the three gay bromance YA novels discussed below.

The Limits of Coming Out in a Bromance

Tim Federle's *The Great American Whatever* demonstrates the restrictions gay boys must internalize and place on their homosexuality when they come out in a bromance. Genre is also implicated when the gay protagonist, Quinn, suggests his life (and thus, the novel), is 'a fairly standard coming-of-age LGBT genre film, with a somewhat macabre horror twist [the death of his sister]' (2016, p. 33). Despite Quinn's apprehension that his life may start 'veering toward romantic comedy' (Federle 2016, p. 33), it nevertheless does, although not just in terms of gay romantic love. The bromance genre adapts the romantic comedy genre and applies it to an intense male friendship, which sees two men develop a friendship, experience a conflict, and then reconcile (Brook 2015, p. 253). This trajectory is evident in *The Great American Whatever*: Quinn and his best friend, Geoff, begin the novel as close friends, but their relationship becomes strained when Quinn begins dating his first boyfriend and, more significantly, when Quinn discovers Geoff secretly dated his late sister. By novel's end, however, the boys reconcile and are once more supportive of each other. That neither boy has a love interest at the end of the novel further demonstrates the extent to which the novel partakes of the bromance genre in privileging male friendship over other intimate relationships.

For a text to be considered LGBTIQ YA, a protagonist's variant sexuality must be made apparent to the reader. This is because such texts circulate within a heteronormative society, and frequently non-heterosexual identities are rendered invisible. This is not to say the process of coming out (and the issues associated with it) is always the central theme of LGBTIQ novels (as it is in Jenkins and Cart's 'homosexual visibility' subgenre of LGBTIQ YA fiction), but one that must be addressed at some point to establish the non-normative sexuality of the protagonist(s). Additionally, coming out should not be considered an individual event; rather, it is an iterative process that LGBTIQ people must constantly negotiate. This coming out process is mediated by both partners in a gay bromance: for a true friendship to develop, the gay friend must first come out, enabling the straight friend to not simply know the 'true' person, but to accept his sexuality and support him in future coming-out episodes. Variations of this pattern are evident in all three novels discussed in this chapter.

Rather than redressing stereotypical aspects of gay sexuality, the depiction of Quinn's homosexuality, including his coming out, reaffirms the negative perspective of effeminacy in men, especially gay men. At the beginning of *The Great American Whatever*, Quinn is not out to his friends, but he alludes to his homosexuality on the second page of the novel. The use of self-deprecating humour demonstrates both the subordination and invisibility of his homosexuality: 'Alas, no fairy. Other than, you know, me' (Federle 2016, p. 2). In many ways, the novel reiterates gay stereotypes as excessive and artistic, as evidenced by Quinn, a budding screenwriter, who is 'Too controlling. Too sensitive. Always just a little *too*' (Federle 2016, p. 109, italics in original). Quinn's feminized positioning as a gay man, though, is disrupted early in the novel when he accidentally shaves his head, which makes him look 'handsome as *whoa*' and 'like a *man*' (Federle 2016, p. 30, italics in original). His physical more masculine appearance negates his somewhat effeminate behaviours, which reaffirms the male body as the site of masculine identity. It also supports Ron Becker's observation that expressions of homosocial male bonding within a bromance are 'no longer structured by the abjection of the gay Other, but they remain firmly structured by the abjection of effeminacy' (2014, p. 252). Becker's observation can be broadened and applied to the enactment of gay masculinity in today's (more) gay-friendly era: to be a valued male member of society, gay men cannot be *too* feminine. On the first night he sports his new look, Quinn establishes a gay love interest. In other words, removing his long brown hair renders Quinn more visible: he is acceptably remasculinized and thus embodies a valued and attractive masculinity, regardless of his sexuality.

Just as Quinn's homosexuality is established for the reader at the beginning of the narrative so, too, is the heterosexuality of his best friend, Geoff. Federle once again reanimates stereotypes—this time gay and straight—to do so. In the first instance, Geoff's penchant for wearing 'outfits [that] never even *fit* right' (Federle 2016, p. 7, italics in original) reiterates the perception that straight men lack fashion sense, while Geoff's naming of his farts maintains the association of scatological and masculine humour. Although scatological humour can be used to 'reduce[] homosexuals both physically and sexually to excrement' (Mauldin 2000, p. 82), Geoff does not use this kind of humour to ridicule or belittle Quinn. Quinn's sardonic remarks, on the other hand, sets him up as a glib voyeur, critiquing life without requiring him to participate in it.[5] Despite these stereotypes, the novel indicates there are shifts in what is considered acceptable in terms of gay and straight masculinities. Quinn struggles with his sexuality and aspects of his homosexuality are constrained in order for him to embody an acceptable masculinity. Geoff, on the other hand, is a sensitive young man secure in his heterosexuality; he is able to negotiate moments of queer tension, thereby expanding what is considered valued straight male behaviour. The adaptability of both Quinn's and Geoff's masculinities demonstrates the reciprocity that exists within masculine gender orders, supporting the idea of 'flexible bodies' (McRuer 2006) within gendered hegemonies.

What is socially acceptable for straight men, though, is not necessarily so for gay men. The willingness of the boys to express their emotions within the narrative demonstrates the shifting boundaries of acceptable masculine behaviours within bromances. Whereas Geoff readily cries, for example, Quinn does not. This may be owing to the novel's attempt to disrupt a heterosexual model of masculinity that permits men to express their emotions. That said, gay or queer men who reside outside the accepted order are frequently associated with the feminine and must regulate their behaviour and appearance to fit within the constraints of acceptable masculinity. Quinn's contemplation about crying in American society reveals the tension that exists between acceptable male behaviours: 'It never dawns on me that as an American, you're legally allowed to cry in front of others. Maybe I've just seen too many old movies. Tough guys never cry in old movies' (Federle 2016, p. 22). The Hollywood tough guy masculinity with which Quinn associates differs from the modern American masculinity that Geoff embodies. Moreover, Quinn alludes to the strict regulation of gender that exists within modern society. His homosexuality positions him outside of the heteronormative framework, and thus any action that is perceived to be feminine—crying, for example—has the potential to further subordinate him within the established gender order. By associating with the tough-guy masculinity, Quinn is able to enact an acceptable masculinity, distancing himself from the feminine and thereby securing a valued masculine position. Geoff, on the other hand, is able to cry and exhibit some traditionally feminine behaviours because his masculinity is already always accepted due to his heterosexuality.

Differences between what is considered acceptable for gay and straight men, however, reveal an underlying instability within the gay bromance. At the beginning of the novel, Quinn believes that straight men will not even get close enough to another guy to knife him as '[t]hat would require a degree of closeness […] they're genetically incapable of' (Federle 2016, p. 8). The corollary to this is that closeness is an inherent and biological characteristic of gay masculinity and gay male relationships. Yet intimacy between men is also fundamental to bromances, and it must be regulated in order to maintain the platonic aspect of the relationship. Although Quinn comes to understand that there can be closeness between male friends, the navigation of the boys' bromantic intimacy demonstrates the way in which heterosexual masculinities are expanded within the bromance genre and gay masculinities are rendered complicit. Geoff readily expresses intimacy towards Quinn; he demonstrates compassion and empathy following Quinn's sister's death, and unquestioningly accepts (and is aware of) Quinn's homosexuality. Moreover, Geoff plays cupid to Quinn and his love interest, Amir, further demonstrating a shift in gay–straight relations in a gay-friendly era. To maintain his bromance with Geoff, Quinn must abide by straight rules, engaging in 'straight-boy half hugs' (Federle 2016, p. 70) and reassuring Geoff that he is not sexually interested in him.

Thus, there are caveats for a gay bromance to function. For Geoff to be accepting, he first needs to be secure in his own sexuality so that he does not feel exposed or threatened by another man's homosexuality. Concomitantly, there is an expectation that Quinn's homosexual desire will not be directed towards Geoff. Despite the asexuality of the boys' friendship being established in the opening chapter when Quinn informs the reader that Geoff is 'not [his] type' (Federle 2016, p. 10), Quinn's coming out nevertheless exposes the inherent threat homosexuality poses to gay bromances:

> 'You know when we were little,' [Quinn says], 'and I used to put your sister's ballet tutus on my head, before we knew it was kind of strange for boys to do that?'
>
> Geoff puts his palm up to [Quinn's] face and stands. 'Quinn, is this about you being gay? I literally don't care at all.[…] I've known for, like, ever. Unless you're confessing that you're in love with me—' He stops. His face goes a little white. 'Oh God, I mean—if you are, I'd be flattered, but—'
>
> 'Ew, Geoff. Please. You name your farts. Seriously.'
>
> We laugh. We laugh hard.
>
> (Federle 2016, p.p 73–74)

Even though the two boys are able to laugh off the queer disruption Quinn's homosexuality causes, it nevertheless demonstrates a moment of straight panic, as Geoff experiences anxiety about how Quinn perceives his sexuality and feels the need to reassert his heterosexuality.

How to Love in a Bromance

The threat homosexual desire poses to gay bromances is a central theme in Will Walton's *Anything Could Happen*. Tretch, the gay male protagonist of the novel, must learn to overcome his infatuation with his straight best friend, Matt. In the opening line of the novel, Tretch declares both his homosexuality and his love for his best friend to the reader: 'Let me tell you about the first time I knew for sure I was in love with Matt Gooby' (Walton 2015, p. 1). While Tretch is secretly in love with Matt, Matt is in love with Amy, a fellow classmate, and Amy's role in the novel supports DeAngelis' (2014, p. 23) observation that although female characters may be confined to secondary roles, they nevertheless serve vital narrative functions. In the first instance, Amy's presence enables Matt to affirm his heterosexuality. In the second, she forces Tretch to come to terms with his unrequited love, given Tretch must also perform the duties of best friend, helping Matt to achieve his romantic heterosexual goal. Tretch states what he believes to be his problem in an internet search: '*i'm gay. how do i fall out of love with my straight best friend?*' (Walton 2015, p. 177, italics in original). His enquiry, though, is not entirely accurate. Tretch does not need to 'fall out of love' with Matt; rather, he must learn how to negotiate his sexual desire for Matt in order to develop a more socially acceptable love for his best friend. My interest in *Anything Could Happen*, then, is in how the experience and enactment of love within a gay bromance regulates the expression of male homosexuality.

An understanding of the Greek types of love is helpful in analyzing appropriate forms of male love within a bromance.[6] If the intimacy between men within a bromance is considered to be akin to *philia*, or brotherly love, then Tretch's homosexual yearning for Matt conforms to *eros*, passion and intense desire. Unlike Quinn in *The Great American Whatever*, Tretch remains in the closet for much of *Anything Could Happen*. Consequently, Tretch's hidden sexuality and unresolved infatuation with Matt is what jeopardizes the bromance. Throughout the narrative, Tretch's desire for Matt is represented as unacceptable homosexual behavior that threatens the platonic aspect of the boys' bromance. Tretch is aware of the danger his erotic desire poses to his bromance, and he constantly restrains his homosexual urges to ensure his friendship remains asexual. To do so, Tretch regulates both his thoughts and body, as evident during his fantasizations:

> My hands are cold, so I slide them into the pockets of my jeans, eyeing Matt's pockets as I do, picturing what it would be like to slide my hands into them, an imaginary moment where he allows it, welcomes it even. No Amy Sinks, just him and me, my hands flattened, passing over the terrain of his hips, the front of his thighs, and finally in between. *Rooftop, through-the-pocket hand job. Is that even possible?* But that's as far as I'll allow myself to go for now. I take my hands from my pockets and cup them together, doing my best to ignore the feathery feeling at the tip of my semi-hard as it tests the bounds of my underwear.
>
> (Walton 2015, p. 109, italics in original)

This is in stark contrast to the supportive relationship that is maintained throughout *The Great American Whatever*, which is made possible by Quinn's early admission that he does not find Geoff attractive, thereby ensuring the boys' bromance remains *philial*.

Walton's use of intertextual references throughout *Anything Could Happen* reiterate the unacceptability of Tretch's infatuation and the threat it poses to intimate male relationships. Walton's passing reference to two novels—Jack Kerouac's *On the Road* (1957) and John Knowles' *A Separate Peace* (1959)—emphasizes his interest in exploring male–male relationships that verge on obsession. Of more import to the narrative's ideology is Tretch's queer reading of F Scott Fitzgerald's *The Great Gatsby* (1925). Tretch explains to the reader:

> I mean, for the whole book Nick Carraway is totally *obsessed* with Jay Gatsby. I mean, that's why the story he's narrating is called *The Great Gatsby* and not something like *Daisy Is Crazy*.
> I'm probably narrating a book right now called *The Great Gooby* and don't even realize it.
>
> (Walton 2015, p. 33, italics in original)

The title of Walton's book, though, is not *The Great Gooby*; rather, it is *Anything Could Happen*, another intertextual reference, this time to an Ellie Goulding song. Whereas Nick in *The Great Gatsby* is unable to move beyond his obsession with Gatsby, the last line of Goulding's song—'But I don't think I need you'—indicates Tretch's ability to move beyond his infatuation and to transition from *eros* to *philia*. Ironically, then, anything cannot happen: Tretch's desire is not reciprocated nor will it be consummated, which once again demonstrates the limits placed on the gay partner of a bromance. More than this, the use of intertextual references reinforces the social function of literature, generally, and the gay bromance novel, specifically, to respond to and shape the implied reader's gendered practices. When Tretch selects the two novels to purchase in the local bookshop, he feels he is meant to read them, that 'Maybe they'll teach me something I don't already know about love, about being in love, or even just about being a person' (Walton 2015, p. 38). Like the novels Walton references, the gay bromance genre functions to teach readers to know something (new) about gay–straight male friendships, sexuality and masculinity, namely how gay boys must limit aspects of their sexuality.

Tretch's regulation of his homosexuality demonstrates the intrinsic conformity of gay masculinity within heteronormative dictates. It also reveals the illusionary instability of heterosexual masculinity and the importance of regulating male desire to maintain heteronormative order. According to David Buchbinder, the idealization of the youthful male body in popular culture renders the male body 'not only an object to be *imitated* by men in the culture, but also, regardless of their sexual orientations or preferences, to be *desired* by them' (2013, p. 144, italics in original). The blurring between imitation and desire creates the potential for slippage between heterosexual and homosexual objectifications of the male body. In the text, gazing at another boys' nudity is permissible in the all-male space of the locker room. This may be because of the imposed disruption between the homosocial and homosexual within Anglo-Western society (Sedgwick 2015, pp. 1–2). If male homosociality depends on the exclusion of homosexuality, as a homosocial space, the boys' locker room can permit male nudity. However, when Matt undresses in the private and intimate space of his bedroom, Tretch's homosexuality permeates homosocial boundaries:

> I want to stop thinking about this.
> I mean, it's not like I haven't seen Matt naked before. I've seen him undress in the locker room loads of times, but that's different, way different, in fact. Being alone with him in a room—*his* room, no less—watching him slide out of his clothes so casually, just talking to me, as if this is part of our routine and shortly we'll be brushing out teeth together, turning off the lights, and crawling into bed.
> (Walton 2015, p. 116–7, italics in original)

Central to Tretch's regulation of his homosexual desire is an understanding of the appropriate ways men are able to look at other male bodies and the spaces within which looking is permissible. Setting is important in terms of both producing and regulating homosexual desire, and Tretch's rumination about the impropriety of his desiring gaze demonstrates how homosexuality must be always already regulated to maintain homosocial order and the asexuality of (gay) bromances.

Fundamental to the boys' bromance is the establishment of a reciprocal platonic intimacy, much as it is in *The Great American Whatever*. In *Anything Could Happen*, Tretch is able to subordinate his erotic desire to support Matt in his romantic endeavours and, in doing so, 'can't help but be happy' (Walton 2015, p. 29) for Matt when he becomes romantically involved with Amy. Matt reciprocates the *philial* love he receives from Tretch, as evident by the concern he expresses about Tretch being lonely once Matt moves back to New York. This leads Tretch to realize that Matt is 'an *actual* best friend. This is him saying, *I care about you, Tretch Farm, and I'll still care about you even after I'm gone*' (Walton 2015, p. 240, italics in original). For both boys, it seems the bromance is more important than their other relationships, which reflects research that shows men find bromantic relationships more emotionally satisfying than heterosexual relationships (Robinson et al. 2017).

Yet, honesty is foundational to any relationship, and Tretch realizes that he must come out if Matt is to have 'the chance to love the full [him]' (Walton 2015, p. 240), even if it might change their relationship. When he does so, Matt unquestioningly accepts Tretch's homosexuality, just as Geoff does Quinn's in *The Great American Whatever*. Unlike Geoff who experiences gay panic, Matt has no such trepidation. Rather, it is Tretch who becomes panic-stricken, evidencing his internalized homophobia. Throughout their friendship, Tretch and Matt have been naked in front of each other and have slept next to each other in the same bed. In making public his homosexuality, Tretch introduces a potential threat to the boys' bromance, and the trepidation he experiences demonstrates the instability homosexuality causes to bromances:

> I want to leave the room before Matt drops his pants. Honestly, I'm not even sure if he *will* drop his pants now that I've told him [that I'm gay]. That would just be disrespectful, right? Or maybe it would be disrespectful for him *not to*, since he normally would? I don't know.
> (Walton 2015, p. 242, italics in original)

Ironically, immediately after coming out to Matt, Tretch finds himself back 'in a closet scrounging around for a sleeping bag' (Walton 2015, p. 243). Both Tretch's return to the closet and the sleeping bag re-establish the boundary between heterosexual and homosexual, precluding the enactment of Tretch's homosexuality.

However, just as *The Great American Whatever* revises gay–straight male relations, so too does *Anything Could Happen*. Yet, in doing so, the novel reiterates the expectation that gay boys must regulate their sexual desires, thereby internalizing heteronormative behaviours in order to maintain a gay bromance. Although Tretch comes out to Matt, he does not admit his sexual desire for him. By keeping his erotic love secret, Tretch maintains the perception that the boys' bromance is reciprocally *philial*. Matt unhesitatingly sleeps next to Tretch, believing there is no chance that Tretch will enact his homosexuality. Problematically, by admitting his homosexuality, Tretch is finally able to reconcile his feelings for his best friend, realizing that he can love Matt 'without the hurt' and that their 'loves are … the *same*' (Walton 2015, p. 245, italics and ellipsis in original). In other words, in coming out, Tretch's love for Matt is no longer erotic; both of the boys' love is appropriately *philial*. Nonetheless, Tretch still feels the need to prevaricate when he later admits to Matt that he had previously desired him, in part because he worries that Matt will '*freak*' (Walton 2015, p. 264, italics in original). The text thus demonstrates the way in which the expansion of straight masculine subjectivities is contingent on the repression of gay masculine subjectivities. Tretch regulates his homosexual desire in order to conform to and maintain accepted gendered orders. By doing so, Tretch enables Matt to dismiss Tretch's feelings as 'puppy stuff' (Walton 2015, p. 265), thereby enabling him to disregard the threat Tretch's erotic desire poses to their bromance.

Without the Bro, It's a Gay Romance

In contrast to the two novels discussed above, the consequences of enacting homosexual desire within bromances are explored in *Openly Straight*. In Bill Konigsberg's *Openly Straight*, the gay protagonist Rafe decides to move across country to attend an all-boys boarding school.

Although accepted in his hometown, Rafe nevertheless experiences a sense of suffocation at being 'the gay kid' (Konigsberg 2013, p. 203). At the new school, Rafe attempts to hide his gay identity in order 'to live a label-free life' (Konigsberg 2013, p. 4) so that he can interact with the other boys without having to navigate the ramifications of his homosexuality. At his previous school, Rafe had been excluded from male bonding because of his sexuality, admitting, 'There was this barrier between me and so many guys. I couldn't take it anymore. You have to understand. I was so tired of feeling different. I just wanted to feel like one of the guys for once' (Konigsberg 2013, p. 290). A talented athlete, Rafe is presumed to be straight by his fellow classmates, and the novel makes evident the pervasiveness of heterosexism in Anglo-Western society, which is succinctly described as being 'assumed to be straight if you're not openly gay' (Konigsberg 2013, p. 135). The novel explores the importance and limitations of male bonding, particularly for men who identify as gay.

Rafe's longing to be accepted as one of the regular (straight) guys and engage in male bonding is an example of homosocial desire. In *Between Men: English Literature and Male Homosocial Desire* (2015), Eve Kosofsky Sedgwick explores the ambivalence of male–male relationships, and defines 'homosocial' as

> a word occasionally used in history and the social sciences, where it describes social bonds between persons of the same sex; it is a neologism, obviously formed by analogy with 'homosexual,' and just as obviously meant to be distinguished from 'homosexual.' In fact, it is applied to such activities as 'male bonding,' which may, as in our society, be characterized by intense homophobia, fear and hatred of homosexuality.
>
> (2015, p. 1)

Rafe's belief that his homosexuality has negatively impacted his ability to interact with other straight men supports Sedgwick's contention that homophobia is an inherent aspect of male homosociality. Homophobia, though, should be considered to be more than simply the fear and hatred of homosexuality. As Michael Kimmel argues, 'it is also the fear that one might be misperceived as gay by others' (2000, p. 211). Throughout the novel, Rafe exhibits internalized homophobia as a result of his homosocial desire. As well as keeping his sexuality secret, he also demonstrates a fear that his homosexuality will become evident, thereby precluding him from male bonding.

In *Openly Straight*, Konigsberg explores the relationship between homosociality and desire more directly than in Walton does in *Anything Could Happen*. Like Sedgwick, Konigsberg seems to believe that 'To draw the "homosocial" back into the orbit of "desire," of the potentially erotic, then, is to hypothesize the potential unbrokenness of a continuum between homosocial and homosexual—a continuum whose visibility, for men, in our society, is radically disrupted' (Sedgwick 2015, pp. 1–2). Primarily through the burgeoning relationship between Rafe and a fellow student, Ben, Konigsberg uses desire to render fluid the boundary between homosocial and homosexual, as evident in the boys' first exchange:

> [Ben] looked me in the eye. His eyes were a translucent blue. He looked kind. I didn't want to look away. I realized that not being the gay kid here allowed me more access. I wasn't supposed to hold eye contact with jocks back in Boulder. It was understood: They accepted me, and I didn't freak them out with eye contact. Here, no such contract had been made. Ben blinked at me, I blinked back, and when it began to feel a bit too close, I averted my eyes.
>
> (Konigsberg 2013, p. 16)

Welcomed as a 'jock', Rafe's sexuality always already threatens his ongoing acceptance, and his presence disturbs the homosocial dictates that regulate the problem of homosexual desire. No matter how much Rafe pretends he is straight, he cannot be anything but gay. In keeping his sexuality secret, Rafe is able to fulfil his homosocial desire, giving him a glimpse into life as a straight man; however, he nevertheless resides outside of the hegemonic order, feeling like 'an anthropologist studying another culture' (Konigsberg 2013, p. 27).

Again, echoing *Anything Could Happen*, Rafe's admiration of the youthful, muscular male body supports Buchbinder's observation that the idealization of the male body in contemporary society blurs the boundary between homosociality and homosexual desire. For Rafe, the 'bunch of big, muscular guys' are 'an Abercrombie & Fitch ad come to life' (Konigsberg 2013, p. 11). If the muscular (straight) male body is something to be admired, the homosexual body is one that must be regulated. The boys' locker room is once again used to expose the instability of male sexuality. Just as Tretch's body threatens to expose his homosexuality in *Anything Could Happen*, so, too, does Rafe's body, as he fears will 'get excited by all the [naked] bodies surrounding [him]' (Konigsberg 2013, p. 144). Rafe's musings about the unspoken homosocial contract that exists between gay and straight men demonstrates both how male sexuality is regulated in an attempt to annex the homosexual from the homosocial and the instability of this bifurcation:

> As I started to get undressed, I saw the first few guys head into the shower area. I felt my heart beat faster as I glimpsed my teammates walking by, some wrapped in towels, some with towels draped over their shoulders. In Boulder, as the gay guy, it was an unspoken rule that I wouldn't gawk at my fellow athletes. That would be considered rude, you know? And, basically, I just figured it was a tradeoff: They accepted me, I didn't stare at them naked. It worked.

Here, no such unspoken pact had been made; why would there be? And I felt a little guilty and a bit tingly, entering the sacred shower room with my fellow straight teammates.

(Konigsberg 2013, p. 46)

Although Konigsberg suggests the boundary between homosocial and homosexual is permeable, sexuality within the all-boys' culture is nevertheless constructed in binary ways, much as it is in wider heteronormative society. Rafe and Ben's vacillation within the space between the homosocial and the homosexual causes both of them angst as they struggle to identify who and what they are. Rafe wonders: 'How [...] straight guys do this? Tiptoe toward the line and then maybe cross it, maybe not, without ever discussing the rules? It was exhausting, and I wasn't even sure if there was a line' (Konigsberg 2013, p. 223). Ben, on the other hand, seeks to label, and thereby justify, their bromance through the lens of Greek types of love. Whereas the bromantic love in *Anything Could Happen* moves from *eros* to *philia*, in *Openly Straight*, the boys' bromance alludes to the fluidity that exists between love and desire. It appears their bromance is a combination of *philia*, *eros* and *agape* (transcendental love). In the private space of Rafe's bedroom, the boys' realization that '*agape* and *eros* are close' (Konigsberg 2013, p. 243) challenges the boundaries that supposedly exist between the forms of love, and they are able to explore their sexuality, momentarily expanding the acceptable ways men can love each other.

Unlike *Anything Could Happen*, which forecloses the enactment of homosexuality, Rafe and Ben act on their sexual desire. In doing so, they are jettisoned from the ambiguous space between the homosocial and homosexual. The boys' fulfilment of their sexual desire is also in opposition to the usual trajectory of Western romantic novels. As Lydia Kokkola (2011, p. 170) suggests, *agape* is traditionally favoured over *eros* and so relationships generally move from erotic love to agapic love. The boys' retrograde movement from *agape* to *eros* not only sees them transgress the asexual precept of the bromance, it also is a defilement of their transcendental love, which maintains the perception that homosexuality is a threat to homosociality. As a consequence, the boys' relationship becomes strained, and they are forced to confront their sexuality. For Rafe, this means finally being open about his homosexuality; for Ben, he must review his supposed heterosexuality.

Seemingly, it is Rafe's dishonesty about his sexuality that causes the rift between the boys. More problematic is the implication that Rafe's homosexuality perverts the boys' exploration of their sexuality. As Rafe argues: 'This is about the label, isn't it? If it's two straight guys playing around, experimenting, that's cool. But if one of the guys is gay, it's not okay' (Konigsberg 2013, p. 289). Ben's retort that 'The barrier isn't straight versus gay; it's real versus bullshit' is undermined by his earlier admission,

'I have to be straight' (Konigsberg 2013, pp. 290, 285), and alludes to the significance of labels and the subordinate position of gay masculinities in heteronormative society. Thrust into the public space where sexuality is constructed in binary terms, Rafe and Ben are restricted in the ways in which they can express and explore their love for one another. While this means Rafe can finally be openly gay, Ben's heterosexuality is not sufficiently secure for him to compensate for the queer disturbance of his relationship with Rafe. Ultimately, Ben chooses not to further explore his sexuality, and the boys' friendship ends. Rafe, on the other hand, joins the school's gay–straight alliance group and begins to develop a new friendship circle. The answer to Rafe's earlier question, 'Why do we have to label everything?' (Konigsberg 2013, p. 186), seems clear: in relation to bromances, labels matter. The fixity of labels facilitates the negotiation of gay–straight relations within the bromance. When the gay partner of a gay bromance is open about his sexuality, it enables both partners to place limits on male homosexuality, reaffirming asexuality and passive homophobia as integral components of bromances.

Conclusion

Over twenty years ago, Roberta Seelinger Trites observed, 'in gay young adult literature, homosexuality seems at once enunciated and repressed' (1998, p. 143). This pattern continues in the gay bromance YA novels discussed in this chapter. In each novel, the gay male protagonist's homosexuality is rendered visible and readily accepted, such that he is able to engage in supportive and positive male–male relationships. However, to enable these relationships, limits are placed on how the gay protagonist can enact his homosexuality. These limitations—or repressions—include the abjection of effeminacy, as seen in the characterization of Quinn in *The Great American Whatever* and the suppression of homosexual desire, as demonstrated by Tretch in *Anything Could Happen*. This limiting of gay subjectivities supports Robert Westerfelhaus and Celeste Lacroix's observation that queer characters may be present in mainstream media 'only so long as they observe certain limits imposed upon them by the conventions of the mainstream's heterosexist sociosexual order' (2006, p. 427). Despite all the novels being narrated by a gay male character, they each must repress their homosexuality in some way to maintain their bromance with their straight male friend, and thereby exist within the represented societies.

Thus, I agree with Trites's assertion that there are 'limits of queer discourse at work in adolescent literature: as a group they show how a genre can become more aware of a social issue without necessarily providing the reader with transformative experiences' (1998, p. 144). Like all LGBTIQ YA novels, the gay bromance novel functions to normalize and accommodate variant sexualities, primarily for readers who may not identify as heterosexual. By focusing on male friendships, the gay bromance novel also revises our understanding of male homosociality and, in doing so, reconfigures both gay and straight masculinities. Ostensibly, the gay bromance demonstrates growing acceptance of non-normative sexualities, yet the dynamics of gay bromances nonetheless limit some aspects of gay subjectivities. While the gay bromance novel engages with and explores contemporary concerns about masculinity, male sexuality and homosociality, it ultimately reinscribes the subordination and compliance of homosexual subjectivities within heteronormative discourses.

The gay bromance genre of LGBTIQ YA literature is limited in the extent to which it revises our understanding of male sexuality and masculinity in response to changes in acceptable constructions of masculinity. The gay bromance expands the enactment of heterosexual masculinity, enabling straight men to engage in intimate relationships with other men, to express emotion and empathy and to be more accommodating of homosexuality. The flexibility of the straight friend's heterosexual masculinity enables him to accommodate the queer disturbances caused by being in a relationship with a gay male, and this revisioning of acceptable masculinity maintains the heteronormative order the gay bromance seems to challenge.

Yet this is only one half of the reciprocal dynamic of the bromance. The gay bromance also imposes new regulations on the enactment of gay masculinities and sexuality in order to maintain the discrete separation between the homosocial and the heterosexual. Gay men must constrain their homosexual desire if they are to fulfil their homosocial desire, as evidenced by Rafe's actions in *Openly Straight*. The question with which I began this chapter, 'Can gay guys have a bromance?', is largely a rhetorical one. The bromance genre is inherently heteronormative; although it redefines some aspects of heterosexual masculinities, it nonetheless limits the ways in which gay men can enact their masculinity and sexuality.

Notes

1 In 2014, Konigsberg's *Openly Straight* won the Sid Fleischman Award for Humor and was a finalist for the Amelia Elizabeth Walden Award and the Lambda Award. In the same year, the book was also listed in the Young Adult Library Services Association's Best Fiction for Young Adults and the American Library Association Rainbow Project Book List.

2 Other novels that depict straight and gay male friends include *Will Grayson, Will Grayson* (Green and Levithan 2010), *Life in Outer Space* (Keil 2013) and *Simon vs the Homo Sapiens Agenda* (Albertalli 2015), to name a few.

3 Literary awards or honours for LGBTIQ children's and young adult fiction (and the year of inception) include: the Lambda Literary Awards (1993), the American Library Association (ALA) Rainbow Book List (2008) and ALA Stonewall Book Awards (2010), the Bisexual Book Awards (2013), the Golden Crown Literary Awards (2014). All three novels discussed in this chapter feature on the ALA Rainbow Book List. Konigsberg's *Openly Straight* and

Walton's *Anything Could Happen* were shortlisted for the Lambda Award (in 2014 and 2016, respectively).
4 Similarly, Kenneth Kidd (1998) noted changes in LGBTIQ YA literature at the end of the 1990s, with homophobia replacing homosexuality as the social problem that was being addressed in this genre of novels.
5 Quinn's positioning as voyeur is fundamental to the narrative developments of the novel. Not only does it reinforce his characterization of a screen writer, but he has also removed himself from the world, retiring to his bedroom following his sister's accidental death. Quinn must learn to act in the world if he is to move on and find happiness.
6 Similarly, in Konigsberg's *Openly Straight*, one of the characters, Ben, tries to understand his bromance through the lens of the four types of Greek love, as discussed below.

References

Albertalli, B 2015, *Simon vs the Homo Sapiens Agenda*, Balzer + Bray, New York.
Becker, R 2014, 'Becoming bromosexual: Straight men, gay men, and male bonding on US television', *Reading the Bromance: Homosocial Relationships in Film and Television*, Ed. M DeAngelis, Wayne State University Press, Detroit, IL, pp. 233–254.
Briggs, CL and Bauman, R 1992, 'Genre, intertextuality, and social power', *Journal of Linguistic Anthropology*, vol. 2, no. 2, pp. 131–172.
Brook, H 2015, 'Bros before ho(mo)s: Hollywood bromance and the limits of heterodoxy', *Men and Masculinities*, vol. 18, no. 2, pp. 249–266.
Buchbinder, D 2013, *Studying Men and Masculinity*, Routledge, New York.
Chen, EJ 2012, 'Caught in a bad bromance', *Texas Journal of Women and the Law*, vol. 21, no. 2, pp. 241–266.
Crisp, T 2009, 'From romance to magical realism: limits and possibilities of gay adolescent fiction', *Children's Literature in Education*, vol. 40, no. 4, pp. 333–348.
DeAngelis, M 2014, 'Introduction', *Reading the Bromance: Homosocial Relationships in Film and Television*, Ed. M DeAngelis, Wayne State University Press, Detroit, IL, pp. 1–26.
Devitt, A 2004, *Writing Genres*, Southern Illinois University Press, Carbondale.
Federle, T 2016, *The Great American Whatever*, Simon & Schuster, New York.
Green, J and Levithan, D 2010, *Will Grayson, Will Grayson*, Speak, New York.
Jenkins, CA and Cart, M 2018, *Representing the Rainbow in Young Adult Literature: LGBTQ+ Content Since 1969*, Rowman & Littlefield, Lanham, MD.
Keil, M 2013, *Life in Outer Space*, Hardie Grant Egmont, Richmond, Australia.
Kidd, K 1998, 'Introduction: lesbian/gay literature for children and young adults', *Children's Literature Association Quarterly*, vol. 23, no. 3, pp. 114–119.
Kimmel, M 2000, *The Gendered Society*, Oxford University Press, New York.
Kokkola, L 2011, 'Virtuous vampires and voluptuous vamps: romance conventions reconsidered in Stephanie Meyer's "Twilight" series', *Children's Literature in Education*, vol. 42, no. 2, pp. 165–179.
Konigsberg, B 2013, *Openly Straight*, Arthur A Levine Books, New York.
Mallan, K 2009, *Gender Dilemmas in Children's Fiction*, Palgrave Macmillan, Basingstoke.

Mauldin, RK 2000, 'The role of humor in the social construction of gendered and ethnic stereotypes', *Race, Gender & Class*, vol. 9, no. 3, pp. 76–95.

McRuer, R 2006, *Crip Theory: Cultural Signs of Queerness and Disability*, New York University Press, New York.

Potter, T 2018, *Books for Boys: Manipulating Genre in Contemporary Australian Young Adult Fiction*, WVT Trier, Trier, Germany.

Robinson, S, White, A and Anderson, E 2017, 'Privileging the bromance: a critical appraisal of romantic and bromantic relationships', *Men and Masculinities*, vol. XX, no. X, pp. 1–22, doi.org/10.1177/1097184X17730386.

Sedgwick, EK 2015, *Between Men: English Literature and Male Homosocial Desire*, Columbia University Press, New York.

Trites, RS 1998, 'Queer discourse and the young adult novel: repression and power in gay male adolescent literature', *Children's Literature Association Quarterly*, vol. 23, no. 3, pp. 143–151.

Walton, W 2015, *Anything Could Happen*, PUSH, New York.

Westerfelhaus, R and Lacroix, C 2006, 'Seeing 'straight' through *Queer Eye*: exposing the strategic rhetoric of heteronormativity in a mediated ritual of gay rebellion', *Critical Studies in Media Communication*, vol. 23, no. 5, pp. 426–444.

Rethinking Sexuality and Girlhood

6 Postfeminism and Sexuality in the Fiction of Sarah J Maas

Elizabeth Little and Kristine Moruzi

Strong female protagonists have become increasingly commonplace in young adult literature in the last two decades. Yet simply including a female hero is 'not enough to overturn' existing patriarchal structures of the fictional world (Clasen and Hessel 2017, p.187). In Sarah J Maas' two bestselling young adult series, *A Court of Thorns and Roses* (2015–2017) and *The Throne of Glass* (2012–2018), two seemingly independent female characters enjoy sexual relationships. In both series, these young women operate as postfeminist heroines as they navigate both 'active and passive forms of recognition and motivation' (Genz 2006, p. 339). In *A Court of Thorns and Roses* series, Feyre's strength is accompanied by stereotypically feminine characteristics that align with patriarchal systems of power and promote the removal of female agency. In *The Throne of Glass* series, Celaena has more power and sexual agency. However, her relationships are also situated within complex – and uneven – relations of power.

In this chapter, we situate these two series within a postfeminist framework to demonstrate how the sexual agency of the protagonists is undermined by patriarchal systems of power. The depiction of sexuality is also informed by elements of the Gothic and fantasy, which have the potential to 'serve as a powerful tool of subverting or perpetuating' dominant social structures, making them particularly relevant to texts for young adults (Stasiewicz-Biekowska 2019, p. 232). This chapter examines the challenges of negotiating female sexuality and femininity in young adult fantasy texts that feature strong female protagonists while also encouraging traditional modes of femininity and sexuality. Power, violence and sexuality intersect in these two series to create postfeminist models of femininity that fail to interrogate existing power structures that inform female experiences in the world.

The Gothic, Fantasy and Postfeminism in Young Adult Literature

By situating these two series as postfeminist texts, we consider how they construct femininity, sexuality and agency. The multifaceted manifestations of postfeminism allow for the examination of 'the plurality and contradictions of contemporary female experience' while also enabling 'a variety of often competing discourses where female agency [is] celebrated by the feminist movement within a patriarchal interest in heterosexual femininity' (Genz 2006, p. 343). Sarah Projansky (2007, p. 68) has observed that 'postfeminism is by definition contradictory, simultaneously feminist and antifeminist, liberating and repressive, productive and obstructive of progressive or social change'. These contradictory impulses require a reconsideration of how girlhood is constructed in literature for young people. Postfeminism can be used in a way that 'moves us from the exclusionary logic of either/or to the inclusionary logic of both/and' (Genz and Brabon 2009, p. 8), enabling an exploration of the nuance in representations of girls, sexuality and feminism. In this chapter, we celebrate the heroines' sexual agency even as we critique the compulsory heterosexuality that privileges male power and experience.

Postfeminism is applicable to young adult literature, particularly texts that include elements of sexuality. While the current cultural moment sees young women as 'sexuality assertive', both 'initiating and influencing a sexual encounter' (McCormick 2010, p. 92), sexual scripts also contradict themselves with 'conflicting expectations' and 'confusion' (Pinquart 2010, p. 440). Young adult literature in this genre typically features some forms of sexual agency for its protagonists, yet the repackaging of sex and sexuality 'as matters of personal choice and individual identity' can potentially be 'as coercive' to girl readers 'as rigid moralities' (Bullen et al. 2011, p. 498). Female sexuality, then, is often positioned ambivalently as either 'freedom from, or submission to, masculine exploitation' (Bullen et al. 2011, p. 498). This ambivalence is apparent in Maas' two series, in which both of the main protagonists are positioned as sexually inexperienced within unequal relationships of power.

Although young adult literature is typically defined by its coming-of-age motifs, one of which is sexual maturity, depictions of teenage sex are relatively uncommon. In fact, teenaged characters who choose to express sexual desire in young adult fiction are frequently labelled as 'deviant' (Kokkola 2013, p. 207). Romantic constructions of childhood as innocent mean that sexual innocence is a prized commodity. Roberta Trites (2013, p. 85) argues that young adult literature is often used 'as [an] ideological tool' to 'curb teenagers' libido' rather than accurately depicting adolescent sexuality. Victoria Flanagan (2017, p. 31) similarly argues that 'when adolescent sexuality is acknowledged or acted upon' in young adult narratives, 'the well-established literary paradigm is to punish teenaged characters for behaving in an "adult" fashion'. That Maas' two series both include sexually active female protagonists mark them as distinct within the genre.

The position of both series within the genres of the Gothic and fantasy help to explain the inclusion of sexuality in these texts. Maas' series are first and foremost popular fantasy series. *A Court of Thorns and Roses* is a modern reimagining of the frequently adapted Scottish ballad 'Tam Lin', expanding on motifs of capture and romance. Echoing the fairy tale 'Beauty and the Beast', teenager Feyre finds herself held captive in the Spring Court by a powerful faerie. She is the High Fae Lord Tamlin's prisoner as a consequence of killing one of his soldiers. Eventually Tamlin allows Feyre some freedom and a friendship develops between them. Their romantic relationship is eventually revealed to hold the key to breaking the curse on Tamlin and his court, a curse that will result in his betrothal to an evil faerie and, until their union, diminishes the Spring Court's power. Feyre risks her life to save him and break the curse. In the *Throne of Glass* series, the assassin Celaena is freed from a brutal prison to compete in a deadly competition to become the King's Champion. This opening gambit begins a seven-book series in which Celaena's true identity as heir to the throne of Terrasen is revealed, along with her half-fae heritage and magical ability. Her world is threatened by Queen Maeve and Erawan, a Valg demon king, and she is fated to die destroying them.

The fantastic worlds of both series enable the depiction of sexually active protagonists. As Jude Roberts and Esther MacCallum-Stewart (2016, p. 2) explain, 'by making a fantasy immersive, the audience is given the illusion of the suspense of the social rules of the society in which they live' and thus this world 'is one in which literally anything could happen'. This idea is indebted to Rosemary Jackson's (1981) argument that fantasy offers possibilities for the subversion of social and cultural norms. The norms for young adult literature and the relative lack of sexually explicit content can be subverted through the fantastic setting, thus enabling sexually active protagonists like Feyre and Celaena within radically unbalanced relationships of power.

Yet the presence of the Gothic in these series simultaneously constrains these fantastic possibilities. Fred Botting (2012, p. 14) writes that the Gothic 'resonates as much with anxieties and fears concerning the crises and changes in the present as with any terrors of the past'. The Gothic elements in these series – especially the presence of the immortal fae – enable the romantic plotlines while also limiting the sexual agency of the female protagonists. With the incorporation of strong romantic plotlines – such as those found in Meyer's *Twilight* series – the terror of the Gothic has been subsumed by the pleasure of the romance (Crawford 2014, p. 5). While Joseph Crawford explores this history to understand the development of the paranormal romance genre, it is relevant to our discussion of Maas' series, which are published in a post-*Twilight* moment when sexuality and sexual desire were brought to the forefront of Gothic young adult fantasy with Bella's determination to have sex with Edward as a human. The Gothic elements of the fantasy, embodied in the male romantic leads who are invested in and representative of patriarchal power, restrict female agency and reinstate power dynamics that position the female protagonists as subordinate.

Sexuality in *A Court of Thorn and Roses* Series

While this chapter critiques the implications of Feyre's romantic and sexual relationships, the positive depictions of female sexuality in the series are significant. Female protagonists like Feyre and Celaena who express sexual desire offer readers a way to 'conceptualise and express the sexuality' of young women (Taylor 2014, p. 396). Diamond (2011, p. 44) suggests that there has been an increase in the 'ownership' of desires in female protagonists of young adult literature, with more young women characterised as embracing and asserting sexual agency. Feyre and Celaena both express their sexuality and desires.

Feyre is sexually independent from the beginning of the first novel in the series. She has been in a relationship with a young man in her village, who she pulls into the barn for 'hungry' sex (Maas 2015a, p. 31). Her agency in initiating this relationship shows her to be sexually aware, and her positive sexuality is empowering. Even in her later relationship with Tamlin, she experiences sexual pleasure and articulates her desires and needs. Feyre feels genuine sexual desire, with the 'heat pounding' in her core and 'between [her] legs' (Maas 2015a, p. 172). She also voices her longings, 'demanding' that Tamlin continue to kiss her by questioning 'that's it?' after he stops (Maas 2015a, p. 172). When they finally have sex, after a lengthy build-up of sexual tension, Feyre explicitly tells Tamlin not to 'stop' but to 'give [her] everything', consenting with passion and desire (Maas 2015a, p. 247). She describes her sexual feelings for Tamlin as 'wild and hard and burning' (Maas 2015a, p. 378). Maas' use of the word 'hard', a term typically used to describe male sexuality, gives powerful connotations to Feyre's sexuality, even equating it to the desire of a man. Feyre's active position in these encounters characterises her as a sexual woman.

However, essentially a captive in Tamlin's household, she has no genuine opportunity to consent to the relationship. Borgia (2014, p. 161) explains that romantic fiction regularly 'justifies women's submissiveness as romance' and promotes the rationalisation of abusive undertones, thereby diminishing its positive aspects. Platt (2010, p. 80) similarly asserts that female protagonists are not always simply 'sexually empowered', but rather become 'perpetual victims of … desires' that keep them within a submissive and patriarchal system. Feyre's sexuality and desire lead her to persist in an oppressive system where her power and agency are limited.

Feyre's relationship with Tamlin is characterised by elements of physical intimate partner violence, which include a 'broad range of behaviours' from the use of weapons to the less extreme acts of 'pushing, grabbing or shoving' (Coyne et al. 2011, p. 56). Their first sexual experience occurs directly against the verbal consent of Feyre and involves grabbing and physical restraint. The encounter occurs on the night of Calamnai, a faerie festival in which Tamlin, as High Lord of the Spring Court, must find 'a maiden' faerie with whom to have sex (Maas 2015a, p. 193). Feyre has been warned to stay in her room and is sick at the 'thought of Tamlin forcing her' as he is transformed by magic that would 'strip away any sense of right or wrong' (Maas 2015a, p. 194). When she accidentally encounters him in the hallway, he grabs her: 'so fast that I didn't see anything until he had me pinned against the wall' (Maas 2015a, p. 197). Feyre sees 'no kindness' in Tamlin's eyes and no evidence of the man she knows (Maas 2015a, p. 198). He refuses to let her go, saying that her scent 'drove [him] mad' (Maas 2015a, p. 198). Tamlin blames Feyre for his uncontrollable sexual desires, and this behaviour is excused because of the 'magic' that was making him 'half wild' (Maas 2015a, p. 198). This explanation is characteristic of some fantasy texts in which the hero's actions are excused because of the influence of supernatural forces beyond his control, at once reinforcing and 'reconceal[ing]' fundamental rape myths (Deffenbacher 2014, p. 925). As Deffenbacher (2014, p. 925) explains, 'in a market that generally no longer accepts undisguised rape in a romantic storyline, the paranormal seems to provide publishers, writers and readers with plausible deniability'. Feyre is held against her will as Tamlin exerts physical strength to restrain her, and although she explicitly denies consent to the interaction, her agency is denied.

The fantastic setting enables the repositioning of this encounter as sexually arousing. Feyre 'couldn't escape' from Tamlin, but 'wasn't entirely sure' that she 'wanted to' (Maas 2015a, p. 196). Feyre transitions from 'shuddering' with fear and feeling 'sick' at the idea of intimacy with Tamlin to going 'taut' as his seductive words 'echoed through [her]' (Maas 2015a, p. 196). This encounter 'naturalises patriarchal dominance' within an intimate relationship and presents this dominance as 'desirable' (Taylor 2014, p. 396), making the romantic and sexual relationship between Tamlin and Feyre problematic. Feyre's non-consent to being bitten by Tamlin renders the act violent, yet her acquiescence to the remainder of the interaction suggest that she complies with his authority.

Patriarchal authority is conveyed explicitly in Tamlin's response to a query from Lucien about the bruise on Feyre's neck. He explains that he bit her because she 'can't be bothered to listen to orders' and that he 'can't be held accountable for the consequences' (Maas 2015a, p. 199). He takes no responsibility for his actions and implicitly blames her for the results of the encounter. The lack of societal consequences for Tamlin demonstrate how 'patriarchal society rewards men who are masculine and assertive enough to take what they want, whenever they want' (Taylor 2014, p. 391). Furthermore, in this interaction between the two men, Feyre is not given a voice to share her experience since the 'female experience is written out and silenced' (Taylor 2014, p. 390). Feyre is not asked to explain what happened, and thus Tamlin's authority over Feyre is further enforced.

Feyre's sexuality is both encouraged and manipulated by the other male lead in the series, the powerful High Lord of the Night Court, Rhysand.

Despite their relationship appearing less problematic than Feyre's relationship with Tamlin, modes of sexuality that are predicated on violence and the absence of consent continue. On their initial meeting, Feyre describes Rhysand as 'radiat[ing] sensual grace and ease' and having a 'magnificent' (Maas 2015a, p. 189) body. However, although he comes from an enemy court, during her time Under the Mountain Feyre is coerced into making a deal with Rhysand to protect herself and save Tamlin. As payment for being healed of a life-threatening injury, she receives a tattoo on her arm, a visible sign of their pact, and becomes Rhysand's 'plaything' (Maas 2015a, p. 354). The tattoo, which magically appears after she makes the deal with Rhys, acts as a symbol of his ownership of her. Feyre is worried about Tamlin's reaction to the tattoo, suggesting that this visible sign of Rhys' deal will threaten Tamlin's own authority over her (Maas 2015a, p. 354). This seemingly simple aspect of the narrative exhibits the patriarchal tendencies of Maas' writing, where the female character is owned and controlled by the men. The sexual undertone to their relationship also demonstrates Rhys' dominance. Feyre sees herself as 'belonging' to him, a belief that is confirmed when he paints her body. He uses magic to ensure that the paint returns to its original design if he touches it so that he can know 'if anyone else touches [her]' as he does not 'like [his] belongings tampered with' (Maas 2015a, p. 348). In the public setting of the throne room, Feyre 'dance[s] for him most of the night' and 'sit[s] in his lap' (Maas 2015a, p. 351). That she does so under the influence of strong faerie wine, which is a strong drug to humans, removes Feyre's agency and demonstrates the shame she feels being sexual with Rhys instead of Tamlin. Yet in the privacy of her cell, a quiet intimacy exists between the two, as Rhys 'ran his finger down [Feyre's] cheek – a gentle caress' (Maas 2015a, p. 349). Despite feeling humiliated for being made to perform for Rhys by night, Feyre's body goes 'taut and loose all at once', and she 'burned' with desire for him when his 'tongue was hot against [her] skin' (Maas 2015a, p. 349). Power and sexuality are inextricably connected in Feyre's experience of pleasure.

In the second novel of the series, *A Court of Mist and Fury* (2016a), sexual desire and intercourse are used as an escape from Feyre's negative experiences at the court that place her in a subordinate position. Feyre uses her sexual relationship with Tamlin to escape from nightmares of what happened with Amarantha where she was forced to endure horrific 'tests' to win Tamlin's life. Feyre is left with the trauma of having to kill another faerie to save Tamlin's life. She 'gasps' and 'begs' for sex until she feels that she is 'nothing, no one' (Maas 2016a, p. 22). Their intimacy occurs amidst arguments, with sex becoming a way for them to reconcile without actually discussing their differences (Maas 2016a, p. 25). Eventually, Feyre's desire for Tamlin wanes as she becomes increasingly aware of feeling trapped by him. As payment for Rhys' healing powers, Feyre visits the Night Court for a week each month. Initially, she is reluctant to go, explaining that she 'didn't want to be stolen away' (Maas

2016a, p. 47). Yet once Feyre realises that Tamlin has 'trapped [her]' in the house and 'locked [her] up' with magic shields (Maas 2016a, p. 123), she flees to the Night Court and refuses to go back. Despite being free from Tamlin's male oppression and control, Feyre exchanges one subordinate position for another. The patriarchal structure of the text remains unchallenged despite the female protagonist's acknowledgement of its negative consequences on her life.

Feyre's time in the Night Court is a journey of self-discovery and healing, in the foundational young adult trope of coming of age. She chooses to stay with Rhysand and his court after the initial compulsory period has concluded and is welcomed as an independent member when she 'accept[s] the offer' to work with Rhys and 'earn [her] keep' (Maas 2016a, p. 179) as an 'emissary to the mortal realms' (Maas 2016a, p. 388). Feyre recovers some of her agency during this novel, with Rhys frequently reminding her that she is 'free' and can choose to leave (Maas 2016a, p. 125). However, his declaration fails to acknowledge the position of power that he holds over her as the most powerful High Lord and her rescuer. Furthermore, while Feyre explains that her decision to stay away from the Spring Court is a 'punishment for [Tamlin]' and 'what *he* had done to [her]' (emphasis in original, Maas 2016a, p. 140), Rhysand's role in her incarceration and pain Under the Mountain with Amarantha receives only minimal discussion. Thus, Feyre remains stereotypically feminine in her desire to remain protected by a powerful man. Although in many ways Rhys is a more positive male protagonist, as he encourages Feyre to expand her knowledge and power and persistently teaches her to read and control her magic, her first-person narration fails to acknowledge her subordinate position.

Despite believing he gives Feyre more freedom, Rhys' authority over her is further evidenced in their first sexual encounter. On a trip to the Court of Nightmares, where Rhys' cousin rules on his behalf, both Feyre and Rhys adopt 'masks' to encounter the cruel members of the court there. Feyre is forced to wear a dress that she describes as 'two shafts of fabric that hardly covered [her] breasts ... and barely covered [her] backside' (Maas 2016a, p. 405). The setting of the Court of Nightmares also reminds her of the trauma she experience Under the Mountain, and she struggles to contain her emotions. The 'role' (Maas 2016a, p. 407) she has to play is as 'the High Lord's whore ... the dangerous new pet' (Maas 2016a, p. 411). Rhysand too takes on a different role at the Court of Nightmares, 'lifting the damper on his power' which 'filled the throne room, the castle, the mountain ... the world. It had no end and no beginning' (Maas 2016a, p. 408). Rhysand assumed the role of 'elegant, cruel High Lord', which enables and requires him to publicly fondle Feyre (Maas 2016a, p. 408). Although this is intended as a game, Feyre's body goes 'loose and tight' and her 'breathing hitched a bit', and Rhys perceives her desire (Maas 2016a, p. 412). The dynamic between the two in this scene is confusing and alarming. Both declare that they do not want to assume these alternative identities as they are connected to memories of Amarantha, yet during their 'performance' they both experience sexual pleasure. Feyre's willingness to be publicly sexually exploited as a part of her job highlights the conflicting nature of her character. She is both sexually empowered yet operating under the patriarchal oppression of her rescuer.

Feyre fulfils the role of postfeminist heroine in the ways that both subvert and conform to expected sexual scripting. While Feyre can understand and reject her containment within the Spring Court, she is unable to see that she has merely exchanged one form of captivity for another and that her sexual choices are not as free as she imagines. As Stamper and Blackburn (2018, p. 63) note, while female protagonists may 'fight for agency in their sexual lives', the 'societal norms are so well ingrained' that they are unable to identify 'all the ways that they conform'. In this series, Feyre's postfeminist sexuality is deployed within Gothic and fantasy generic conventions that restrict her agency and reinforce patriarchal hierarchies of power.

Sexuality in the *Throne of Glass* Series

The postfeminist framework in the *Throne of Glass* series is embodied through the figure of Celaena, an assassin and the true heir to the throne of Terrasen. Like Feyre, Celaena's postfeminist sexual agency is contained within power structures that insist on her subordinate position throughout much of the series. Celaena is a postfeminist heroine in so far as she must work within patriarchal structures to reach her potential as a powerful being, with her romantic and sexual relationships inextricably linked to her ability to save her country and her people. Her sexual desire is positive and explicit, but is at times conflated with violence, and her inexperience is juxtaposed with a much older, wiser male partner.

Celaena's identity as the heroine in the *Throne of Glass* series includes stereotypical femininity and experiences of violence as equally as overt as Feyre's. As a highly trained assassin who has spent over a decade training, she is well situated to defend herself, and thus the threat of sexual violence is minimal. Although this strength and skill is vital to her success in becoming the King's Champion, Celaena's femininity is reinforced through her love of reading and pretty clothes. Her role as both a strong and violent female protagonist who maintains this normative femininity 'hints at a somehow innate female nature just waiting for the right trigger' (Clasen and Hassel 2017, p. 188). Kennedy (2018, p. 429) also discusses the 'appropriate' femininity displayed by 'postfeminist princesses' in young adult fantasy, contrasting it to those female characters who demonstrate the 'type of femininity to avoid'. Celaena is able to reinforce her feminine (and heterosexual) identity through this passion for clothes and books, yet the violence surrounding her ensures she is not weakened by this. As a heroine, then, Celaena is postfeminist in so far as she interacts with what Genz and Brabon (2009, pp. 31, 191) call 'competing and conflicting forms of agency' as well as 'multiple subject positions' in which she can be a neoliberal consumer of fashion while also occupying a position as a physically strong and capable young women.

However, like Feyre, Celaena's captivity informs her sexual agency. She is only freed from the slave labour camp to enter the competition to become the King's Champion and her captivity, though less violent, continues. If she succeeds in the competition, she will eventually be freed. This lack of freedom is the main motivation behind many of her decisions and a common theme throughout the series. It complicates her first sexual relationship with Chaol, in which his humanity enables their nominally more equal relationship. Despite occupying a position of power as the Captain of the Royal Guard, his first sexual encounter with Celaena is 'tentative' (Maas 2013, p. 188) since his sexual experience, like hers, is limited. This perpetuates the postfeminist dynamic in the novel, as Chaol is not positioned as holding the power.

Celaena's reaction and subsequent loss of identity demonstrates the influence the relationship has on her. Chaol's kiss 'obliterate[s] her', and she describes it as 'like coming home or being born or suddenly finding an entire half of herself that had been missing' (Maas 2013, p. 188). With Chaol there is 'no doubt, no shred of fear or uncertainty' about having sex, and she explicitly gives consent when she tells him that 'I've never been so sure of anything in my life' (Maas 2013, p. 189). She expresses her desire and agency in this relationship as she gives him 'everything she had' (Maas 2013, p.189) when she has intercourse with him. Nonetheless, Celaena fails to consider the unequal power dynamic between them: Chaol's main job in the first book is to ensure Celaena remains captive inside the palace. Their romantic relationship is postfeminist in that Celaena is empowered and sexually assertive. Yet, her consideration of the implicit pressures is not present. In this way, Celaena and Chaol's relationship occurs among persistent gender discourses and norms, whereby Celaena's 'empowered' sexuality 'reproduces the terms ... set by heteronormative discourses' (Burkett and Hamilton 2012, p. 817). Although her consent is freely given, their unequal circumstances remain an issue. She seemingly has nothing to give Chaol except for her body.

Celaena's subsequent relationship with the immortal Fae Prince Rowan is characterised by similar unequal power relationships and demonstrates the tension the postfeminist heroine experiences in forging her own destiny. Rowan – as an experienced male magical warrior – fulfils the role of male advisor and romantic lead in the *Thrones* series, and the violence he brings to both of these positions echoes the dynamic between Feyre and Tamlin in the *Court* novels. By this point in the series Celaena has been revealed to be Aelin, the Queen of the country of Terrasen, and she is working towards her 'true' identity. Banet-Weiser (2012 p. 5) asserts the postfeminist nature of revealing the authentic self. The postfeminist heroine is expected to be true to herself, yet also choose from a range of identities that are pre-approved as societal constructs and are 'distinct and regulated types of femininity' (Banet-Weiser 2012, p. 5) Aelin is expected to work on herself, to bring out her natural state, yet she experiences constant surveillance as she does this work and still requires male assistance to truly be 'authentic' (Kennedy 2018, p. 427).

Aelin is forced to submit to training from Rowan in order to obtain the answers she seeks and reveal this authentic self. This 'male' (Maas 2014, p. 13) – he is explicitly othered as non-human to justify some of his behaviours – trains Aelin by repeatedly attacking her in order to motivate her to produce a magical shield to protect herself. Not only is she incapable of reaching the pinnacle of her power without his assistance, but she experiences violence at his hands. Indeed, Aelin feels that she deserves this violence because she failed to save her friend earlier in the series. She is, she thinks, 'barely passable as a human being' and that she 'deserved' (Maas 2014, p. 65) to be punched. This type of 'victim blaming' is precisely what Storer (2017, p. 294) highlights as a dangerous aspect of postfeminist young adult fiction. In this case the postfeminist neoliberal worldview that positions Aelin as responsible for harm and deserving of punishment negates the 'structural and systemic inequalities' that are truly the cause (Storer 2017, p. 295). Aelin literally invites the violence in a confrontation with Rowan when she says 'it might be better if you just slapped me instead … of reminding me again and again how rutting worthless and awful and cowardly I am.… So just hit me' (Maas 2014, p. 275). Moreover, this lack of self-worth is exacerbated by Aelin's continued lack of freedom, despite her role as Queen. She contemplates the 'horrible realization' that 'she could not remember what it was like to be free' (Maas 2014, p. 87). The conflation of self-worth and violence at the hands of her male trainer is enabled through the generic opportunities offered by the fantastic that would be unlikely in realist fiction.

The *Throne of Glass* series also includes possessive and violent aspects in the romantic and sexual relationship between Rowan and Aelin. Initially much of the violence is explained away by the fact that Rowan is training her. Like the ancient immortal fae appearing in the *Court* series, he is much older, stronger and wiser than she is. He takes control of her body not only in training, but also in other ways. For instance, he 'grabbed her by the chin – not hard enough to hurt, but to get her to look at him' (Maas 2014, p. 340). When she is ill following an overuse of magic, he 'scooped her up, blanket and all' and tells her 'You're staying with me from now on' (Maas 2014, p. 367). She does not have the energy to object and easily acquiesces, thereafter sleeping in Rowan's room instead of her own. While this is intended to be out of care for Aelin, her lack of consent to the change of circumstance is telling. Further, Rowan's changed behaviour is prompted by his newfound knowledge that she has been viciously whipped while at the slave camp. Now that he knows she has suffered, she is somehow more deserving of care and attention. The physical marks of violence inscribed on her body define her as more vulnerable, but also more desirable. Rowan's kindness and comfort are juxtaposed with the violence of training, however, which makes these texts especially troublesome for their intended young adult audience. Aelin admires the training regime that Rowan devises even as she suffers under it as 'each morning [brings] something new, something harder and different and miserable' (Maas 2014, p. 389). Readers are supposed to be reassured that this violence is no longer 'from malice, not like it had been before' (Maas 2014, p. 389). Instead, it is intended to keep her safe from her enemies. This idea of violence as a form of protection produces a model of femininity in which girls can expect to be hurt and that violence is an expression of care and concern.

As the tense and volatile relationship gradually shifts into a romantic and sexual one, the violent and possessive dynamic between them does not dissipate. Rowan as a romantic lead differs from what Ananya Mukherjea (2011, p. 3) observes in her examination of vampire–human romances that 'present us with old-school gentleman-vampires who are, certainly, sensitive and evolved in some ways, but who also offer the security and stability of old-fashioned gentlemen'. In contrast, Rowan is undoubtedly not a gentleman. Instead, he is the definition of an ancient warrior who is powerful, loyal and deadly. He agrees to take a 'blood oath', which is defined by 'complete and utter submission ... He would yield everything to her – his life, any property, any free will' (Maas 2014, p. 516). Although Aelin initially rejects his offer to take the oath, he simultaneously 'claims' (Maas 2014, p. 516) her. The blood oath should in theory give Aelin much greater control in their relationship, yet it paradoxically exacerbates the power imbalance between Aelin and Rowan, as he becomes more assertive in controlling her. She attempts to resist this control, saying that 'Just because you're older and stronger doesn't mean you're entitled to order me around' (Maas 2015b, p. 306). He counters this assumption explicitly: 'It's exactly because of those things that I can do whatever I please' (Maas 2015b, p. 307). The sexual tension in this encounter becomes overt when he grabs her hand and drags her a step closer to him. She tilts her head to look up at him and 'For a moment ... she allowed herself to take in his face, those green eyes, the strong jaw. Immortal. Unyielding. Bloodied with power' (Maas 2015b, p. 307). His physical control over her body is arousing to her, even as he resists their sexual attraction when he tells her: 'Don't touch me like that' (Maas 2015b, p.371). She assumes it is because she is 'young and inexperienced' while he is 'three hundred years old, and immortal' (Maas 2015b, p. 371). While she is acting on her sexual and romantic desires, Rowan controls this encounter by rejecting her and leaving her embarrassed that she has offered herself to him. This tension between a strong position as the powerful Queen of Terrasen and yet subordinate to Rowan further establishes Aelin as the postfeminist heroine.

Despite the apparent sexual empowerment of young women, McCormick (2010, p. 93) writes that 'the traditional sexual script, depicting men as dominant and women as submissive, remains ingrained at the deepest cognitive level'. We see this reflected in Maas' heroines. Not long after Rowan has rejected her, he apologises for not keeping her safe, and she offers her exposed neck in 'a silent invitation' (Maas 2015b, p. 435) to demonstrate her continued trust in him. His role as a predator is explicitly contrasted to her role as prey, yet the implicit sexuality of the scene is reminiscent of vampire fiction in which the vampire bite is akin to sexual penetration. Aelin is aware of the risk he poses: 'One bite, one movement, was all it would take for him to rip out her throat' (Maas 2015b, p. 435). She not only submits to his control, but also reassures him that he will be the only one to ever receive this invitation. She will 'never allow anyone else at her throat' and visibly demonstrates this so that the 'predatory, Fae side of him would comprehend' (Maas 2015b, p. 435). His male otherness requires assurance that she will always be his, even though he makes no such reciprocal commitment. Rowan retains control of the encounter by pulling back from the brink of this penetration, with his 'powerful body trembling with restraint above her' (Maas 2015b, p. 436). Aelin is both desiring and desirable, but her agency as a desiring subject is contained by Rowan's decision that it is 'not yet' (Maas 2015b, p. 436) time for them to consummate their relationship.

Their decision to have intercourse is prefaced by mutual declarations of love and heightened by the equality of their magical powers. Aelin wonders whether the sexual encounter will be different, but Rowan admits that he has never been with 'an equal' and has never allowed himself 'to be that unleashed' (Maas 2016b, p. 350). Aelin is moved to tears by Rowan's declaration that he will love her 'when the world is a forgotten whisper of dust between the stars' (Maas 2016b, p. 350). Nonetheless, the scene is initially focalised through Rowan to position Aelin as a desirable body. Rowan says that she is 'so beautiful', and he tracks 'every movement' of her body, with his gaze lingering on her breasts and the apex of her thighs (Maas 2016b, p. 351). Importantly, however, Aelin's consent is explicit and obvious in this scene, especially as the focalisation shifts to her perspective. She lifts a hand to his chest which 'halt[s] him dead' (Maas 2016b, p. 352). This pause is an opportunity for her to reassert their equality: 'If we're equals, then I don't understand why you're still half clothed' (Maas 2016b, p. 352). Her sexual attraction to Rowan is also overt: 'He was the most beautiful thing she'd ever seen' (Maas 2016b, pp. 352–353). This sexual experience is characterised by equality and mutual desire. Although it is seemingly unmarred by the violence that marked their earlier encounters, Maas nonetheless alludes to the potential for danger 'at the touch of those lethal teeth against her, the death that hovered nearby' even as Rowan's hands 'would always be gentle with her, always love her' (Maas 2016b, p. 356). Love and violence remain intertwined in this sexual encounter that is premised on equality and reinforces Aelin's sexual agency.

Conclusion

This chapter has demonstrated the ways in which postfeminist approaches to texts for young adults offer female protagonists agency, but only within heterosexual and patriarchal norms. Although postfeminism seems to suggest that heroines can be active and agential in the world and in their sexual experiences, only certain girls are able to take up these opportunities and only if they remain within established patriarchal and heterosexual systems of oppression. The two series by Sarah J Maas seemingly present opportunities for independence and choice, but they ultimately fail to critique heterosexual norms that merge violence with love, romance and sexual desire. The protagonists are offered only an illusion of freedom, one that fails to critique definitions of femininity and sexuality. Although both Aelin and Feyre engage in sexually active relationships, these relationships are situated within structures of heteronormativity and male-dominated sexual control.

Genre plays a crucial role in enabling this postfeminist containment. The fantastic worlds of both series offer an imaginary setting in which the possibilities of postfeminism are celebrated. Both young women are seemingly freed from contemporary cultural norms and have special qualities that enable their heroism. Yet the Gothic tropes of the texts play into postfeminist ideologies in which the patriarchal power structures are reinforced through unquestioning adherence.

Critical work in the area of young adult literature tends to elide the political and pedagogical implications of the representations of female sexuality, ignoring the broader cultural contexts of postfeminist and popular culture. The popularity of both of Maas' series may, in part, be owing to their combination of postfeminism with patriarchalism and sexuality in which female sexuality is not only celebrated but also contained by patriarchal norms and where violence is romanticised and normalised. Female consent is not always freely and explicitly given, and sexual desire is unerringly depicted as heteronormative. Aelin, though an incredibly powerful being herself, relies on her male counterparts for guidance, persists through violent encounters and positions herself as subordinate in sexual relationships. Feyre too is willing to be submissive to her lovers, does not resist or question violence shown to her, and appears to give little consideration for the removal of her agency. Both women exist in a tension where they are free to explore their power and sexuality within a hierarchy that maintains their subordination and offers them limited opportunities to resist. Furthermore, these postfeminist heroines are constrained by the definitions of femininity being mobilised in the texts, including stereotypically feminine preferences and limited agency. These series demonstrate the limits of current young adult literature in challenging societal norms, and they deserve more interrogation for the ways in which they reproduce models of femininity and sexual agency for young adult readers.

References

Banet-Weiser, S 2012, *Authentic™: The Politics of Ambivalence in a Brand Culture*, New York University Press, New York.

Borgia, D 2014, 'Twilight: the glamorization of abuse, codependency, and white privilege', *The Journal of Popular Culture*, vol. 47, no. 1, pp. 153–173.

Botting, F 2012, 'In gothic darkly: heterotopia, history, culture', *A New Companion to the Gothic,* Ed. D Punter, John Wiley & Sons, Chichester, pp.13–24.

Bullen, E, Toffoletti, K and Parsons, L 2011, 'Doing what your big sister does: sex, postfeminism and the YA child lit series', *Gender and Education*, vol. 23, no. 4, pp. 497–511.

Burkett M and Hamilton K 2012, 'Postfeminist sexual agency: young women's negotiations of sexual consent', *Sexualities,* vol. 15, no. 7, pp. 815–833.

Clasen T and Hassel H (eds.) 2017, *Gender(ed) Identities: Critical Rereadings of Gender in Children's and Young Adult Literature*, Routledge, New York.

Coyne, S, Nelson, D, Graham-Kevan, N, Tew, E and Olsen, J 2011, 'Media depictions of physical and relational aggression: connections with aggression in young adults' romantic relationships', *Aggressive Behaviour*, vol. 37, no. 1, pp. 56–62.

Crawford J 2014, *The Twilight of the Gothic? Vampire Fiction and the Rise of the Paranormal Romance*, University of Wales Press, Cardiff.

Deffenbacher, K 2014, 'Rape myths' twilight and women's paranormal revenge in romantic and urban fantasy fiction', *Journal of Popular Culture*, vol. 47, no. 5, pp. 923–936.

Diamond F 2011, 'Beauty and the beautiful beast: Stephenie Meyer's Twilight saga and the quest for a transgressive female desire', *Australian Feminist Studies,* vol. 26, no. 67, pp. 41–55.

Flanagan, V 2017, 'Representations of adolescent female sexuality in the digital age', *Gender(ed) Identities: Critical Rereadings of gender in Children's and Young Adult Literature*, Eds. T Clasen and H Hassel, Routledge, New York, pp. 28–40.

Genz, S 2006, 'Third way/ve', *Feminist Theory*, vol. 7, no. 3, p. 333.

Genz, S and Brabon, BA 2009, *Postfeminism: Cultural Texts and Theories*, Edinburgh University Press Edinburgh.

Jackson, R 1981, *Fantasy: the Literature of Subversion,* Methuen, London.

Kennedy, M 2018, '"Come on, […] let's go find your inner princess": (post-)feminist generationalism in tween fairy tales', *Feminist Media Studies*, vol. 18, no. 3, pp. 424–439.

Kokkola, L 2013, *Fictions of Adolescent Carnality: Sexy Sinners and Delinquent Deviants*, John Benjamins Publishing Company, Amsterdam.

Maas, SJ 2012, *Throne of Glass*, Bloomsbury, London.

Maas, SJ 2013. *Crown of Midnight*, Bloomsbury, London.

Maas, SJ 2014. *Heir of Fire*, Bloomsbury, London.

Maas, SJ 2015a, *A Court of Thorns and Roses,* Bloomsbury, London

Maas, SJ 2015b, *Queen of Shadows*, Bloomsbury, London.

Maas, SJ 2016a, *A Court of Mist and Fury,* Bloomsbury, London.

Maas, SJ 2016b, *Empire of Storms*, Bloomsbury, London.

McCormick N 2010, 'Preface to sexual scripts: social and therapeutic implications', *Sexual and Relationship Therapy,* vol. 25, no. 1, pp. 91–95.

Mukherjea, A 2011, 'My vampire boyfriend: postfeminism, "perfect" masculinity, and the contemporary appeal of paranormal romance', *Studies in Popular Culture*, vol. 33, no. 2, pp. 1–20.

Pinquart M 2010, 'Ambivalence in adolescents' decisions about having their first sexual intercourse', *Journal of Sex Research*, vol. 47, no. 5, pp. 440–450.

Platt CA 2010, 'Cullen family values: gender and sexuality politics in the Twilight series', *Bitten by Twilight: Youth Culture, Media and the Vampire Franchise*, Eds. M Click, J Aubrey Stevens and E Behm-Morawitz, Peter Lang, New York, pp. 71–86.

Projansky, S 2007, 'Mass magazine cover girls: some reflections on postfeminist girls and postfeminism's daughters', *Interrogating Postfeminism: Gender and the Politics of Popular Culture*, Eds. Y Tasker, and D Negra, Duke University Press, Durham, NC, pp. 40–72.

Roberts, J and MacCallum-Stewart, E 2016, 'Introduction', *Gender and Sexuality in Contemporary Popular Fantasy: Beyond Boy Wizards and Kick-Ass Chicks*, Eds. J Roberts and E MacCallum-Stewart, Routledge, London, pp.1–7.

Staciewicz-Bienkowska, A 2019, 'Lustful ladies, she-demons and good little girls: female agency and desire in the universes of Sookie Stackhouse', *Continuum: Journal of Media and Cultural Studies*, vol. 33, no. 2, pp. 230–241.

Stamper CN and Blackburn MC 2018, '"I will not be a 17 year old virgin": female virginity and sexual scripting in graphic narratives for teenagers', *Journal of Graphic Novels and Comics*, vol. 10, no. 1, pp. 47–66.

Storer, H 2017, 'A year of bad choices: the postfeminist "restorying" of teen dating violence', *Affilia*, vol. 32, no. 3, pp. 292–307.

Taylor, J 2014, 'Romance and the female gaze obscuring gendered violence in the Twilight saga', *Feminist Media Studies*, vol. 14, no. 3, pp. 388–402.

Trites, RS 2013, *Disturbing the Universe: Power and Repression in Adolescent Literature*, University of Iowa Press, Iowa.

7 Graphic Sexualities

Visual Negotiations of Queer Girls' Sexuality and Desire in Graphic Narratives

Lara Hedberg and Rebecca Hutton

Over the past two decades, girls who desire girls have come to openly populate a range of young adult (YA) graphic narratives. Gwen Tarbox and Michelle Ann Abate (2017) observe that YA graphic narratives have grown into a publishing phenomenon and this medium is increasingly being taken up by creators producing queer narratives. Writers and illustrators have mobilised the visual and narrative conventions of the medium to 'expand the range of narratives depicting young female characters and their same-sex relationships' (Gillingham 2018, p. 1). This boom coincides with significant movement in contemporary representations of queer young people, with the ever-growing corpus forming a collective site for examining how queer girlhoods are remembered, imagined, and represented for young readers.

The graphic narrative medium offers young readers myriad queer engagements, not just in terms of queer characters and stories, but in reading experience(s) as well. Scott and Fawaz suggest there are multiple 'locations where queerness – understood variously as a social force, a complex network of erotic and affective ties, or an entire shared culture – appears intimately bound up with the formal and narrative capacities of the comics medium' (Scott and Fawaz 2018, p. 200). In particular they cite the 'representational capacity' of the form to offer infinite possibilities in visually representing expressions of diverse sexualities and genders; the role the iterative nature of serialised panels and images can play in refusing to (borrowing from Sedgwick) 'signify monolithically'; and the ways that readers 'construct their relationships to these texts on the basis of the medium's marginality and often their own sense of disconnection from the expectations of normative social life' (Scott and Fawaz 2018, pp. 200–203). In this chapter, we focus on YA graphic narratives featuring queer female protagonists. We have selected three texts that demonstrate the productive capacity of the graphic narrative form in amplifying representations of adolescent girls' negotiation of desire and their sexual identities: Maggie Thrash's memoir *Honor Girl* (2015), Carol Maurel's time-travel romance *Lusia, Now and Then* (2018), and Tillie Walden's space adventure *On a Sunbeam* (2018). We argue these texts model the queer potential of the graphic narrative form and showcase the medium's capacity to present nuanced visions of queer adolescence.

Each text employs vastly different intersections of genre, form, narration and visual technique to offer young readers ways to witness and engage with queer desire and sexuality. In the memoir *Honor Girl*, authorstrator Maggie Thrash shares her experience of falling in love with an older camp counsellor at an American all-girls Christian camp when she was fifteen. The pastel illustrations and first-person narration detail the complexities of coming out in an environment that does not welcome queer sexuality. *Luisa, Now and Then* bends time and space to unite Luisa's younger and older selves as both struggle with facets of their sexual identities. Translated into English from French, Maurel's narrative takes advantage of the capacity of the form to undermine linear, traditional thinking that delineates between adult awareness and childhood 'innocence' of sexuality. In blurring distinctions between 'now' and 'then', child and adult, the text suggests equality between young person and adult in their capacity to be sexual beings. And set in a future where same-sex relationships are the norm, *On a Sunbeam* draws readers into a protracted adventure, crossing galaxies in the name of same-sex love and friendship. The vibrant illustrative style of this text comingles with a fluid reading style that encourages active, participatory reading and contributes to the text's many queerings of the normative. These texts are part of a continuously growing body of works that privilege compelling queer girl protagonists and utilise the complexities of the comics medium to depict queer desire and sexual exploration.

Honor Girl tells the story of fifteen-year-old Maggie as she falls in love for the first time with an older camp counsellor, Erin, at an all-girls Christian summer camp, Camp Bellflower. The artistic style is roughly drawn and coloured, with blocky, sharp-edged bodies, minimal detail in faces, and imprecise colouring, while the strategic use of panels, gutters and framing throughout the narrative highlight moments of queer desire. Maggie's story is told through the voice of her seventeen-year-old self, but readers are predominantly shown the experiences via fifteen-year-old Maggie. The text's status as 'memoir' is declared prominently on the cover in conjunction with an evening watercolour landscape and the dark silhouette of the teen protagonist sitting away from the camp, which is rendered in colour. Bauer suggests that lesbian comics produced in English 'tend to be autobiographically inspired' (2015, p. 221) and *Honor Girl* sits within the tradition of queer autobiographical graphic narratives such as Alison Bechdel's *Fun Home* (2006). Whereas *Fun Home* is centred on adult Alison's reflections about her youth, *Honor Girl* features two teen versions of Maggie to tell the 'past' and 'present' of this story. This locates the protagonist's engagement with her burgeoning queer subjectivity wholly in the domain of adolescence.

Thrash deploys various graphic narrative conventions throughout the text to highlight moments of desire or sexual possibility. Significant shifts in layout and framing focus and elongate Maggie and Erin's interactions, inviting the reader to linger in these moments. The comics medium offers narratives that are both written and drawn, and in the deployment of framing and layout strategies, graphic narratives have the ability to direct a reader's spatiotemporal experience. As Chute and DeKoven note, graphic narratives are able to call 'a reader's attention visually and spatially to the act, process, and duration of interpretation' (2006, p. 767). Scholars have noted how the 'doubled narration that visually and verbally represents the self, often in conflicting registers and different temporalities' (Chute 2010, p. 5), can offer complex and queer possibilities for representing diverse subjectivities (Chute 2010, Scott and Fawaz 2018). Throughout *Honor Girl,* Thrash uses a conventional comic layout for the majority of the text, each page offering a series of panels that are read left to right. However, in moments of sexual longing or physical connection between Maggie and Erin, Thrash disrupts these conventions by deploying unconventionally shaped panels, full-page illustrations with inset panels, and sequences without dialogue or narration to slow and complicate time so the reader is positioned to linger on moments of queer desire.

The first key moment of Maggie and Erin's relationship, when Maggie finally summons the courage to hold hands with Erin, is shared with the reader via a double page of scattered panels of varying sizes (Thrash 2015, pp. 98–99). With the inclusion of vertical, open, horizontal, inset and overlaid panels, this sequence breaks with the previous layout structure that had offered a consistent left to right series of panels in linear sequence. As Maggie realises her blossoming attraction to Erin, the destabilisation of narrative consistency offers young readers a complex textual space where they can read and experience Maggie's nerves through a fractured and disassembled layout. As Chute writes, gutters are the 'rich empty space between the selected moments', where readers 'project causality' within the 'punctual moments of the frames' (Chute 2010, p. 8). In this moment, the previous evenly spaced and consistent use of gutters is disbanded for large, uneven and complex space between frames. To glance at these pages, this is a sequence where two girls are depicted holding hands, but the strategic deployment of panels and gutters creates a feeling that reflects Maggie's nervousness. The sequence concludes with an open (unframed) image of Maggie and Erin centred at the bottom of the page, both girls smiling as they look at their interlaced fingers. The repeated depiction of interlaced fingers across eight panels over the two-page spread emphasises the electricity of Maggie's first physical connection with another girl.

Visualisations of fifteen-year-old Maggie's desires and fantasies purposefully complicate reality in this text. Maggie's desire to touch Erin plays out further in a later dream sequence, with the two girls meeting serendipitously in the middle of the night. The colour scheme of the text – previously dominated by sunny pastels – now features only blues, purples and greys. As they sit together, knees touching, Erin makes her desire clear: 'I'm just going to pretend I can't see you. Because if I see you, you'd be in huge trouble' (Thrash 2015, p. 109). As readers turn the page they encounter another moment of visual disruption from the conventional layout where a triangle panel is centred. This unusual panel emphasises the moment that Erin pulls Maggie toward her. This is followed by a sequence of three panels that show their hands entwined, a mid-shot of Maggie kissing Erin, and then a close-up of their lips locked together. The opposite page features a full-sized image of the yellow moon reflecting on the surface of the river. The full-page image here acts as a pause, a moment that encourages readers to take time to imagine further what actions might be taking place on the bank of the river (pp. 110–111). This four-page narrative sequence is then violently disrupted, as over the page Maggie's bunkmate is seen yelling her name and asking if she is awake. As Chute highlights, the medium of the comic is 'centrally occupied with experiments in spatiotemporal representation' (2010, p. 17), and these 'experiments' position readers to align with particular experiences. A chronic sleepwalker, Maggie realises that her foot leash (used to limit her sleep walking) has been removed, and the sequence ends with Maggie looking back to an empty riverbank. The queer potential of this moment is not just the visual depiction of fifteen-year-old Maggie's fantasy, but the lack of clarity in the text as to whether or not the moment between them actually happened.

As the narrative progresses and Maggie and Erin come closer and closer to kissing, it is made clear that Maggie's fantasies about kissing and touching Erin were in fact dreams. The reality of the situation is that Erin is significantly older than Maggie and so their desire is considered taboo. This is especially so within the Christian camp setting where same-sex attraction is discouraged, as Maggie discovers later in the narrative. Before their attraction to each other is discovered and ended by the camp director, there is a moment when Erin lifts Maggie onto a large tree root and the full-page image of them arm-in-arm again provides a break for readers to focus on the possibility that a real kiss will eventuate (Thrash 2015, p. 148). The following double page offers two large mirror images of Maggie and Erin, with external narrative from seventeen-year-old Maggie reflecting on how she knew that if they were to kiss she would have to be the one who initiated it because of the age difference. But the four small panels that appear below reveal that fifteen-year-old Maggie could not act and the moment was over. The mirror images of Maggie and Erin, as they anticipate their kiss, gestures to the complexity of enacting queer desire for the first time. After fifteen-year-old Maggie's narrative ends, the text returns to the 'present' where seventeen-year-old Maggie faints as Erin goes to kiss her. When Erin then retreats from their interaction and drives her back to her hotel, Maggie is devastated by what has happened. However, in their final scene together, Maggie recognises that the age gap and power dynamic between them is problematic and that she would be better off without Erin. The possibilities offered throughout the graphic narrative visualise and highlight the complexities of young love, queer desire and coming to terms with sexuality. Localising this learned knowledge within Maggie's adolescence means that young readers are given a picture of youth as capable of introspection and agency.

Western discourses attached to youth can work to justify the delegitimisation of queer sexual identity, with one of the 'dominant' narratives expecting pre-adolescent youth to be disconnected from sexual desires while simultaneously 'officially, tacitly' heterosexual (Bruhm and Hurley 2004, p. ix). In terms of the transition into adolescence, young people continue to be positioned as 'interminably outside adulthood', existing in 'a temporary state of being that one is expected to move through and leave behind' (Owens 2015, p. 133). These notions of adolescence enmesh with more targeted assumptions about adolescent negotiations of queer sexuality: 'For those who identify as queer, their desires may be delegitimized by adults who insist they are just going through a phase' (Kokkola 2013, p. 109). Overlapping discourses like these suggest that to be 'not adult' is to be uncertain and incapable of engaging with the complexities of sexuality – particularly queer sexuality. Carol Maurel's *Luisa, Now and Then* offers a counternarrative that presents adolescent sexuality and adult sexuality as entwined and reciprocal. Through visually breaking down demarcations between past and present, as well as adolescent and adult bodies, Maurel's graphic novel challenges boundaries often tacitly instated between adolescence and adulthood concerning awareness of, and engagement with, queer sexualities. In doing so, the text rejects demarcation between what is deemed 'adult' matters and the level of knowledge and understanding of queer desire that is supposedly acceptable for young people.

Originally published in French then adapted to English by Mariko Tamaki, *Luisa, Now and Then* features a double incarnation of the queer protagonist. In this 'time-traveling queer romance' (Maurel 2018, back matter), fifteen-year-old Luisa boards a bus in 1990s France only to disembark years later in contemporary Paris where a disillusioned adult Luisa now lives. The two meet and the narrative takes on a somewhat Dickensian twist, whereby adult Luisa becomes young Luisa's glimpse into her possible future and young Luisa is adult Luisa's haunting from the past. But where literature, including literature for young people, has a history of marginalising queer desires through associating them with ghostly figures (Kokkola 2013, pp. 122–124), young Luisa is far from this. Both Luisas are equally tangible, physical beings who clash first intellectually, then physically, over their conflicting perspectives about the trajectory that adult Luisa's life has taken. In fact, even when young Luisa is threatened with disintegrating, she refuses to be wholly subsumed into adult Luisa's body, as will be discussed further below. The double incarnation of Luisa generates for readers an opportunity to see myriad expressions of queerness play out across bodies that are simultaneously (and paradoxically) both adolescent and adult, the same person but different.

Comics are particularly well-suited to a reading experience that can enable young people to scrutinise queerness – be it bodies, desires, experiences or ideologies – and attend to this in whatever ways they desire. Hilary Chute (2010) describes how strategies employed when reading graphic narratives offer readers agency in determining their areas of focus and the intensity with which they attend to a topic, an idea, or a moment. She suggests that this form 'avoids the manipulation often associated with film – in which the camera might linger on an image of atrocity for too long, on the one hand, or wash over it too casually, on the other – by allowing a reader to be in control of when she looks at what and how long she spends on each frame' (Chute 2010, p. 9). The freedom to move at will around the page – to ignore the conventions of Western reading practices that rely on left-to-right and top-to-bottom movements across each page – opens up possibilities in how each image can be interpreted. Concurrently, the reader's ability to study at their own discretion any aspect of the page affords agency and can encourage participatory rather than distanced engagements with queer adolescent desire in a text like *Luisa, Now and Then*. For example, in a sepia flashback chronicling young Luisa's accidental first kiss with her friend Lucie early in the book, readers are met with a spread featuring a set of six panels that sequentially present how an accidental loss of balance leads to the two girls kissing passionately. At the top of the page, a horizontal panel spans the width of the page depicting a hand catching and bracing another. At the centre of the page two square panels juxtapose the wide-eyed moment their lips press together, immediately followed by their withdrawal from each other. Finally, a tryptic strip sits at the bottom of the page where a second, intentional kiss is initiated and prolonged, with the last panel of the trio a close-up of the two girls kissing with eyes closed. To read sequentially is to follow a linear path from accident to intention in this scene, with the subsequent page turns revealing that Luisa soon breaks away then leaves abruptly.

However, the potential for non-linear, queer engagements exists for readers here. Chute suggests:

> The movement of the eye on the page instantly takes in the whole grid of panels and its particular opening elements at once; comics suggest we look, and then look again. In this sense, it builds a productive recursivity into its narrative scaffolding.
>
> (2010, p. 8)

The spread in question lends itself to multiple rereadings prior to the page turn that can allow young readers opportunities to linger within, scrutinise and repeatedly reconstruct this moment between the two girls before moving on if they so choose. Each panel is borderless and separated by white space, allowing for easy movement between each square or rectangular panel in whatever direction is desired. Likewise, the lack of dialogue and written narration removes the need to attend to a strict chronological reading to understand verbally directed contexts. But even beyond that, the ordering and construction of the images facilitates more fluid movements around the page. In the final strip, which offers three slices charting the two girls' bodies moving closer, the eye can move back and forth to re-engage with the different aspects of intimacy on display; from the direct eye contact in the first panel, to the emphasis on the closeness of their bodies and intimate touch in the second, to the kiss itself in the third. The second and third of these panels in particular can coexist – they do not have to be read as one act after another but can instead be simultaneous as their proximity allows for both to be witnessed at once. The relationship between the first panel of the middle strip and the last panel of the bottom strip also encourages a non-linear return. The images are quasi-mirrored, with the same grey background and Luisa positioned to the left and Lucie to the right. Both also feature the girls kissing, with the similarities and differences between the body language during each kiss drawing the eye to repeatedly move horizontally to engage in somewhat of a 'spot the difference'. Those differences are key, as the key divergences are in the girls' expressions and the proximity of their bodies. The ability for young readers to plot their own trajectory around any given page, and to play with the way time moves in intimate moments like this, affords opportunities to take control of the way they can connect with queer bodies, desires and experiences that appear on the page.

More broadly, *Luisa, Now and Then* uses the meeting of young and adult Luisa to assist both characters in negotiating their sexuality; for young Luisa this means recognising the legitimacy of her feelings for Lucie, while for adult Luisa it prompts her to acknowledge her repressed desires for women, particularly her neighbour, Sasha. This unusual meeting is possible through a bending of time and space that goes unexplained throughout the narrative, even at the conclusion when young Luisa simply returns home via a similar bus trip. But it is the graphic narrative form that particularly transforms this scenario into an opportunity to disrupt ingrained assumptions about young people's capacity to be queer sexual beings. Chute argues that the ability of graphic narratives to represent 'time as space on the page' enables a unique 'palimpsesting [of] past and present moments together in panels that are traditionally understood to represent only one temporal register' (2010, p. 7). The text uses the visual narrative and the premise of an unexplained meeting across time to literally blur distinctions between now and then, adult and child. While at first it is the striking visual similarities, shared name and memories that evidence the two Luisas as the same person, this evolves throughout the narrative to a point where the two Luisas start to merge. During her time in contemporary Paris, young Luisa begins to age rapidly, while adult Luisa notices that her skin, body shape and eyesight are all becoming more youthful. This visual representation of non-linear time – of being present, past and future on a single page and even in a single body – queers understandings of conventional time and starts to unravel the Western assumption that the 'emergence of the adult from the dangerous and unruly period of adolescence [i]s the desired process of maturation' (Halberstam 2005, p. 4).

Rather, *Luisa, Now and Then* troubles easy demarcations of adolescent and adult through its undoing of temporal logic, with young Luisa's merging with adult Luisa sparking the evolution of both in the way that they think about their sexual identities and desires. At the climax of the narrative both Luisas engage in a physical brawl that culminates in the two disintegrating and merging into a single figure. As the combined young/adult Luisa races to meet her mother, the visual narrative shows alternating or sometimes combined images of the two. Young Luisa's body sits in the backseat of a taxi, but adult Luisa is visible in the rearview mirror. Likewise, their reflection in car windows and on a shiny floor reveals both in mirrored poses. These visual representations underpin an understanding of the negotiation of sexual awareness – and disclosure of sexuality – as neither wholly the domain of young person nor adult, nor a singular moment. Rather, it is an iterative process, as both young Luisa and adult Luisa must face their mother to have a conversation that interweaves their memories of the past, their understanding of the present, and how they will proceed forward from the point where Luisa discloses that she is 'able to fall in love with women' (Maurel 2018, p. 260). In doing so, the text establishes a counternarrative around the coming-out process to present it as something that recurs across a lifetime. There is no single 'coming out' for Luisa, as even though young and adult Luisa were concurrently present for the conversation with their mother in contemporary Paris, the text then closes with young Luisa back on the bus in the past (her present), returning home to face her mother who – at this point in Luisa's timeline – has yet to be present for the disclosure. Furthermore, Luisa's acknowledgement that she is 'able to fall in love with women' also gestures to the text's openness around sexuality as a spectrum, while affirming both Luisas' same-sex desire through the emphasis not on an inability to 'like *men*' (as her mother puts it) but instead on the *ability to* 'fall in love with women'. By positing these desires in relation to potential rather than deficit, the text not only acknowledges queer sexual desire but also refuses to binarise sexuality for this character who simultaneously embodies adolescence and adulthood. That each Luisa is both the same and different in terms of their experiences of non-hegemonic sexuality suggests an equality between young person and adult in terms of their capacity to understand and experience queer sexual desire.

Tillie Walden's 2018 science fiction space western, *On a Sunbeam*, takes this further, utilising the capacity of comics to offer an immersive reading experience where queer bodies, desires and communities are naturalised and accessible. In theorising the potential inherent in the graphic narrative form, Scott and Fawaz contend that:

> comics function [...] as queer orientation devices, productively directing readers towards deviant bodies that refuse to be fixed in one image or frame, toward new desires for fantasy worlds that rebel against the constraints of everyday life, and toward new kinds of counterpublic affiliations among readers who identify with the queer, deviant, maladjusted form called comics.
>
> (2018, p. 203)

On a Sunbeam projects multiple overlapping naturalised and unchallenged visions of queer desires across all ages. Quite literally 'rebel[ling] against the constraints of everyday life', the text reimagines entire galaxies in order to reorient the ways young readers can engage with queer female sexualities. The narrative weaves together two timelines: in one, nineteen-year-old protagonist Mia journeys through space after she joins the crew aboard the spaceship *Aktis*; in the other, readers witness fourteen-year-old Mia's exploits at an elite space-based boarding school and her budding love with transfer student Grace. The narrative shifts swiftly from present to past just as Mia and the team move swiftly between restoration jobs. Like Mia, who must learn quickly on the job, the reader is placed in a similar position in which there is often work to be done to produce connections within the story, as well as to slowly recognise that this is a universe where same-sex relationships are the only relationships and cisgender men do not seem to exist anymore. A rescue/romance narrative, Mia works closely with Captain Char, Char's partner Alma, unruly bunkmate, Jules, and gender non-binary and non-verbal engineering specialist, Ell, who are employed to rebuild architectural space ruins throughout the galaxy. As the narrative progresses, Mia and the crew embark on a mission to search for Mia's lost first love, Grace.

Walden's visual style of fried egg shaped, fluid space and wind-kissed planetary landscapes produces an aesthetic of a space that is in constant flux. This aesthetic condition – with its malleable boundaries, fluid panels and vertical transitions – queers ideas of a stable, linear development of queer subjectivity while simultaneously creating a vision of queer sexuality uncontained and unchallenged. The social condition in this narrative, alongside this visual aesthetic, offers readers the possibility for imagining queer futures. As José Muñoz puts it, queerness may be a condition that is not yet upon us:

> Queerness is that thing that lets us feel that this world is not enough, that indeed something is missing. Often we can glimpse the worlds proposed and promised by queerness in the realm of the aesthetic.

The aesthetic, especially the queer aesthetic, frequently contains blueprints and schemata of a forward-dawning futurity.

(2009, p. 1)

On a Sunbeam functions as one such vehicle for 'forward-dawning futurity' as the convergence of aesthetic, form and narrative posit infinite possibilities. The vibrant, expansive aesthetic of Walden's style and the ambitious revisioning of societal structure renders an imagined future of queer community and acceptance of same-sex desire far beyond our contemporary world. Cart and Jenkins (2006) note that the finding of a queer community is one of the three main narratives regularly depicted in gay and lesbian young adult fiction. However, the intergalactic world of *On a Sunbeam* moves beyond queer community, as displayed through Mia's newfound crew, toward a queer female 'utopia'. When the intergalactic worlds featured in the narrative are only comprised of women and those who are non-binary – with the absence of men not even addressed in the narrative[1] – same-sex desire operates as a social condition rather than being defined and measured in relation to heterosexuality. Rendering heteronormativity non-existent for the protracted span of the narrative consequently removes many of the complications inherent in the notion of coming out, in particular its association with young people that both Maggie and Luisa must negotiate in *Honor Girl* and *Luisa, Now and Then*. There is no coming out in *On a Sunbeam*, no pushback from figures demanding adherence to heteronormative traditions, and no anxiety around same-sex desire. Readers are instead offered visions where same-sex desire, intimacy and connection are valid and productive across all stages of life, with Mia's bourgeoning relationship with Grace when she was fourteen years old and Alma and Char's strong, long-term relationship in Mia's present-day life equally vibrant in the narrative.

First published online, then published in print form as a 533-page graphic novel, *On a Sunbeam* features twenty chapters. In the online form, these chapters are located through circular icons that allow the reader to scroll vertically through the science fiction world created by Walden's filmic illustrative style and vast lunar landscapes. Our analysis here focuses on the online publication as the vertical scrolling function adds considerably to the way the reading experience can be interactive, immersive and varied. When read online in the form offered in full on the author's website, each chapter scrolls vertically so the reading process shifts from a traditional left-to-right series of panels (McCloud 1993) to block horizontal panels, quadrilateral panels, or fluvial gutters that swirl across and down the page, drawing readers into a downward and animated reading experience. Distinct colour palettes further demarcate Mia's past and present, with blues and greys that frame her young romance with Grace suggestive of distance and discomfort, while a palette of purple and lilac signal her present difficulty with emotionality years after her separation from Grace. As Mia's dual narratives progress and readers see her come to terms with the events of her past, the colour palette swirls with oranges and yellows signalling the interconnection between Mia's past and present selves. As with *Luisa, Now and Then*, this cue to perceive past and present as coexistent rather than mutually exclusive contributes to the work the text does in disrupting static, linear notions of sexual understanding. Mia's past romance with Grace is not something concluded at the 'end' of childhood/youth, but instead something that blends with her ongoing development and shapes her future.

This is reinforced when these separate narratives visually come together at the midpoint of the story through a literal bleeding of colour and framing as Mia tells the crew her history with Grace. Mia sits cross-legged on a pink floor with purple shading behind her as she begins her story. The floor acts as a faux half-page border that then drips down into the bottom half of the page. The pink and white of the cascading floor disappears into the two-tone blue landscape of Mia's school narrative. The merging of the two time periods signals the interconnected navigation of love, friendship and regret experienced by both past and present Mia. These intertwined narratives are visually depicted as the text progresses with a reduction in panelled pages, and more full-page illustrations showcasing transient landscapes and the vastness of space, as Mia and the crew fly into the dangerous world of 'The Staircase' to attempt to reconnect with Grace. When Grace and Mia do reconnect, the narrative continues to destabilise assumptions. Grace may be happy to see Mia, but she does not seek to rekindle their relationship, which has been such a focal point throughout the extensive narrative. Both remain content with friendship, and Mia offers Grace a place on the *Sunbeam*. Through this, readers are offered yet one more example of a powerful queer connection that resists conventional assumptions of romantic or monogamous coupling as the natural and inevitable narrative end point. The text closes with the crew of the *Sunbeam* working together to fix a broken wing; a vision of a young queer collective existing in a world that can offer seemingly limitless expressions of queerness, particularly queer girlhoods.

In 2017, Gwen Tarbox identified the 'medium of comics' as 'an integral part of the young adult category' (p. 233). Contemporary YA graphic narratives like the ones addressed here present an apt site for excavating visions of queer girlhoods and the shifting ways the relationships between young people and sexuality are conceived in, and through, these narratives.

Note

1 That is not to say that this world operates without spectres of the existence of men. Mia attends 'Cleary's School for Girls', with the inclusion of 'for Girls' in the formal school title implying that this institution sits in contrast to other institutions (whether they exist in the past or present is unclear). Likewise, Jules declares Ell to be 'non-binary' early in the narrative, with the verbalisation of

this term likewise indicating a shared understanding in this world of binarised gender identities. Jules and Mia's offhand use of 'dude' and 'man' to refer to each other in dialogue also gestures to a history that included men.

References

Bauer, H 2015, 'Comics, graphic narratives, and lesbian lives', *The Cambridge Companion to Lesbian Literature*, Ed. J Medd, Cambridge University Press, New York, pp. 219–236.

Bechdel, A 2006, *Fun Home: a Family Tragicomic*, Mariner Books, Boston & New York.

Bruhm, S and Hurley, N 2004, *Curiouser: on the Queerness of Children*, University of Minnesota Press, Minneapolis & London.

Cart, M and Jenkins, C 2006, *The Heart Has Its Reasons: Young Adult Literature with Gay/Lesbian/Queer Content*, 1969–2004, Scarecrow Press, USA.

Chute, H 2010, *Graphic Women: Life Narrative and Contemporary Comics*, Columbia University Press, New York.

Chute, HL and DeKoven, M 2006, 'Introduction: graphic narrative', *MFS Modern Fiction Studies*, vol. 52, no. 4, pp. 767–782.

Gillingham, E 2018, 'Representations of same-sex relationships between female characters in all-ages comics: *Princess Princess Ever After* and *Lumberjanes*', *Journal of Lesbian Studies*, vol. 22, no. 4, pp. 1–12.

Halberstam, J 2005, *In a Queer Time and Place: Transgender Bodies, Subcultural Lives*, New York University Press, New York & London.

Kokkola, L 2013, *Fictions of Adolescent Carnality: Sexy Sinners and Delinquent Deviants*, John Benjamins Publishing, Amsterdam.

Maurel, C 2018, *Luisa, Now and Then*, adapted by M Tamaki, Life Drawn, Los Angeles, CA.

McCloud, S 1993, *Understanding Comics: the Invisible Art*, HarperPerennial, New York.

Muñoz, JE 2009, *Cruising Utopia: the Then and There of Queer Futurity*, New York University Press, New York.

Owens, G 2015, 'Toward a theory of adolescence: queer disruptions in representations of adolescent reading', *Jeunuesse: Young People, Texts, Cultures*, vol. 7, no. 1, pp. 110–134.

Scott, D and Fawaz, R 2018, 'Introduction: queer about comics', *American Literature*, vol. 90, no. 2, pp. 197–219.

Tarbox, GA 2017, 'Young adult comics and the critics: a call for new modes of interdisciplinary reading', *Children's Literature Association Quarterly*, vol. 42, no. 2, pp. 231–243.

Tarbox, GA and Abate, MA 2017, 'Introduction', *Graphic Novels for Children and Young Adults: a Collection of Critical Essays*, Eds. MA Abate and GA Tarbox, University Press of Mississippi, Jackson, pp. 3–16.

Thrash, M 2015, *Honor Girl*, Candlewick Press, Somerville, MA.

Walden, T 2018, *On a Sunbeam*, Digital comic, retrieved 31 October 2020, www.onasunbeam.com/.

8 'Are You Sure We're Witches and not Puritans?'

Sexual Flexibility and Unrealised Desire in Netflix's *Chilling Adventures of Sabrina*

Debra Dudek

Sabrina the Teen-age Witch first appeared in Archie Comics in 1962. Even then, Sabrina straddled human and witch worlds, trying simultaneously to defy and belong to both. Since that time, Sabrina reappeared in a sitcom in the 1990s, in Archie Horror comics (2018-), and, more recently, in the Netflix television series *Chilling Adventures of Sabrina* (2018–). In each manifestation, Sabrina embodies a liminal state inherent in young adults and witches alike. In *Chilling Adventures of Sabrina*, however, this liminality is situated between troubling binaries about human and witch sexuality, with humans leaning towards heteronormativity and witches towards sexual flexibility. Although Sabrina repeatedly advocates for power in liminality, ultimately the series defaults to heteronormative monogamy rather than sexual flexibility by denying Sabrina the opportunity to realise her desire fully.

Aesthetically and ideologically, Netflix's *Chilling Adventures of Sabrina* draws upon Sabrina's first appearance in Archie Comics in 1962 and more fully upon her recent horror-inflected re-emergence in 2018. The opening credits animate key beats of Roberto Aguirre-Sacasa and Robert Hack's *Chilling Adventures of Sabrina* comic and acknowledge that the series is based upon the Archie Comic character by replicating the first panel in which Sabrina appeared. She was introduced in *Archie's Mad House* #22 (October 1962) and became so popular that she became star of her own comic book series—*Sabrina the Teen-age Witch*—in January 1972 (Gorelick 2017, p. 4).

Sabrina the Teen-age Witch Comic

The original *Sabrina the Teen-age Witch* comic introduces Sabrina's witch identity as one that trades love for power, a dynamic that infuses her most recent manifestation, as I shall discuss shortly. In the October 1962 issue of *Archie's Mad House* that introduced Sabrina, Sabrina directly addresses readers' expectations about witches by debunking stereotypes:

they do not live on a 'dreary mountain top' or wear 'grubby old rags' or make 'some nasty old brew' (Gladir et al. 2017, p. 11). Instead, modern witches 'believe life should be a ball' (Gladir et al. 2017, p. 12) and can be identified by their familiars, who are animals that assist with their witchcraft; their inability to cry; and their incapacity to sink in water. Most relevant to *Chilling Adventures*, however, is that witches can make other people fall in love, but they are not 'permitted to fall in love [themselves] … . that would make the head witches very angry' (Gladir et al. 2017, pp. 12–13). *Chilling Adventures* draws most heavily upon this last characteristic, as well as on Sabrina's uncertainty about the trade-off of love for power.

The final four panels of the five-page 1962 introduction to Sabrina suggest a power–love binary about which Sabrina is undecided. While Sabrina is an object of desire and has the power to make other people fall in love, she herself does not experience love. As she narrates in text boxes, 'Everywhere I go the boys are simply wild over me! But you'll never catch me falling in love … that would mean I would lose my powers and become human' (Gladir et al. 2017, p. 15). The narrative switches from text boxes to speech bubbles—a change that implies a move from a distant narration to a personal reflection—in the final two panels when Sabrina continues, 'and that would be bad! … I think!' (p.15). Sabrina's cool demeanour in the second last panel, as she looks in profile at a couple cuddling on a park bench, changes in the last panel. In this close-up panel of her face, Sabrina looks directly at the reader, her index finger touching her lip in a gesture of uncertainty.

Although this first introduction to Sabrina's character—and to witches more generally—focuses upon witches' commitment to power and not to love, the main narrative arc that repeats throughout the early *Sabrina the Teen-age Witch* comics is Sabrina's attraction to various young men, and, beginning in December 1969, her relationship with her boyfriend Harvey. In other words, even the earliest Sabrina stories, running from 1962 to 1971, depict Sabrina as a witch who defies witch authority and exists in a liminal space between humans and witches. She stays committed to her witch duties, casting spells that wreak havoc, while also dating the human Harvey against her Aunt Hilda's wishes. Aguirre-Sacasa's *Chilling Adventures of Sabrina: Book One* (2018) comic pulls threads from these stories and weaves them into a horror version.

Chilling Adventures of Sabrina Comic

In *Chilling Adventures of Sabrina* comic, a human and witch opposition begins with clashing ideologies expressed by Sabrina's witch father and mortal mother. The comic opens on Halloween day 1951, one year after Sabrina's birth. Sabrina's father, Edward Spellman, High Priest of the Church of Night, prepares to deliver Sabrina to Satan, the Dark Lord. Sabrina's mother Diana, however, has taken Sabrina and run away with her to save her from Edward and the coven. Edward catches Diana, takes the baby, casts a spell basically to lobotomise Diana, and has her committed to a clinic for the mentally unwell. The comic then fast forwards through Sabrina's life from a baby to a six-year-old to a twelve-year-old and then slows down time to focus on Sabrina as a teenager. This cross-over with the earlier *Sabrina the Teen-age Witch* comic includes the main characters of: Sabrina; her two aunts Hilda and Zelda, with whom she lives; her cousin Ambrose; and her love interest Harvey Kinkle. The comic also contains two key ideologies that the Netflix series embeds and problematises: witch law forbids witches to 'consort with mortals' (Aguirre-Sacasa 2018, np) as Aunt Zelda states; and mortals can know true love but witches cannot.

In the comic, when Sabrina develops a crush on Harvey, however, she shuns witch law to pursue her desire. Sabrina and Ambrose cast a spell to encourage Harvey's heart to come to Sabrina metaphorically and, by one week before her sixteenth birthday, Harvey and Sabrina are dating. They express their desire through public displays of affection, kissing on the high school bleachers and in parking lots. When Harvey verbally pressures Sabrina into having sex with him on her sixteenth birthday, however, Sabrina tells him she cannot, even though it is frustrating for her too. My chapter takes its title from a flashback conversation between Sabrina and Aunt Hilda, which occurs six months before Sabrina's sixteenth birthday. Hilda explains to Sabrina that with the privilege of being a witch comes certain rules:

> Hilda: there will no defilement, of any kind, before a young witch's confirmation at the age of sixteen… I understand, I do, so many challenges facing young women during these tumultuous times, but on this one **extremely** specific point, there's no middle-ground. If you plan on writing your name in the Dark Lord's book, you _must_ be pure of mind and body.
>
> Sabrina: Are you sure we're witches and not Puritans, Aunt Hilda?
>
> (Aguirre-Sacasa 2018, np)

This conversation condenses a key aspect of Sabrina's character: while Hilda claims there exists no middle ground, Sabrina questions rules that refuse her desire for liminal subjectivity and sexual flexibility. Sabrina's question to her aunt also implies that Sabrina rejects an innocence/experience dichotomy, as well as the notion that sex constitutes defilement of her body.

Chilling Adventures of Sabrina Netflix Series

Netflix's television series *Chilling Adventures of Sabrina* combines elements from its comic source material with aspects of other paranormal screen romances—such as those depicted in *Buffy the Vampire Slayer*,

Twilight, and *The Vampire Diaries*—which feature a romance between a supernatural and a human being. While *Chilling Adventures* pays homage to these earlier screen stories, the romance between witch-human Sabrina and fully human Harvey informs, but does not drive, the narrative. The central conflict is not that a witch loves a mortal, but rather that Sabrina is pressured to choose between a future as a human or as a witch, at least in season one. Sabrina frames this decision as a choice between living as a human and keeping her mortal boyfriend and her best friends or living as and gaining the powers of a witch, as her two aunts say she must. Sabrina repeatedly questions why she must choose between human and witch and argues that she wants to inhabit both worlds.

At the time of writing this chapter, Netflix's *Chilling Adventures of Sabrina* comprises two seasons, or two parts, with each part containing ten episodes or chapters. In other words, the format of the television series mimics the structure of a book. Part one introduces fifteen-year-old half-witch Sabrina Spellman, who lives in Greendale with her father's sisters, witches Zelda and Hilda. Sabrina's parents, Edward, a warlock, and Diana, a human, died in a suspicious airplane crash when Sabrina was a baby, leaving her to be raised by her aunts. Edward's marriage to Diana nearly resulted in his excommunication from Satan's Church of Night—the witches' church—where Edward was High Priest because, under witch law, witches and mortals are forbidden from marrying. As High Priest, Edward petitioned the church and received special dispensation to marry Diana. Sabrina frequently uses her parents' marriage as precedence for her own challenges to church law, claiming their mixed marriage stands as an example of the interrelationship between mortals and witches, in opposition to the seemingly entrenched laws that the church enforces under the current leadership of the patriarchal misogynist Father Blackwood.

Sabrina's resistance to Father Blackwood's ideologies also situates *Chilling Adventures* within a broader genre of young adult paranormal romance in which personal coming of age narratives feature metonymically as challenges to an established power structure. In *Chilling Adventures*, for instance, church law dictates that, in order to obtain full powers, witches (and warlocks) must sign their name in the Dark Lord's book on their sixteenth birthday to show their dedication to Satan and his laws. Chapter one of the series introduces Sabrina in the week before her sixteenth birthday divided between her human and witch identities: in her life at Baxter High School with her friends, Susie and Roz; her boyfriend, Harvey; and at home with her aunts and her warlock cousin, Ambrose. Her mortal friends initially do not know Sabrina is a witch, and Sabrina's family encourages her to lie to her friends and to tell them she is transferring to a new school. Once she signs her name in the Dark Lord's book, she must—or will want to—sever all ties to the mortal world because she will grow older at a slower rate than them and her witch powers will distance her from them emotionally.

Sabrina's continued resistance to being pressured to abide by dichotomous patriarchal ideologies results in her occupying a liminal pedagogical space. When Sabrina refuses to sign her name in the Dark Lord's book, she strikes a compromise with the Church of Night by agreeing to attend both the mortals' Baxter High and the witches' Academy of Unseen Arts. At the academy, Sabrina meets the three Weird Sisters—Prudence, Dorcas, and Agatha—and Nicholas/Nick Scratch, who in season two/part two becomes Sabrina's boyfriend. When Sabrina first arrives at the academy, the Weird Sisters bully and abuse her, saying they hate her because she is a half-breed who will eventually betray witches, just as her father did by marrying her mortal mother. Over the course of the series, however, the relationship between Sabrina and the Weird Sisters becomes informed less by hatred and more by comradery, as the Weird Sisters—and especially Prudence—learn from Sabrina that the most powerful threat to their wellbeing is the patriarchal Church of Night.

Witches—such as Sabrina, her aunties, and the Weird Sisters—embody contradictions about power. On the one hand, for instance, they can cast spells that bring people back from the dead, but, on the other hand, they (mostly) abide by witch law, which controls the amount of power they have and puts them at the mercy of a patriarchal Dark Lord and his High Priest, Father Blackwood. In his essay, 'Figuring the witch', David Punter argues that witches' powers contain an 'ancient wisdom which we ignore at our peril' but that this power has historically been shown 'to be ineffectual, incapable of resisting authority' (2017, p. 67). This struggle between being powerful and yet having that power repeatedly questioned and punished seems core to the narrative arc of *Chilling Adventures of Sabrina*, as her aunties pressure Sabrina to sign her name in the Dark Lord's book, which serves as a metaphor for both gaining and losing power: Sabrina gains witch powers but loses power to the Dark Lord, to whom she is indebted once she signs her name in his book. The tension in the first season rests upon Sabrina's decision and indecision about whether or not to go through with her Dark Baptism, the ritual in which she signs her name in the Dark Lord's book on her sixteenth birthday in order to become a full witch.

Sabrina frequently pushes against the binaries implicit in the witch world. Witch law stems from one basic binary, which Sabrina's aunts articulate in the first episode of the series, 'Chapter one: October country'. Sabrina asks her aunties if she can postpone her Dark Baptism because she does not want to end her human relationships. When her aunties ask Sabrina why she wants to postpone her baptism, the following conversation occurs:

SABRINA: I admit, I have reservations about saving myself for the Dark
    Lord. Why does he get to decide what I do or don't do with my body?
AUNT ZELDA: Because it is witch law. Covenant.
SABRINA: Okay, but why?
    ...

AUNT ZELDA: It is our sacred duty and honor to serve the Dark Lord. The extraordinary delicious gifts he bestows on us in return for signing his book.

... ...

AUNT HILDA: Sabrina, do you not want to join the Church of Night as a full member, my love?

SABRINA: I think so. I just don't know why I have to give up everything in my life that's human to do it.

AUNT ZELDA: Witch law. The Path of Night or the Path of Light.

SABRINA, HILDA, AND ZELDA TOGETHER: But not both.

I quote this scene at some length because it establishes three basic binaries upon which the series rests: witch/human; night/light; and purity/defilement. This last binary is the one that most explicitly relates to Sabrina's— and perhaps all witches'—personal and political power. Sabrina rightly questions why the Dark Lord has dominion over her sexuality, and Zelda's pedantic response is less than convincing. That all three witches say 'But not both' together suggests it is an oft-quoted mantra.

Sabrina's response to Hilda's question about wanting to join the Church of Night points to Sabrina's desire not to choose one or the other side of the binaries but to embody both. This state of undecidability is a position that Punter connects to a witch's subjectivity:

> the witch comes to remind us ... . that we are frequently in the presence not of firmly maintained binaries but rather of the undecidable... ... the 'question of the witch' is not one of those questions susceptible to a permanent answer ... but rather to do with transient, becoming, halting, temporary, liminal states: what might it be like, not to *be* a witch, but rather to experience a moment of 'witch-becoming', being able to think and feel with the intelligence and the sense of a witch?
>
> (2017, p. 68)

Sabrina seems intent upon existing in a liminal state in which she can embody both the human and witch aspects of her personality, and viewers are positioned to align and agree with her vehemence.

The show suggests that every moment leading up to a witch's baptism contributes to her witch-becoming. Sabrina's aunties make this point explicitly in the first episode after Sabrina tells them that she has chosen her baptismal name to be Edwina Diana in order to honour both her parents. Hilda responds: 'Your parents would be so proud of the young woman you've become'. Zelda admonishes her: 'Correction Hilda! They would be so proud of the witch she is becoming.' Zelda's response reflects Punter's notion that the process of becoming a witch should be embraced as a movement towards empowerment in opposition to human ideas of development, which suggest that a girl's identity reaches an end point with womanhood. While Hilda and Zelda often feature in opposition to one another, their dichotomy also weakens throughout the series as Hilda flexes her witch powers and Zelda empathises with humans. One of Sabrina's defences against having to choose between witch and mortal rests upon her parentage, that is, her witch father marrying her human mother, so her choice of name may be seen as another way of rebelling against a witch–human binary and of embodying both.

While Sabrina's aunties use the language of becoming, Sabrina addresses not what the future holds but what she is leaving behind—her friends, her boyfriend, and her girlhood. As a way of trying to live in both worlds and to be honest with Harvey, Sabrina decides to go against her cousin's recommendation to lie to Harvey and instead takes him into the woods to show him where she was born and where she will be reborn. In a scene that visually references the moment in *Twilight* when Bella leads Edward into the woods to confront him about being a vampire, Sabrina describes her Dark Baptism to Harvey and equates it to a bat mitzvah or a *quinceañera*, a ritual in which, as she says to Harvey, she will leave her 'girlhood behind' ('Chapter one: October country'). Harvey responds by asking her if leaving her girlhood behind is a metaphor. It is, but in more ways than Harvey knows. The implication is that she is leaving her human life, her virginity, and her girlhood behind in order to become a sexually active, womanly, witch.

Perhaps the most confounding aspect of Sabrina's liminal state, of experiencing witch-becoming, is how it relates to Sabrina's sexuality. Sabrina's choice between human and witch is underpinned by an ambiguous, unstable, and problematic dichotomy about sexual identity. To be human supposedly means agreeing to be monogamous, identifying as straight, and being able to fall in love. Witches, on the other hand, apparently cannot fall in love, believe in polygamy, and express sexual flexibility. In their article 'Malleable identities, leaky taxonomies: the matter of sexual flexibility', Susanna Paasonen and Sanna Spisak advocate for taking 'seriously the openness and diversity' with which young people define their sexual self-identifications: 'Rather than presuming that their self-definitions will become at some point fixed along the binary categories of straight versus lesbian/gay/queer, we suggest that the openness … disrupts … identity categories' (2018, p. 1375). They conclude that 'there seems to be newness to how younger people approach and disclose their non-binary palates outside the framings of either humour or shame' (2018, pp. 1375–1376). This notion of sexual flexibility seems to align with an idea of witch-becoming in that both concepts refuse binaries and posit a liminal space that provides more freedom to explore and embrace a variety of sexualities, especially for young people.

The series seems to advocate for sexual flexibility, at least for witches and warlocks. For instance, Ambrose's first lover is the warlock Luke ('Chapter three: The trial of Sabrina Spellman'). Later, he engages in an orgy with Luke, the Weird Sisters, and Nick ('Chapter seven: Feast of feasts'), and in the sexual frenzy of Lupercalia ('Chapter fourteen:

Lupercalia'), he partners with Prudence. Similarly, in the past, Nick dated the three Weird Sisters at the same time and he, too, engages in the orgy. At one point, Nick says to Sabrina, 'You have two natures, go to two schools, why not date two guys? I'm down with sharing' ('Chapter six: An exorcism in Greendale'). Sabrina's response to being invited by Nick to participate in the orgy or to date two guys is never more judgmental than a raised eyebrow or an exit from the situation, so the first nine episodes of part one suggest that, although Sabrina is committed to her straight, monogamous relationship with Harvey, sexual flexibility is part of witch culture, and therefore part of her witch-becoming identity.

Although Sabrina and Harvey are straight, monogamous virgins, the way Sabrina expresses her sexuality *is* on a sexual flexibility spectrum. While Harvey and Sabrina do not engage in sexual intercourse, they do have a very sensual relationship. Roz and Susie tease them about their public displays of affection in which they kiss passionately, and Sabrina and Harvey show no shame in being naked together. One of the most erotic scenes between Sabrina and Harvey occurs when she asks him to check her body for a birthmark, which she believes she does not have. In 'Chapter three: The trial of Sabrina Spellman', the High Priest charges Sabrina with breach of promise for not signing the *Book of the Beast* and summons her and her aunties to trial. One way of defending herself is to prove that she is not a witch and therefore should be tried under mortal and not witch law. To prove she is not a witch, the witch's court demands Sabrina strip naked in front of the court to search for a witch's mark. To prepare for court, Sabrina takes Harvey into the woods and asks him to look for a birthmark. Facing him, Sabrina slowly unbuttons and removes her top and Harvey does the same. She then unclips her bra, holds the front of it against her, turns her back to him, and leans her neck down to expose her back and neck flesh. In a series of slow close-up shots, Harvey trails a finger down Sabrina's back, neck, shoulders, spine, causing goosebumps to rise on Sabrina's flesh. Sabrina then turns to Harvey and says, 'Before you keep looking …' and kisses him, their bare chests pressed against each other. Although the scene ends here, the implication is that they shed the rest of their clothes and continue intimately touching each other without engaging in intercourse.

The sensuality of this scene suggests an already established intimacy between Harvey and Sabrina that will grow throughout the first season, but, instead, they drift apart and never again do more than kiss. This dynamic sets up another potentially problematic binary that places love in opposition to sex, or perhaps passion. In the season one finale, Sabrina and Harvey break up, and Sabrina tells Nick about the end of the relationship:

NICK: You really love him, don't you? [Sabrina nods.] That's the one thing
       I envy. The way [mortals] can give themselves to each other. I mean

witches are aces at passion and lust, but when it comes to love, true love, not so much.

SABRINA: Why is that?

NICK: Our Dark Lord is a jealous lord. He wants us to love him and only him. Selfish, isn't it?

SABRINA: Yeah, but it might be easier in some ways.

NICK: Nah, I'd trade all the witch orgies in the world for what you and the mortal have.

('Chapter ten: The witching hour')

Nick's words suggest an ideological—and perhaps physiological—tension that infuses the series. Initially, it seems witches are unable to experience true love between each other; they feel passion and lust, but not love. When Sabrina asks why witches cannot feel love, Nick's response shifts from physiology to ideology. The reason is not one of inability, but rather that when they pledge themselves to the Dark Lord, they deny themselves the possibility to love anyone more truly than they love him, or perhaps the witch power he bestows upon them also binds their love to him.

With the relationship between Harvey and Sabrina waning and the sexual tension between Sabrina and Nick waxing, viewers are positioned to expect that Sabrina's witch-becoming corresponds to an emerging sexual flexibility, or at least to a more sexually active relationship with Nick, in which her virginity is no longer linked to her value to the Dark Lord. This expectation is heightened in the closing scene of the part one season finale, when Sabrina finally decides/is coerced to sign her name in the *Book of the Beast* in order to access enough witch power necessary to save her friends and family, and, indeed, all of Greendale. After Sabrina signs her name and defeats the witches and angel of death that threaten the town, she goes to Harvey to say goodbye, and he asks for one last kiss. She kisses him softly, and then disappears. This kiss between Harvey and Sabrina functions as a farewell to her human life and to her girlhood. Like the relationship between Matt and Elena in *The Vampire Diaries*, the relationship between Harvey and Sabrina reads like a first love with the boy next door, rather than as a passionate, more fully reciprocal and robust partnership. Although sexual flexibility and being sexually active are not the same, Sabrina's movement away from Harvey and towards Nick, who has repeatedly demonstrated his sexual flexibility, suggests that Sabrina is open to this possibility.

Sabrina's trajectory to sexual flexibility becomes more apparent in the final scene of the episode, when she reappears with the Weird Sisters, her hair and clothing changed to align her with their aesthetic. As Harvey, Roz, and Susie sit on a couch discussing Sabrina and trying to convince themselves that 'She's still Sabrina … still the girl we know', Harvey is not convinced: 'Something had changed, and not just her hair.' The background music, 'A Little Wicked', by Valerie Broussard, fades into and informs the scene. The scene shifts through flames from the couch in Baxter High to the Academy of Unseen Arts. In slow motion, Sabrina walks with the three Weird Sisters towards the viewer holding a direct gaze. The shot shifts back and forth from Sabrina walking towards the viewer and towards Nick, who sits on the bottom of a staircase. As Sabrina draws closer and closer to Nick and to the viewer, she walks to the beat of the music, a slight smile tugging up the corner of her mouth. The final shot of the season is a close-up of Sabrina's face, a teasing smile upon her lips. As she winks into the camera, the music ends with the lyrics, 'I am a little wicked'.

Sabrina's alignment with the Weird Sisters and her movement towards Nick sets up the second season to feature Sabrina's witch-becoming as a sexual-becoming. Now that Sabrina has pledged herself to the Dark Lord, received full witch powers, and seemingly left her mortal life and friends behind, sexual pleasure with Nick seems to be the next step in Sabrina's emerging sexual identity, and the first episode of part two/season two satisfies this expectation. In an outfit-change montage, Sabrina decides what to wear to her first day of full-time school at the Academy of Unseen Arts. She blasts Devo's 'Girl U Want' and spins in front of the mirror, trying on outfit after outfit, wiggling her butt and shaking her hips. She finally decides on a black turtleneck and short tartan skirt, just as Devo sings, 'You know you're headed for the pleasure burn'. Confirming how her new look links to a new identity, Aunt Zelda asks Sabrina at the breakfast table, 'Since when do you wear black? Trying to be edgy, are you? 'Loosen up, Aunt Zee', responds Sabrina. 'It's a new year, a new cycle ('Chapter twelve: The epiphany'). By taking an indefinite leave of absence from Baxter High, Sabrina elects to emerge herself in witch culture and education, which also suggests a sexual immersion. Indeed, when she first sees Nick at school, he tells her he is glad she stayed with her new hairstyle because it 'looks hot'.

If season one unfolded around Sabrina's liminal position between mortal and witch worlds, then season two shifts this liminality to focus upon the intersection between gender politics and sexuality, challenging a male–female binary in which men have power and privilege and women do not. For instance, in the Academy of Unseen Arts, Sabrina challenges 'one of the Academy's grand traditions' ('Chapter twelve: The epiphany') of the customary election of a new top boy, by running for the position, which is usually held by a male student. Thwarted and excluded by Father Blackwood and the male students (except Nick) at every step during the three challenges leading up to the election, Sabrina gains support from Prudence and the other Weird Sisters, therein solidifying the division between men and women that Sabrina seeks to overturn. At the end of the episode, Nick and Sabrina combine forces, which results in their exclusion from the election, so Father Blackwood selects Ambrose as top boy. Although Nick and Sabrina align to challenge Father Blackwood's patriarchal tradition, ultimately the male–female binary holds with Ambrose becoming top boy. Ambrose, however, is the best worst option as Sabrina's cousin, who was not involved in the competition.

Over in Baxter High, Susie throws down a similar challenge to entrenched patriarchy by trying out for the boys' basketball team, in part because there is no girls' team. When the male basketball teacher refuses to let Susie try out for the team, Susie calls Principal Mary Wardwell, who supports Susie and asserts, 'There shall be absolutely no gender discrimination at Baxter High under my regime.' Susie's challenge to change Baxter High's sexist structure begins her overt transition to defy binaries more fully for, at the end of the basketball tryouts, Susie tells Harvey and Roz that their name is Theo now. Roz and Harvey accept Theo literally with open arms as they all engage in a group hug, forecasting the strength of the trio that continues to build throughout the season.

Young mortals and witches challenge structures of patriarchy to forecast season two as a season of rebellion against oppressive ideologies perpetuated mostly by adults. Sabrina, Nick, and Prudence defy Father Blackwood's rules and regulations at the Academy of Unseen Arts, leaving space for Sabrina to ascend to the role of High Priestess. Roz, Harvey, and Theo support Theo in their bid to join the boys' basketball team and to self-identify as male. These challenges to patriarchy and binary ideologies exist alongside a parallel narrative that seemingly defies witch practices. While Aunt Zelda and Father Blackwood engaged in sexual trysts while Lady Blackwood was alive, after Lady Blackwood's death, Zelda tells Blackwood that their relationship will be all business until he makes their romantic relationship legitimate. On one hand, Zelda's insistence on monogamous marriage deviates from witch polygamy and implies that young witch passion and sexual flexibility is a phase they move through before choosing one partner. On the other hand, once Zelda and Blackwood are married, he casts a spell on her, which ensures she follows his commands. This spell may be read as a metaphor for the dangers of losing one's sense of self in a marriage, but more overtly it reinforces Blackwood's patriarchal villainy. Although Sabrina is unaware of this situation, at least initially, viewers are positioned to see young people resisting oppressive gender politics while adults like Zelda actively keep them in place.

In both the mortal and witch worlds, tragic love stories suggest prevailing ideologies about romantic love while providing space for young people to perform their potential sexualities. For instance, in episode two, 'Chapter thirteen: The passion of Sabrina Spellman', Baxter High drama students are required to select and perform a scene from *Romeo and Juliet*. Harvey and Roz pair together, and Harvey suggests they enact the scene in which Romeo and Juliet first meet. When Roz asks Harvey, 'Uh, would that be the kissing scene?' Harvey says, 'I think so. Would that be weird?' The conversation then cuts to Roz's vision/imagination of her and Harvey kissing deeply, signaling her desire for him, and their desire for each other. She responds in the negative to Harvey's question about whether kissing him would be weird, but then asks him if he has spoken with Sabrina. Harvey replies, 'No, not in a while. We're still figuring things out', to which Roz mumbles to herself, 'Hm, aren't we all … Yes, I'll be the Juliet to your Romeo.' Roz's response about everyone trying to figure things out may be read as another liminal space between her desire for Harvey and her concern about Sabrina's response to the potential romance between Harvey and Roz. Harvey's desire for both Roz and Sabrina invokes *Romeo and Juliet*, as does Rosalind's very name, which sounds close to Rosaline, Romeo's beloved before Juliet. In this version of *Romeo and Juliet*, however, Roz embodies both Juliet and Rosaline, Romeo's first and second beloveds.

Both Rosaline and then Sabrina's desire is unrealised, however, ostensibly due to the Dark Lord's actions, which may be read as an assertion of his patriarchal control over their sexual expression. Sabrina returns to Baxter High briefly in an attempt to thwart the attention of the Dark Lord, who has been telling her she must follow his commands because she signed her name in his book. The commands start off small, such as stealing a pack of gum, but Sabrina fears that if she succumbs to his demands, then she will be under his power completely. In retaliation, the Dark Lord gives Roz the chickenpox, so she can no longer be Juliet to Harvey's Romeo. Instead, the drama teacher partners Sabrina and Harvey together, which leads to a passionate kissing session in the library and then in Harvey's bedroom. When Sabrina moves from kissing Harvey on the lips to unbuttoning his shirt and kissing his chest, however, she notices three raw red gashes, the same sign of the devil's claw she herself has on her back, which literally marks their bodies as infused with evil. Sabrina interprets these marks as a threat from the Dark Lord, so she abruptly jumps off the bed and ceases their kissing session, which, in effect, also ends any future possibility of a reunion between them because she does not want to put Harvey in danger. This scene anticipates several other instances in which Sabrina's expression of her desire is thwarted by outside circumstances, usually relating to Satan's power over Sabrina.

These moments of interrupted desire may be seen as throwbacks to what Linda Williams calls *osculum interruptum* (2006, p. 303). In her essay, 'Of kisses and ellipses: the long adolescence of American movies', Williams discusses how kisses were frequently interrupted in the era of the Hollywood Production Code, which encompassed the years 1934 through 1966 approximately. The code prohibited movies from representing 'low forms of sex relationship[s]' that might infer such relationships as accepted or common occurrences (p. 298). Although *Chilling Adventures of Sabrina* is not as explicit about its temporality as its comic source material—which takes place primarily in the 1960s, the same time period as the first appearance of Sabrina in 1962—its indeterminate temporality both invokes and resists these screen politics of the 1960s.

Indeed Sabrina, through whom the series is focalised and with whom viewers are seemingly aligned, repeatedly is unable to fulfill or articulate her desire. For instance, while watching a rehearsal of *The Passion of*

Lucifer Morningstar, the witch drama that parallels Baxter High's *Romeo and Juliet* performance, Prudence attempts to tease Sabrina into admitting her desire for Nick. Initially, Dorcas is cast as Lilith to Nick's Lucifer with Sabrina serving as the understudy and, when Prudence finds Sabrina watching Nick and Dorcas rehearse, she taunts Sabrina and urges her to admit her attraction to Nick:

PRUDENCE: You're jealous aren't you? That Dorcas is playing the romantic lead opposite Nick… … Didn't you break up with the mortal so you could be with Nick?

SABRINA: No, I broke up with Harvey because … . None of your business. As for Nick, he's … .

PRUDENCE: A friend. Yes, yes, we've all heard that refrain. But come on, Sabrina. In the dark, late at night, between the sheets of your virgin's bed are you telling me you've never had the odd, stray thought about Nick? Imagined him slipping through the window? Between your legs?

SABRINA: Eww! You're like one of my Aunt Hilda's bad Harlequin romance novels.

PRUDENCE: Lust isn't a sin, Sabrina. It's an emotion.

This exchange begins as a playful teasing, but when Prudence asks Sabrina if she thinks about Nick in bed, the camera zooms in to a profile of Sabrina's face, with Prudence whispering in her ear like the Dark Lord. In this way, lust and sex become equated with evil temptation rather than with passion or desire. Part of the tension of the series and this scene, however, is that Sabrina listens intently to Prudence, and her 'eww' response of disgust sounds more like disdain at the way Prudence articulates desire rather than about desire and sex more generally. In other words, Sabrina feels desire, but her passion is never allowed full expression.

The most overt instances of Sabrina's unrealised desire occur as sexual tension builds between Sabrina and Nick in this episode and the next one. Prudence and Sabrina's exchange analysed in the previous paragraph serves as titillation and suggestion, for as the episode progresses, so does the sexual tension between Sabrina and Nick. They rehearse lines together, drawing closer and closer, but Sabrina interrupts the rehearsal remembering her intimacy with Harvey. When Dorcas also contracts the chickenpox, Sabrina plays the role of Lilith for the performance. Love, power, and desire intertwine as Nick playing Lucifer asks Lilith to stay with him to educate the people about Morningstar's teachings and to rule beside him as queen. Inside and outside the play, Lucifer asks Lilith to give herself to him, and he will make her worthy of her power as queen. On stage, Nick and Sabrina, as Lucifer and Lilith, kiss passionately, and Sabrina plays at giving herself to the Dark Lord, prostrating herself before him, an act that binds Lilith to Lucifer eternally. Sabrina's performance earns kudos from the coven and from the Dark Lord, who especially notes the chemistry between Nick and Sabrina. In her role as Lilith, Sabrina performs passion—as made overt in the title of the episode 'The passion of Sabrina Spellman'—but Sabrina's passion is linked more to the suffering contained in the word's etymology rather than to sexual pleasure.

This conjoining of Sabrina's suffering and pleasure meets its apex when her desire is again unrealised during the witch festival of Lupercalia designed explicitly for the expression of lust. The building sexual tension between Sabrina and Nick seems set to climax when Lupercalia provides an opportunity for Sabrina and Nick to have intercourse. After confiding in Roz about Lupercalia and asking her advice about how she knows if she is ready to become sexually active, Sabrina strategises with Nick to ensure that, instead of a random pairing, they will be paired with each other. The episode builds an expectation that Nick and Sabrina will actively participate in the ritual of Lupercalia as a couple rather than in the orgiastic carnality Zelda so gleefully describes. The episode, however, takes a strange twist by introducing Nick's familiar, a wolf who goes rogue out of wild jealousy in response to Sabrina and Nick's relationship. Each time they start kissing passionately, and before it has a chance to move beyond kissing, Amalia, Nick's wolf familiar appears, snarling and howling, seemingly threatening the two of them. In desperation, Nick goes into the woods and brings back a wolf's heart, saying he killed Amalia. During the final event of Lupercalia, however, Sabrina and Nick are in the woods when Amalia again appears, and Nick admits he killed another wolf because he could not bring himself to harm her. In a heart-wrenching act of violence, Sabrina repeatedly stabs Amalia in the back to save Nick from being mauled. Hands covered in blood, wearing a red cape, Sabrina resembles Little Red Riding Hood, who kills the wolf and sheds its blood in lieu of metaphorically—and perhaps literally—bleeding herself during intercourse ('Chapter fourteen: Lupercalia'). When Sabrina kills Amalia, Sabrina seemingly destroys her own desire, for rather than building upon the sexual desire interrupted in Lupercalia, the remaining six episodes of the season shift away from a drive towards sexual pleasure and instead focus on overthrowing patriarchal power.

These final episodes of season two suggest that sexual desire and political activism cannot coexist when Sabrina seemingly sets aside her desire in order to save Aunt Zelda and the Church of Night from Father Blackwood's misogyny. In an unexpected twist, the season finale features the return of Lucifer to his human form and the revelation that Sabrina is not the daughter of Edward Spellman but of Lucifer himself, destined to rule by his side as queen in a world in which the doors of hell open to release demons who will populate earth. In a resolution that pays homage to the season two finale of *Buffy*, in which Buffy sends Angel to hell in order to save the world, so *Chilling Adventures of Sabrina* features a conclusion in which Nick becomes the vessel for containing the body of Lucifer, who Lilith then carries into hell. Sabrina's final words of the season, 'Let's go to hell, and get my boyfriend back' ('Chapter twenty: The Mephisto waltz'), anticipate a third season in which Sabrina's desire drives the action but may not result in sexual satisfaction.

Netflix's *Chilling Adventures of Sabrina* features a powerful sixteen-year-old, who occupies a liminal space between witch and mortal, adult and child, pleasure and suffering, sexual experience and innocence. Although undecided in relation to her sexual desire, she rarely wavers in her decisions to try to help others, especially when identifying an injustice against a marginalised group. Sabrina's witch-becoming features loyalty to her family and friends and resistance against patriarchal power. The series represents a tension between sexual flexibility for young witches and warlocks and a desire for monogamy based upon love rather than power. Ultimately, the series seems undecided upon its own stance regarding young people's desire and sexuality, but perhaps the third season will allow Sabrina to experience her desire more fully, even if she has to go to hell to do so.

Postscript

While finalising the edits for this chapter, Netflix released season three/part three of *Chilling Adventures of Sabrina*. In the first of eight episodes, Sabrina goes to hell and rescues Nick, who still functions as the vessel that imprisons Lucifer. In exchange for releasing Nick and in order to maintain cosmic balance, Sabrina agrees to take her place as Queen of Hell. Sabrina's liminality in season three finds her negotiating identities both on earth and in hell. The season ends bizarrely with a time loop that allows two versions of Sabrina to exist simultaneously: one as a teenager on earth and the other reigning as queen in hell. As with the first two seasons, characters that constellate around Sabrina express sexual flexibility and fulfill their sexual desire, but Sabrina's desire remains unsatisfied, especially after Nick ends their romance in episode five. Although show creator Aguirre-Sacasa states that the forthcoming part four will clarify the identity of Sabrina's 'endgame' lover (Maas 2020), the season finale of part three does not promise sexual fulfillment for Sabrina: the Greendale version of Sabrina sits with her aunties and Ambrose in the kitchen; while Lilith dresses Sabrina in hell as a version of the Virgin Queen and tells her to 'gird your loins, let nothing touch you, let no man hold power over you', once again problematically equating virginity with political power.

References

'A Little Wicked', 2016, V Broussard, song, House of Artemis.

Aguirre-Sacasa, R 2018, *Chilling Adventures of Sabrina: Book One*. Illus. R Hack. Archie Comics, USA. Kindle.

Buffy the Vampire Slayer, 1997–2003, television series, Creator J Whedon.

'Chains of Love' 1988, Erasure, song, Sire Records.

Chilling Adventures of Sabrina, 2018, 'Chapter one: October country', television episode, Netflix, 26 October.

Chilling Adventures of Sabrina, 2018, 'Chapter three: The trial of Sabrina Spellman', television episode, Netflix, 26 October.

Chilling Adventures of Sabrina, 2018, 'Chapter six: An exorcism in Greendale', television episode, Netflix, 26 October.

Chilling Adventures of Sabrina, 2018, 'Chapter seven: Feast of Feasts', television episode, Netflix, 26 October.

Chilling Adventures of Sabrina, 2018, 'Chapter ten: The witching hour', television episode, Netflix, 26 October.

Chilling Adventures of Sabrina, 2019, 'Chapter twelve: The epiphany', television episode, Netflix, 5 April.

Chilling Adventures of Sabrina, 2019, 'Chapter thirteen: The passion of Sabrina Spellman', television episode, Netflix, 5 April.

Chilling Adventures of Sabrina, 2019, 'Chapter fourteen: Lupercalia', television episode, Netflix, 5 April.

Chilling Adventures of Sabrina, 2019, 'Chapter twenty: The Mephisto waltz', television episode, Netflix, 5 April.

Chilling Adventures of Sabrina, 2020, 'Chapter twenty-eight: Sabrina is legend', television episode, Netflix, 24 January.

'Girl You Want', 1980, Devo, song, Warner Brothers.

Gladir, G, DeCarlo, D, Lapick, R and DeCarlo, V 2017, 'Presenting Sabrina the Teen-age Witch', *Sabrina the Teenage Witch Complete Collection: Volume 1 1962–1972*, Archie Comics Publications, Pelham, NY, pp. 11–15.

Gorelick, V 2017, 'Introduction', *Sabrina the Teenage Witch Complete Collection: Volume 1 1962–1972*, Archie Comics Publications, Pelham, NY, pp. 5–6.

Maas, J. 'Sabrina boss says season 4 will be a demonic version of the Crown with an HP Lovecraft vibe', *The Wrap*, 26 January 2020, retrieved 5 February 2020, www.thewrap.com/chilling-adventures-of-sabrina-season-4-details-season-3-ending/.

Paasonen, S and Spisak, S, 2018 'Malleable identities, leaky taxonomies: the matter of sexual flexibility', *Sexualities*, vol. 21, no. 8, pp. 1374–1378, retrieved 26 November 2018, JSTOR database.

Punter, D, 2017, 'Figuring the witch', *New Directions in Children's Gothic: Debatable Lands*, Ed. A Jackson, Routledge, New York, pp. 67–80.

Twilight, 2008, film, Director C Hardwicke.

The Vampire Diaries, 2009–2017, television series, Creator J Plec.

Williams, L, 2006, 'Of kisses and ellipses: the long adolescence of American movies', *Critical Inquiry*, vol. 32, no. 2, pp. 288–340. Retrieved 1 May 2019. JSTOR database.

The Politics of Sexuality and Desire

9 'You Two Seem to be the Same Person'

Death, Sexuality and Female Doubles in Chinese Young Adult Fiction and Film

Cathy Yue Wang

This chapter focuses on female Chinese writer Anni Baobei's (the pen name of Li Jie) novella 'Qiyue and Ansheng' (2000) and its cinematic adaptation *Soul Mate* (2016), as well as other similar narratives, to examine the theme of the double and its implication for sexuality and maturation for young female characters.[1] These narratives employ the theme of the double as a metaphor to depict the distorted and fluid identity of girls who come of age in post-socialist China, where its young female members face both the plights and chances brought by the neoliberal capitalist economic system and authoritarian political structure in the new millennium. In the context of the complicated negotiation of progressive and conservative gender ideologies in contemporary China, sex and sexuality become a key battlefield for younger generations. On the one hand, girls who come of age in post-socialist China are probably the only child of their families, enjoying rising economic power and intellectual opportunity; on the other hand, the traditional Confucian patriarchy and its sexual norms still linger. For example, in today's China, premature dating is regarded negatively. Many secondary and primary schools instruct rules and regulations against premature dating, with adolescent violators get verbal and official warning, or even be expelled from school (Shen 2015). Tracing its historical roots to the early twentieth century, Shen argues that *zaolian* (premature dating) as a social problem arose in the 1980s China with three institutions that had been well-established in China: modern marriage against early marriage, family planning policy against early childbirth, and the modern educational system. In this official discourse against premature love, girls are the main targets and victims (Evans 1997). With these interferences from schools and parents, the formation of sexual identities and free expressions of sexual desires of young girls are far from autonomous.

This chapter will first contextualize these stories about two girls amid the changing values and attitudes towards gender and youth in contemporary China, and then examine the thematic significance behind the representations of two girls as similar yet differing doubles. The paradigmatic framework for female doubling is 'angel and monster' (Gilbert and Gubar 2000, p. 76), or 'asexual Madonna and over-sexed whore' (Sencindiver 2010, p. 66); both are framed through a masculine perspective. The texts examined in this chapter simultaneously conform to and depart from this framework. Their subversion of this masculine framework indicates feminist potential, but the realization of this potential is repressed by the threatening patriarchal order. The chapter ends with an effort to discover the queer possibilities hidden behind the friendship and antagonism between the two girls. Although a male character as the love interest of the two girls and the consequent heterosexual love triangle jeopardize the female erotic undercurrent, his marginalization and objectification in the narrative foregrounds the ambiguity of the homosocial and homosexual distinction in the female-centered relationship.

Coming of Age as Girls in Post-socialist China

Chinese young adult literature, in the broader sense, can be divided into three categories in regard to authors and each category has its own strategy in relation to sex and sexuality. The first group consists of works written by established authors of children's literature whose target audience is young adult readers. In China, young adult literature appeared much later than works targeting younger readership. Not until the 1980s did adolescent literature become a visible genre in the Chinese literary scene (Wang 2006, p. 36). In the Chinese context, considering the long history of children's literature as a didactic and educational tool since its germination in the early twentieth century, as well as the less tolerant views on sex in mainstream society, novels for young readers that touch the thorny topics of sex and sexuality are relatively rare. However, the picture is changing—gradually and slowly. According to Lisa Chu Shen:

> Until the 1990s, sexuality had been a sensitive topic in Chinese adolescent literature [...] In the 1990s, children's authors, most notably Cao Wenxuan and Yin Jianling, began to address male and female sexualities respectively and explicitly in their adolescent novels, with the coming-of-age narrative as the representative genre.
>
> (2020b, 65)

For example, Yin Jianling's works touch on themes such as pre-marital sex, teenage pregnancy and homoeroticism. In these works, adolescent heterosexual relationships and sex are usually depicted as perilous and to the physical and mental health of girls. The stories tend to caution against pregnancy, abortion, suicide and premature sex (Shen 2020a). These negative depictions of sex correspond with Kokkola's (2013) observation that Anglophone young adult fictions shed often depict adolescents' sexuality and carnal desires in troubling ways.

The second group are works written by mainstream writers and marketed as adult literature but feature young adult characters as protagonists. Narratives centering on young female protagonists can be found in modern and contemporary Chinese literature, especially when written by female authors (Xu 2011). Xu observes that a certain kind of melancholy is pervasive in these coming-of-age stories of girls written by female authors born in the 1950s and 1960s. Representations of 'melancholic girls' give ways to 'bad girls', introduced by a new group of women writers born in the 1970s. Referred as 'beauty writers', female authors such as Wei Hui and Mian Mian are well known for their exposure of personal experience and for the 'explicit expressions and representations of female sexuality' in their writings (Zhong 2006, p. 655). They also use their youth and beauty as a marketing tool to achieve fame and financial success.

The last group of writers and works belongs to a remarkable new literary phenomenon in new millennium China. These novels are written by adolescents and newly adults themselves. Writers born between 1980 and 1989 belong to the first generation who grew up under the one-child policy and during the economic reform and opening-up period. Their writings are refreshing compared to Chinese literary tradition, freely expressing their inner feeling and paying no attention to social issues or moral philosophy (Coats 2011; Fumian 2010). Their writings deal with themes such as adolescent friendship, love, sexuality, discontent towards school and parents, and feelings of loneliness and isolation, and thus elicit emotional resonance with readers of a similar age. In these novels, dating, romantic relationships and sex are indispensable aspects of the growing-up process of their protagonists, but they seldom include graphic depictions of sexual behaviors. *Cherry Trees in the Distance* (2004) by female author Zhang Yueran (born 1982) and *Enchanted City* (2003) by male writer Guo Jingming (born 1983) are representative examples of the post-1980s writing group.

Anni Baobei, as an author, should be positioned in between the second and third group of writers discussed above, namely, post-1970s beauty writers and post-1980s youth writers. Born in 1974, she does not belong to the post-1980s generation in the strictest sense, but her writing is representative of both groups. Beauty writers and post-1980s youth writers share many similarities in their writing as well as in their public marketing strategy. They both favor first-person narration, and their novels are semiautobiographical. The popularity of these authors shows the rising power of women and adolescents in contemporary China. However, as Kong (2004, p. 96) argues, although women and adolescents are empowered by the burgeoning cultural market to make their own voices heard, they are also exploited by the capitalist market and consumerist culture. In other words, the newly gained autonomy enjoyed by the female and young members of society is limited.

Anni Baobei has a more restrained writing style compared to the daring beauty writers of Wei Hui and Mian Mian, and her writing remains influential for some post-1980s writers. Much of Anni Baobei's fiction, such as 'Goodbye Vivian' (2000) and 'Qiyue and Ansheng' (2000), features two female protagonists who typically have either parallel or opposite personalities. The narratives of the dual protagonists in her writings are usually intertwined, indicating the multiple dimensions of women in the face of seemingly plural possibilities in the postmodern city (Yang 2011, p. 184). The novella 'Qiyue and Ansheng', first posted online and then published in 2000, is one of her most popular stories. It has subsequently been adapted into a manga (2002), a drama (2011), a film (2016) and a TV drama (2018). The story touches on the theme of female doubling, depicting the love and friendship between a docile and obedient girl, Qiyue (literally means July), and a wilder and more unrestrained girl, Ansheng (literally means 'peaceful life'). The two girls grow up as close friends but choose different paths in their adulthood: Qiyue fulfills the traditional female role of good daughter and good wife, whereas Ansheng leads a vagrant and wayward life. The story ends with the death of the bad girl Ansheng, and leaves Qiyue in a state of everlasting mourning. The cinematic adaptation radically rewrites the plot of the original novel, but also ends in the death of one of the two girls.

The theme of the double is also one of the distinctive features of post-1980s writers' narratives, as represented by *Cherry Trees in the Distance* and *Enchanted City*. *Enchanted City* features brothers Kasuo and Shi as doubles, who 'symbolize a traumatic splitting of the ego' (Fumian 2010, p. 405). The rivalry between the two brothers ends when Kasuo dies by the hand of his more ambitious brother, Shi. Similarly, in Zhang's *Cherry Trees in the Distance*, which explicitly alludes to Polish director Kieślowski's film *The Double Life of Veronique* (1991), two girls—the poor orphan Xiaomu and middle-class Wanwan—are mysteriously connected through sharing each other's sensations. Their relationship is initially defined by hatred and then culminates in reconciliation. However, Xiaomu dies from congenital heart disease, and her spirit saves Wanwan from an attempted suicide. Both novels end with the death of one of the pair.

The double is also a recurring theme in young adult novels, where two protagonists represent each other's alter ego. As McCallum notes, as a widespread motif in Western fantasy fiction, the double is 'frequently used to represent selfhood as fragmented and plural', but it is also 'used in realist fiction to explore the social construction of subjectivity' (1996, p. 17). The deeper understanding of the prevalence of the double in contemporary Chinese adolescent fictions and films can only be achieved with the consideration of the broader social and cultural context.

Fumian (2010), inspired by Rank's psychoanalytic study (1914), views the theme of double as a symptom of the post-1980s writers' narcissism self-pitying sentimentalism. This narcissistic sentimentalism is not caused simply by spoiling and over-indulgence from the only-child's parents, as suggested by public opinion, but is also a result of a repressive educational system. In their formation of subjectivity, the post-1980s generation is trapped in a complex position between freedom and limitation, between the individual and society, and between old and new ideologies. The promotion of a market economy in China lauds competition and efficiency, and material wealth becomes the symbol of success. The mentality of competition seeps into all aspects of society, including the education system. Teachers as well as parents urge students to work harder and play less, to achieve more and conform to the rules, with emphasis on the intellectual achievement of students while neglecting their mental and emotional development. Self-pity has been born from the conflict between competition and affection (Fumian 2010, p. 406). Zhang (2007, p. 368) also explains the appearance of imagined kin in Chinese films as the result of dissolution of family and the lack of human connection. Both link the representation of the double in literature and film with the enforcement of one-child policy.

The sociocultural perspective from Fumian and Zhang overlook the essential role of gender. In modern and contemporary novels on female doubles, compared to their male counterparts, girls often face sharper conflict and dilemma, especially in regard of sexuality. Confucian morals and its sexual norms promote chasteness and virginity and the repression of female sexual desires. The emergence of the female double therefore can be viewed as the expression of the silenced female sexual desire. In other words, the double 'represents another possible position that the character might occupy' but cannot achieve under the rigid sexual norms (McCallum 1999, p. 77). It is necessary to the developmental process of female identity and sexuality.

The Good Girl and the Bad Girl

In Chinese literature, the paradigm for the female double is the selfless and self-sacrificing good women and the individualistic and hedonistic bad girls (Lee 2016, p. 354). At first glance, the two protagonists from Anni Baobei's novella fit within this paradigm. Qiyue is a good girl with loving middle-class parents, and she is beautiful and talented. She is obedient to her parents and beloved by her classmates. She has conservative attitudes towards romantic love and marries her first love. All these qualities are associated with conventional models of femininity. Qiyue's sweet and demure femininity contrasts sharply with Ansheng's unruliness and transgression. Ansheng is wild and reckless. As the illegitimate daughter of an unmarried woman, she does not have a father in her life, and her mother stays overseas without fulfilling her maternal duty. She quits school early and leaves her hometown before she is eighteen years old. Afterwards, she lives a kind of nomadic lifestyle, wandering from one place to another and constantly changing jobs. She frequently changes sexual partners and has an affair with a rich married man.

In Anni's novella, Ansheng rebels against conformist society primarily through her sexual promiscuity. Ansheng's 'badness' is also demonstrated by her immoral affair with Qiyue's boyfriend, Jiaming. However, the text does not indicate that Ansheng enjoys sex, nor does it suggest that she gains a sense of empowerment from this promiscuity. Instead, she feels guilty. Ansheng dies giving birth to a child fathered by Jiaming. On her death bed, Ansheng views the difficult labor as the judgment for her sin. Death as a narrative solution indicates that sexual promiscuity and immorality as transgression of phallocentric notions of female sexuality are problematic and guarantees punishment. More importantly, the two girls willingly surrender to this patriarchal standard. For Ansheng, she is grateful to Jiaming for giving her a baby, since being a mother can redeem her sins. For Qiyue, she forgives the unfaithful Jiaming and marries him. The unfaithfulness of Jiaming receives no punishment. Instead, he and Qiyue adopt Ansheng's daughter, and a 'happily ever after' life seems to be a reality. Such a closure reaffirms the limitation of the rebellious and alternative expression of female sexuality and subjectivity.

The distinctive life trajectories of Qiyue and Ansheng represent two modes of female development, the traditional and the postmodern. These two modes diverge on their conventional and radical attitudes towards female sexuality. Qiyue remains chaste before marriage, and she prefers plain asexual clothing and makeup. She resembles heroines from fiction of the eighteenth and nineteenth centuries, exchanging one domestic sphere (her parents' home) for another (her own family with Jiaming), where she is either protected or taking care of others (Abel et al. 1983, p. 8). In a period between childhood and adulthood normally marked by fluidity, liminality and transformation, Qiyue's life is singularly fixed. She does grow up biologically and she does physically move among several places (university, workplace and home), but her daily routine is very stable and her life is described as 'quiet', 'ordinary' and 'same'. As Trites observes, the spatial metaphor of the journey, which connotes mobility, is often used to refer to adolescent growth (2014, p. 21); in this sense, Qiyue hardly experiences any growth other than physical maturation, for she is geographically restrained to a limited space.

In contrast with Qiyue, Ansheng is the postmodern atomized individual, who travels constantly and engages actively with the broader society and the world, but never settles down in one place. Her relationships with men are unstable. She often dresses in a sexual way that emphasizes her femininity, such as black lace tops and scarlet lipstick. She also explores different modes of creation, including painting and writing. Sexual potency and creativity are common metaphors for empowerment, but Ansheng gains limited agency from this freedom. She is unhappy and depressed, and the expression of her sexuality leads to her objectification through the male gaze. Although Ansheng enjoys great freedom to travel and explore the world, an activity usually associated with male characters in classical *Bildungsroman*, she longs for a home. Home is metonymically connected with the mother and, whenever Qiyue thinks of home, she thinks of radish with ribs cooked by her mother. Both food and domestic space are associated with maternal femininity in the patriarchal family. Qiyue enjoys this maternal nutrition and is thus tied spatially to her hometown, while Ansheng is marked by the lack of a maternal figure and thus becomes a vagabond. She incessantly seeks a relationship that can replace her lost mother–infant bond, first with Qiyue, then with Jiaming, and finally with her own daughter. Feminist psychoanalytic theorists point out that 'female identity is shaped primarily by the fluctuations of symbiosis and separation from the mother' (Abel et al. 1983, p. 9). On her death bed, Ansheng tells Qiyue it is only with pregnancy that she 'finally can transform' (Anni 2008, p. 235). By transformation Ansheng means she can get rid of her bruised and corrupted body and give birth to a new and pure life. In other words, her formation of identity is achieved by becoming a mother, even at the cost of her own life. Under the bad girl's disguise, Ansheng's longing for family affirms the desirability of the good girl.

The relationship between the two girls diverges from the paradigmatic mode of female doubling, since they are not represented by pure opposition and rivalry, but by mutual longing. Ansheng always wants to be like Qiyue, who is surrounded by family and friends, whereas Qiyue is attracted by Ansheng's freedom and unrestraint. The film adaptation visualizes this desire for an 'exchanged life'. In the latter part of the film, which differs drastically from the original novella, Ansheng marries and settles down, working as a white-collar worker—a scene showing her husband cooking for her implies a happy family life—while Qiyue escapes from her wedding with Jiaming, and embarks on a wandering life just as Ansheng had previously done.

In this film the motif of short hair is used to represent the transformation. After Qiyue escapes from her wedding ceremony, she cuts her long hair and starts to travel around the world. After this exchange, it seems that both heroines have finally achieved their dreamt of lives. However, a plot reversal exposes this happy ending as fictional, and as coming from the online novel written by Ansheng, and she is as unreliable a narrator. The truth is that Qiyue does indeed escape from her wedding and plans to start a free and independent life, just like Ansheng has led, but she finds herself pregnant with Jiaming's child and dies in childbirth. Here we see the pre-marital sex is punished once again. The grieving Ansheng chooses to give Qiyue a happy ending through her writing. Ansheng remains single and adopts Qiyue's daughter. Although the complicated *mise-en-abyme* narrative of the film innovatively rewrites the novella, the endings of both texts endorse the path chosen by the good girl. In the postmodern world, characterized by uncertainty and high risk, and with the highly competitive economic system of contemporary China, returning to home and family may express the nostalgic longing for a more stable and secure life. Yet this traditional way of being and living undermines female subjectivity and reaffirms the patriarchal order, in which transgression from the conventional good girl role leads to self-destruction and death.

Between the Homosexual and the Homosocial

In spite of their different backgrounds, personalities and life trajectories, Qiyue and Ansheng build a genuine friendship. The two girls meet at the age of thirteen and immediately become intimate friends. From thirteen to sixteen, they are extremely close, to the extent that 'sometimes Qiyue was Ansheng's shadow and sometimes Ansheng was Qiyue's shadow' (Anni 2008, p. 208). Later, they keep in contact through postcards. Wherever Ansheng goes, she sends a postcard to Qiyue, telling her friend how she is going. After Ansheng dies, Qiyue adopts Ansheng's daughter and decides not to have her own child. In many senses, the friendship and sisterhood between the two titular protagonists are strong and solid, and this intimacy is not without queer connotations. As both Rich (1980) and Sedgwick (1985) explain, the opposition between the homosocial and homosexual is less complete and visible in relation to women than it is for men. This lack of distinction between the homosocial and the homosexual makes lesbian possibilities invisible under the cover of passionate friendship between women.

Anni's novella provides many ambiguous descriptions of this passionate friendship between Qiyue and Ansheng. The physical intimacy between the two girls is evident throughout the novel. From thirteen to sixteen, they two girls are extremely close: 'On weekends Ansheng would come to Qiyue's home to have dinner with her family and the two would sleep together. When they walked on the road they would hold each other's hands' (Anni 2008, p. 208). When Ansheng's mother leaves her to live abroad, the heartbroken Ansheng goes to Qiyue for comfort. 'Suddenly Ansheng held her [Qiyue] tightly. She buried her head in Qiyue's arms and whimpered like a wounded animal. The warm and wet tears slid down Qiyue's neck (Anni 2008, p. 211).' These two excerpts describe intimate gestures such as holding hands and hugging. Although holding hands and sleeping together are common means by which adolescent girls express their close friendship and do not necessarily imply a lesbian identity, these gestures rightly belong to Rich's lesbian continuum, 'which is unconfined to any single part of the body or solely to the body itself' (1980, p. 650).

The friendship between the two girls is not asexual nor purely spiritual. Sometimes they look at each other through an erotic eye: ' "Ansheng, now you look like a Vietnamese woman", Qiyue hugged her with a smile, "and I like your new look so much." "But you look like a freshly dried peanut; I wish to take a bite", Ansheng smiled' (Anni 2008, p. 219). As the bad girl, Ansheng is bolder in her expression of desire for Qiyue, while the conventional femininity embodied by Qiyue makes her more firmly constrained by heteronormality. In the film, this desire between the two girls is depicted in two bedroom scenes. In the first, when they are still high school students, they lie together on the bed in a small room rented by Ansheng, who asks Qiyue to lie on her arm. Qiyue refuses by saying 'you are not a boy'. For Qiyue, cuddling on bed is the proper gesture between heterosexual couples. It is also in this scene that Qiyue tells Ansheng that she has a crush with a boy named Jiaming. After hearing this confession, Ansheng shows a heartbroken expression. Years later, the pregnant Qiyue escapes from her wedding, and the two women meet again. As they lie on the bed, Ansheng reaches out her arm again and repeats the line to 'come to lie on my arm'. This time Qiyue willingly lies on her arm. By juxtaposing Qiyue's refusal of marriage and her acceptance of same-sex intimacy, this scene is significant in its affirmation of the good girl's liberation from heterosexual romance.

As the two bedroom scenes show, the intimate friendship between the two girls and its queer possibilities are not just 'a passing phase', temporarily associated with female adolescents who will eventually grow out of it (Monaghan 2016, p. 40). The love between Qiyue and Ansheng lasts into their adulthood. As the novella describes, when they were young, 'Ansheng was the first person she [Qiyue] had loved' (Anni 2008, p. 230). After they grow up and Qiyue marries, Ansheng confess to her that '[Jiaming] is the man we love. I love you, Qiyue' (Anni 2008, p. 235). The same word 'love' is used to designate both heterosexual romance and same-sex friendship, and these descriptions blur the boundary between friendship and romance. In their shared love, Jiaming functions as a conduit through which the mutual desires of the two girls can be openly expressed. These descriptions also make clear the continuation and longevity of the passionate friendship between the girls. The closeness and intimacy formed during adolescence do not give way to heterosexual marriage, as some researchers observe happens in similar texts which also feature indeterminate relationships between girls (Martin 2003; Monaghan 2016; Shamoon 2012). The relationship between Qiyue and Ansheng is not just part of a nostalgic past, but rather has the chance to be future-oriented.

The film adaptation includes a scene depicting Qiyue and Ansheng dreaming about a queer family life in the future. After Qiyue successfully delivers her child and is resting on the hospital bed, Ansheng suggests:

> I will not marry. We two together will raise the baby. You will be the good mother, and I will be the bad mother. I will teach her how to do make up and attract boys, while you will teach her how to study and get high scores in exams.

The frail Qiyue replies with a smile, 'If so, then I will be the bad mother.' Sadly, this vision of a queer family is not to be realized, because Qiyue dies of postpartum hemorrhage several hours later. Her death implies that queer kinship as a more radical way to structure the family can be imagined, but difficult to realize.

The conventional plot of the love triangle, with two girls fighting for one male, serves to sabotage female solidarity. However, the male character, Jiaming, as both girls' love interest, is a flat and shallow character. He is a functional symbol through which the two female characters can strengthen their mutual bond. Jiaming develops no subjectivity throughout the narrative. The third-person narrator repeats several limited adjectives in describing him, and he is always seen from the perspectives of the two girls. His own point of view is never fully expressed, nor are his family, friends, hobbies and career mentioned. Mostly, Jiaming remains silent and, on the rare occasions when he speaks, he talks about the two girls and the female doubling: 'both of you are such good girls, and you two seem to be the same person' (Anni 2008, p. 229). Jiaming is a purely abstract symbol, a necessity in the compulsory heterosexual structure. The attraction and desire between the two girls are only expressible through a relationship that is mediated by the male lover. This triangular structure reminds us of the homosocial relationships Eve Sedgwick identifies in English literature in *Between Men*, only with a gendered twist.[2]

In addition, a large part of Jiaming's attraction for Ansheng comes from his affinity with Qiyue. Jiaming and Qiyue share certain traits, from an attractive appearance to a mild personality, and both are model students. If we see Jiaming as the male version of Qiyue, then Ansheng's desire for him can be viewed as a way to legitimatize her homosexual desire for Qiyue. Similarly, Qiyue shows little jealousy or anger about the affair between Jiaming and Ansheng (at least in the novella). Their love triangle is defined by the complicated and subtle interconnection between identification and desire, and female doubling and cross-gender mirroring make each relationship among the three non-exclusive. The coexistence of heterosexual love, homosocial bond, and homosexual relation renders this triangle ambiguous and queer. The feedback and reviews from readers and film audience reinforce this ambiguity. In the websites such as Douban (the Chinese version of Goodreads and IMDB) and Zhihu (the Chinese version of Quora), discussions and debates on whether 'Qiyue and Ansheng' is a queer story are abundant.

Conclusion

In Chinese young adult narratives, it seems the explicit expression of sexual desire from female protagonists always leads to death, and it is always the bad girls who are punished (Bai 2017). As Wu and Dong's study on Chinese feminist trends and its social and cultural contexts illustrates, on the one hand, 'market reforms have drastically changed gender representations, with previously suppressed gender and sexual expression now allowed, both legally and socially', while on the other hand, an anti-feminist backlash is formulated among the masses (2019, p. 16). Anni's novella and its filmic adaptation, which build upon the paradigm of good and bad girls, is reflective of this broad gender dilemma. The emergence of the female double represents a split between conventional and radical modes of femininity, onto which different gender ideologies are projected. In spite of their mutual longing, the path chosen by the good girl is emulated as the more desirable model. Death therefore signifies the punishment of bad girls' transgressions through sexual promiscuity. As James notes, death in contemporary adolescent literature is associated with 'violence, teenage pregnancy, homosexuality, sexual abuse … and disease' (2009, 7). In both the novella and the film, the death of the female protagonist is caused by childbirth. Ansheng in the novella dies of obstructed labor, while Qiyue in the film dies of postpartum hemorrhage. The perilous childbirth not only functions as a warning of the negative consequences of pre-marital sex, it also indicates a refusal of motherhood, which marks conventional female adulthood.

Under its ostensibly heterosexual plot, homoerotism is evoked implicitly in both the novella of Anni and its film adaptation, which also invites a queer reading position from its audience. More radical imaginations of female sexuality as lesbian desires appear occasionally in mainstream literature and film of contemporary China (Sang 2003), but narratives for children and young adults are generally restrained by heteronormativity.

As Trites (2014) notes, growth is a metaphorical concept that has dominated and even hegemonized adolescent narratives, and it is hard to imagine 'other ways of being, other epistemologies, that would help young readers understand literature—and life—in less goal-oriented ways' (p. 148). Death before adulthood is the extreme refusal of growth, but the cost is too high. Chinese young adult narratives with two female protagonists provide an appropriate example to reflect on different modes of female development, and we are left to ask whether, apart from death as the refusal of conventional female adulthood as characterized by marriage and motherhood, there are alternative paths of female growth, alternative ways of expressing female sexuality, and how these alternative imaginations can be realized.

Notes

1 All the translations in this chapter are mine except otherwise noted.
2 The symbolic function of Jiaming is also manifested through his name. 'Jiaming' (which literally means 'family bright') is a common male name appearing frequently in popular romance novels authored by Hong Kong writer Yishu. All the Jiamings in these romance novels are similar; as the stereotypical middle-class Prince Charming, they are handsome, rich and gentle. To name the male protagonist Jiaming in this novella indicates that he is an embodiment of the inherited romantic conventions of Prince Charming.

References

Abel, E, Hirsch M and Langland, E (eds.) 1983, *The Voyage in: Fictions of Female Development*, Dartmouth College Press, Hanover, NH.

Anni Baobei 2008 [2000], 'Qiyue and Ansheng', *Good Bye Vivian [Gao bie wei an]*, Beijing October Arts and Literature Publishing House, China.

Bai, HY 2017, 'The death of Nezha: mirror, fantasy and suture as cultural symptoms in recent Chinese girl movies' [Nezha zhisi: jingxiang, huanxiang yu fenghe, jinnian zhongguo shaonü dianying de wenhua zhenghou], *Literature & Art Studies*, no. 10, pp. 25–34.

Coats, K 2011, 'Young Adult Literature', *Handbook of Research on Children's and Young Adult Literature*, Eds. SA Wolf, K Coats, PA Enciso and C Jenkins, Routledge, London, pp. 315–329.

Evans, H 1997, *Women and Sexuality in China: Dominant Discourses of Female Sexuality and Gender Since 1949*, Polity Press, Cambridge.

Fumian, M 2010, 'The social construction of a myth: an interpretation of Guo Jingming's parable', *Oriental Archive*, vol. 78, no. 4, pp. 397–419.

Gilbert, SM and Gubar, S 2000, *The Madwoman in the Attic: the Woman Writer and the Nineteenth-Century Literary Imagination*, Yale University Press, New Haven, CT.

Guo, JM 2003, *Enchanted City [Huancheng]*, Chunfeng Art and Literature Press, Shenyang.

James, K 2009, *Death, Gender and Sexuality in Contemporary Adolescent Literature*, Routledge, New York.

Kokkola, L 2013, *Fictions of Adolescent Carnality: Sexy Sinners and Delinquent Deviants*, John Benjamins, Amsterdam.

Kong, SY 2005, *Consuming Literature: Best Sellers and the Commercialization of Literary Production in Contemporary China*, Stanford University Press, Redwood City, CA.

Lee, A 2016, 'From "good women" to "bad girls"? China's (not-so-new) new generation of female writers', *Contemporary Women's Writing*, vol. 10, no. 3, pp. 354–372, https://doi.org/10.1093/cww/vpw018.

Martin F 2010, *Backward Glances: Contemporary Chinese Cultures and the Female Homoerotic imaginary*, Duke University Press, Durham, NC.

McCallum, R 1996, 'Other Selves: Subjectivity and the 'Doppelganger' in Australian Adolescent Fiction', *Writing the Australian Child: Texts and Contexts in Fictions of Children*, Ed. C Bradford, UWA Publishing, Perth, pp. 17–36.

McCallum, R 1999. *Ideologies of Identity in Adolescent Fiction: the Dialogic Construction of Subjectivity*, Garland Publishing House, London.

Monaghan, W 2016, *Queer Girls, Temporality and Screen Media: Not 'Just a Phase'*, Palgrave Macmillan, London.

Rank, O 1971[1914], *The Double: a Psychoanalytic Study*, University of North Carolina Press, Chapel Hill, NC.

Rich, A 1980, 'Compulsory heterosexuality and lesbian existence', *Signs*, vol. 5, no. 4, pp. 631–660, retrieved 20 May 2019, www.jstor.org/stable/3173834.

Sang, TL 2003, *The Emerging Lesbian: Female Same-Sex Desire in Modern China*, University of Chicago Press, Chicago, IL.

Sedgwick, EK 1985, *Between Men: English Literature and Male Homosocial Desire*, Columbia University Press, New York, NY.

Sencindiver, SY 2010, 'Sexing or Specularizing the Doppelgänger: a Recourse to Poe's Ligeia', *Fear Itself: Reasoning the Unreasonable*, Eds. S Hessel and M Huppert, Rodopi, Amsterdam, pp. 63–84.

Shamoon, D 2012, *Passionate Friendship: the Aesthetics of Girl's Culture in Japan*, University of Hawai'i Press, Honolulu.

Shen, LC 2020a, 'Femininity, homoeroticism and heterosexuality in Yin Jianling's female coming-of-age narratives', *Children's Literature in Education*, retrieved 10 October 2020, https://doi.org/10.1007/s10583-020-09417-6.

Shen, LC 2020b, 'The effeminate boy and queer boyhood in contemporary Chinese adolescent novels', *Children Literature in Education*, vol. 51, pp. 63–81, retrieved 10 October 2020, https://doi.org/10.1007/s10583-018-9357-7.

Shen, YB 2015, 'Too young to date! The origins of zaolian (early love) as a social problem in 20th century China', *History of Science*, vol. 53, no. 1, pp. 86–101, retrieved 20 May 2019, https://doi.org/10.1177/0073275314567437.

Soul Mate [*Qiyue yu Ansheng*] 2016, film, Jike Film, Shanghai.

Trites, RS 2014, *Literary Conceptualizations of Growth: Metaphors and Cognition in Adolescent Literature*, John Benjamins, Amsterdam.

Wang, QG 2006, 'On juvenile novels in modern China' [Shaonian Xiaoshuo de Dangdai Sikao], *Journal of Hunan University of Science and Engineering*, vol. 27, no. 9, pp. 36–40.

Wu, AX and Dong, YG 2019, 'What is made-in-China feminism(s)? Gender discontent and class friction in post-socialist China', *Critical Asian Studies*, retrieved 10 October 2020, http://doi.org/10.1080/14672715.2019.1656538.

Xu, LJ 2011, 'Constructing girlhood: female adolescence, depression and the making of a female tradition in modern Chinese literature', *Frontiers of Literary Studies in China*, vol. 5, no. 3, pp. 321–349, retrieved 10 October 2020, http://doi.org/10.1007/s11702-011-0132-z.

Yang, X 2011, 'Configuring female sickness and recovery: Chen Ran and Anni Baobei', *Modern Chinese Literature and Culture*, vol. 23, no. 1, pp. 169–196, retrieved 20 May 2019, www.jstor.org/stable/41491044.

Zhang, YR 2004, *Cherry Trees in the Distance* [*Yingtao zhi yuan*], Chunfeng Art and Literature Press, Shenyang.

Zhang, Z 2007, 'Urban Dreamscape, Phantom sisters, and the Identity of an Emergent Art Cinema', *The Urban Generation: Chinese Cinema and Society at the Turn of the Twenty-First Century*, Ed. Z Zhang, Duke University Press, Durham, NC pp. 344–387.

Zhong, XP 2006, 'Who is a feminist? Understanding the ambivalence towards Shanghai Baby, body writing and feminism in post-women's liberation China', *Gender & History*, vol. 18, no. 3, pp. 635–660, retrieved 20 May 2019, https://doi.org/10.1111/j.1468-0424.2006.00459.x.

10 Intoxicated Masculinity, Allyship and Compulsory Heterosexuality in Young Adult Rape Narratives

Amber Moore and Elizabeth Marshall

Did you drink with dinner? No, not even water? When did you drink? How much did you drink? What container did you drink out of? Who gave you the drink? How much do you usually drink?

(Miller 2019)

In January 2015, Brock Turner sexually assaulted an unconscious Chanel Miller behind a Stanford University dumpster.[1] Initial media coverage repeatedly referred to Miller as an Emily Doe and focused on her drunken state the night of her attack which spilled into the trial; Turner's attorney focused on her drinking history, presenting her as 'practically an alcoholic' (Baker 2016, unpaginated)—indeed, the law is often unkind to women (Gilmore 2001. In contrast, the lawyer characterized Turner as a good boy who succumbed to Stanford's 'drinking culture'. Turner was eventually released after three months from an already light sentencing. While Miller's case exceeds a straightforward reading, it makes clear how compulsory heterosexuality, white male privilege,[2] and rape culture coincide with chilling effects. Miller quickly became symbolic of the horror of sexual violence and of facing a justice system rigged to doubt her (Gilmore 2017). In mainstream press coverage, the twin temptations of alcohol and hetero-femininity rather than male entitlement and violence came to dominate the reasons for Turner's assault, yet the case also reveals how victim survivors make rape culture visible through their testimonies 'going viral' to broader communities of witness. For example, when Miller published her victim impact statement on *BuzzFeed*, 18 million people read it (Brown and Miller 2019). This testimony modeled ally behaviour because she communicated her experience and perspective, engaged in public rhetoric to voice social justice views, and initiated dialogue about rape culture (DeTurk 2011). Miller also powerfully challenged Turner to 'show men how to respect women, not how to drink less' (Baker 2016), troubling a familiar rape script through which she was blamed for drinking too much, and made clear that sexual violence is ordinary (Hall 2004) rather than the result of too much liquor.

Ultimately, she asked readers to consider the relations between alcohol, compulsory heterosexuality, and sexual violence and simultaneously demonstrated the importance of feminist allyship.

As scholars who study rape culture in texts for and about youth, we take Miller's case as a jumping-off point to examine how drinking and sexual violence as well as allyship (or a lack thereof) are represented in young adult (YA) fictions. In general, the cultural script that organized the Turner trial—that drunk young women are responsible for sexual violence—circulates in YA literature, including Laurie Halse Anderson[3] and Emily Carroll's *Speak* (2018), EK Johnston's *Exit, Pursued by a Bear* (2016), Aaron Hartzler's *What We Saw* (2015), Courtney Summers' *All the Rage* (2015), Louise O'Neill's *Asking for It* (2016), Chris Lynch's *Inexcusable* (2005) and Ashley Herring Blake's *Girl Made of Stars* (2018).[4] We have selected these texts for analysis because each one features a male protagonist who rapes a young woman at an unsupervised party where she either chooses to drink alcohol or is given a substance that causes her to black out. When she returns to school, she has no allies and her previously close friends desert her. Throughout this chapter we are particularly interested in: (1) how intoxicated hetero-masculinity presents when drinking and rape cultures collide; (2) the ways in which heterosexual girls are cast as 'good' or 'bad' after their rapes at parties; and (3) how allyship both sinks (especially with straight girls) and surfaces (especially among queer girls) as the victim survivors navigate the fallout from their trauma. Drawing on feminist theories of rape culture (for example, Ahmed 2017; Buchwald et al. 2005; Gay 2014; Gruber 2016; Rodier et al. 2012; Wunker 2016), we analyze all of these YA texts in conversation with one another to highlight the discursive entanglements of rape culture, alcohol consumption, heteronormativity, and feminisms within YA fiction.

Ultimately, we move through these materials to demonstrate the ways in which the authors make rape visible and yet simultaneously reinforce compulsory heterosexuality in two central ways: first, alcohol is represented as the primary issue rather than male violence. Next, girls' friendships are portrayed as places where rape culture is compounded because these relationships are often fraught with dysfunction. As a result, the allyship that, for example, Miller demonstrates, rarely surfaces in these stories and instead rape scripts reign. However, one of our most compelling findings is that gender and sexually diverse characters offer rare and resistant solidarity to the victim survivor characters. As such, YA literature about rape generally sticks to conventional and gendered scripts and serve as cautionary tales, even as authors seek to make visible the violence of rape culture and how it operates. In what follows, we examine the complex relationships between male violence, compulsory heterosexuality, and alcohol in YA rape narratives.

Rape Culture and #MeToo

The novels in this chapter can be read against the backdrop of rape culture as well as feminist resistances against it.[5] First used in the 1970s, the term 'rape culture' names systemic violence against girls and women and is defined as 'a complex set of beliefs that encourages male sexual aggression and supports violence against women … a society where violence is seen as sexy and sexuality as violent' (Buchwald et al. 2005, p. xi). A major consequence of rape culture that is taken up in the stories under discussion in this chapter is that women's testimonies about sexual violence are often dismissed through tactics such as shaming and discrediting female victims: 'when the witness is a woman, and especially when the harm includes sexual violence, she will be subjected to practices of shaming and discrediting that pre-exist any specific case' (Gilmore 2017, p. 5). Alcohol consumption is often a key element used to discredit women's testimony about rape and used to blame and shame girls and YA authors often draw on such actual cases that involved teen girls, alcohol, and sexual assault. *What We Saw* is based on the Steubenville High School rape case in the US—a 'familiar enough' (Dean 2013, unpaginated) 'nearly text-book example of peer sexual assault among teenagers' (Pennington and Birthisel 2015, p. 2436)—while *Asking for It* references that same case as well as '#SlaneGirl' in Ireland.

The YA novels in this chapter can also be read through the lens of the global #MeToo movement. Established in the US in 2006 by Tarana Burke, MeToo focused on supporting women of color victim survivors of sexual assault. The movement garnered international attention in 2017 when US actress Alyssa Milano tweeted about it in response to the anniversary of Trump's 'grab 'em by the pussy' video and the exposure of Hollywood producer Harvey Weinstein's sexual violence. Burke remains a pivotal leader of the movement as #MeToo continues to evolve as not only an outcry against rape but to the complexity of rape culture as a whole.[6] Although #MeToo has undoubtedly inspired activism and shifted conversations about patriarchy, privilege, and power, much work remains to be done with respect to better understanding the communities, contexts, and cultures where sexual violence is perpetuated in particular ways (Gay 2018).

(In)toxic(ated) Heteromasculinity

In each of the texts under examination, heteromasculinity is claimed by the rapists through sexual violence. This is a toxic form of masculinity, 'characterized by homophobia and the subjugation of weaker men and women' (Creighton and Oliffe 2010, pp. 414–415). In these novels, heteromasculinity is presented as consistently aggressive when adolescents drink at unsupervised parties, resulting in rape despite the diverse relationship dynamics between young boys and girls portrayed across the stories. Casual friends, committed romantic partners, and complete strangers attack when one or both parties are intoxicated. Here, we use the term '(in)toxic(ated) masculinity' to highlight intersections between toxic heteromasculinity and drinking culture.[7] Thus the heteromasculinities of the rapists in the texts under discussion are both toxic and hegemonic as they include scenes of inebriated sexual violence.

The rapists in *Inexcusable* and *Girl Made of Stars* are each romantic partners of the girls that they take to isolated locations post-drinking. Propelling a particular kind of pain due to previous romantic intimacy between these characters who were in romantic relationships, the male characters act shocked at the accusations of rape, claim they had consensual sex, and betray the girls they had previously been affectionate with. In *Inexcusable*, the only text in the sample written from the perpetrator's perspective, the narrator Keir wakes up the night after a party with his girlfriend Gigi. He is incredulous when she screams that he raped her. Keir denies the rape, tells Gigi he loves her, and starts kissing her. She falls limp, horrifying him with her resistance to his affection—her refusal to return intimacy. His attack establishes a pattern of intoxicated masculinity that comes after a drunken confrontation with his sisters, who skipped his graduation due to his increasing 'frat boy antics' that made them 'dread' (Lynch 2005, p. 150) seeing him. In *Girl Made of Stars*, Owen rapes girlfriend Hannah in the woods during a field party. Like Keir, Owen is 'a total miscreant frat boy when he drinks' (Blake 2018, p. 28). He holds Hannah's hands above her head during the rape, spraining her wrist. The boys in each of these novels demonstrate their presumed entitlement to girls' bodies as they physically pin them down. Both Keir and Owen repeatedly deny their violence, hide behind the romantic relationships, insist upon reciprocity rather than rape, and blame alcohol.

The victim survivors, Gigi and Hannah, immediately seek allies in response to being attacked by someone they once felt affection for. The violence they experience as a result of the (in)toxic(ated) masculinities of their boyfriends is compounded by their emotional involvement with their attackers. Perhaps in response to this particular betrayal of trust, Gigi insists on telling her ex-boyfriend and her father while Hannah goes straight to a hospital where the police are called. The girls then largely temper further trouble by successfully blocking repeated viciousness and violence being waged directly against them such as Owen spreading rumours about Hannah in her absence to 'taint' her testimony (Gilmore 2017). Said another way, because the girls immediately seek adult allies to help them following their assaults, the fallout from their attacks is mitigated as compared to other characters we analyze whose suffering is exacerbated because they deal with the consequences of their rapes alone. One reading of these rapist romantic partners is that neither wholly believed that they were guilty of assault but, rather, that they were constructing their heteromasculinities in accordance with hegemonic understandings of what that means. They pursued sexual conquest in a dominating fashion and believed in their entitlement to girls' bodies—a feature of rape culture.

In contrast, in *All the Rage* and *Speak*, survivor protagonists Romy and Melinda are assaulted by classmates who are largely strangers to them. Rapists Kellan and Andy are acquaintances who follow or lure the girls away from drinking parties to isolate them, rendering the attack invisible. This invocation of stranger danger discourse particularly emphasizes the presumed precarity of girls; that is, girls are frequently represented as victims in perpetual danger hidden in plain sight (Marshall and Gilmore 2015). For example, Kellan violates Romy in the back of a pickup truck. Left on the side of a dirt road, Romy is forced to crawl home. In *Speak* Andy follows Melinda outside after she downs three beers and starts to feel ill. At first, drunken Melinda is thrilled that Andy wants to kiss; however, in the unnumbered pages that follow, Carroll visually emphasizes both Melinda's drunken confusion and isolation by losing her in the unpaginated text itself and her characterization of Andy as 'beast' (Anderson and Carroll 2018, p. 255) and 'wolf' (p. 169) is foregrounded. Andy's eyes darken, literally drawn as though they are scratched out in the illustration by his intoxicated masculinity as the story spills out in a graphically slurred font. Melinda's body is fragmented on the page as she disassociates, remembering a time she previously felt safe—in a friendship, crimping her hair with a girl who will soon also turn on her. Later, a sober Andy attempts to attack Melinda again, challenging the idea that alcohol is the instigator of his violence. Indeed, because she has threatened his reputation and relationship with his girlfriend by warning others, his toxic masculinity informs his response to be violent again and brazenly do so in the middle of the day, at school. This second attack also demonstrates his arrogance—his entitlement to Melinda's body as a site for expressing his anger.

Across the two texts the viciousness of the attacks extends beyond the attempted and actual sexual assaults. Kellan successfully influences his male friends to harass Romy. Classmate Brock stalks her spewing taunts about 'crying rape' and trips her, aggressively shoulders her in the hallways, stares at her like she's 'meat' (Summers 2015, p.183), drugs her, and plays an extraordinarily violent 'practical joke' on her. Andy consistently stalks and harasses Melinda the following year, taunting her by blowing in her ear, dating her former best friend, sneaking touches, winking, and whispering 'fresh meat' (Anderson and Carroll 2018, p. 148) as he passes. There are also rumors that Andy is aggressive with other girls, chronicled in the cautionary graffiti of the girls' washroom. In this way, the violence waged against the girls is relentless as the rapists turn from relative strangers to sadistic stalkers.

Expanding on the violent themes in *Speak* and *Inexcusable*, *Asking for It* and *What We Saw* each reference especially horrifying, publicized rapes inspired by real events. O'Neill and Hartzler base their novels on the Steubenville high school rape case in Ohio in the US where members of the Steubenville high school football team sexually assaulted a sixteen-year-old girl and chronicled the attack on social media.[8] YA authors balance representing the actual violence of this case, the brutal sexual assault and public defilement of a sixteen-year-old girl, with writing for an adolescent audience. However, these authors do not soften the realities of the real-life events; indeed, O'Neill and Hartzler place violence front and center and through their stories, demonstrate the horror of rape and rape culture. Victim survivor characters Emma in *Asking for It* and Stacey in *What We Saw* are gang raped by casual school friends, publicly humiliated at parties and then repeatedly online via social media. Emma devastatingly receives over 600 notifications that she has been deemed 'Easy Emma' after pictures chronicling her assault hit the Internet. In them, she is blackout drunk, undressed, and her classmates are on top of her. In one photograph the boys wrench her legs open, their fingers inside her. In another, they grimace, pretending she smells. Reminiscent of the details of Steubenville, Emma finds images of the boys urinating on her head and vomiting onto her face and hair.

O'Neill links toxic heteromasculinity to compulsory heterosexuality throughout *Asking for It* to demonstrate the broad scope of rape culture and how toxic masculinity can unfold horrifically, particularly because of the ways in which young men feel entitled to access girls' bodies. For example, before the gang rape, twenty-eight-year year-old Paul assaults Emma, warning her not to be 'a fucking cock tease' (O'Neill 2016, p. 101). Paul wraps her hair in his fist, yanks her head back, bites her, calls her a slut repeatedly, and pins her down. She feigns enjoyment, hopeful that it will end quickly. He represents a particularly pernicious form of toxic masculinity due to his near pedophilic propensity for young girls (Emma is just eighteen), violence, and overall disrespect for women. After, he complains about his girlfriend to her, demonstrating how he feels not only entitled to her body but her mind and compassion as well. There is something remarkably different about this attack, particularly because as Emma implies, she has been raped before while drunk. 'It happens all the time … you regret it or you don't remember what happened exactly, but it's easier not to make a fuss' (p. 84)—but not like this, with the added emotional labor and public shaming.

Like O'Neill, Hartzler references the Steubenville case to highlight the reality and perniciousness of intoxicated heteromasculinity. In *What We Saw*, Stacey is raped while blacked out at a party in front of her classmates—all of which is videotaped and uploaded to social media with the hashtag #r&p, meaning 'rape and pillage'. After downing tequila with the protagonist who is then safely escorted home for being too drunk, Stacey ends up in the basement. There, boys cheer the cameraman with their beers before taking turns raping Stacey while onlookers point and laugh. The humiliation continues online as both Emma (*Asking for It*) and Stacey contend with the visibility of their rapes going viral. Both assaults ultimately make the news and consequently function to largely turn their small communities against them as the public and their peers battle over the significance of the violence they experienced because of their drinking. In this way, visibility compounds the pain of their assault as they are rendered social pariahs, irresponsible drunkards, mortified, and muted while the boys' dominant and inebriated heteromasculinities are validated via their sexual violence going viral. Alcohol consumption in these texts is key to compulsory heterosexuality and it cuts two ways as the rules of rape culture are communicated through drink: girls who consume too much alcohol are 'asking for it' and boys are made more masculine through alcohol consumption.

Good Girls/Bad Girls

In the wake of their rapes at parties where they experience alcohol and assault, the protagonists of these YA novels are made or unmade as good or bad girls. The Madonna–whore dichotomy 'denotes polarized perceptions of women as either good and chaste or as bad and promiscuous' (Kahalon et al. 2019, p. 348) and in these stories, 'good' girls are sober and 'bad' girls are drunk: an understanding taken up by both male and female characters. In fact, this good/bad binary is especially damaging because of how it impacts relationships between girls. As such, the young men exercising toxic heteromasculinity through assault, the young women surrounding the victim survivors, as well as their communities all largely buy into the Madonna–whore dichotomy and use it as a measure of believability and validation for their own responses to these rape narratives. More specifically, we take the feminist view that while sexist attitudes such as those inherent in the Madonna–whore dichotomy or understandings of 'good' and 'bad' girls have negative consequences on heterosexual relations, they also frequently destroy female bonds in YA rape texts.

After the rapes, the majority of the girls in these texts (save for *Exit*'s Hermione and *Inexcusable*'s Gigi) are made out to be 'bad' girl 'boozy' whores in the narratives. However, two were previously known as 'good' girls—happy and well-liked: *Girl Made of Stars*' Hannah and *Speak*'s Melinda—and so they experience a particular kind of whiplash when they are recast. Such recasting is convenient for their respective communities because then the girls are rendered responsible for their own rapes rather than anyone critically addressing and confronting their local rape cultures. This recasting is also particularly painful because it destroys or threatens their relationships with other girls. Hannah, for example, is described by protagonist Mara (Owen's twin and Hannah's best friend) as 'all laughter and horoscopes, a wild hum running just underneath everything she does and says' (Blake 2018, p. 10). However, after her boyfriend Owen rapes her, Hannah stays away from school to recover, and Owen takes advantage of her absence to spreads rumors about what happened between them. At first, the rape accusation leaves Mara conflicted, creating a chasm between Mara and Hannah for a time. However, Mara eventually believes Hannah, standing by her during her return where her recasting as a 'whore' is swift. The boys terrorize Hannah with a planned slut-shaming campaign, but Mara and a few other girls defend her. Indeed, while *Girl Made of Stars* does represent encouraging moments of female solidarity—particularly with the queer female characters as we will go on to illustrate—unfortunately, Hannah's connections with other women are compromised when she is constructed as a 'bad girl' whore who drank too much and 'cried rape' as revenge for her boyfriend breaking up with her.

In *Speak* a similarly bleak narrative emerges as Melinda's close friends abandon her after Andy rapes her. Still drunk and stunned, Melinda stumbles back to the party and dials 911. Her friends catch her and scream at her for ruining the party—Carroll illustrates the page shattering into glass-like fragments with glimpses of angry eyes and Melinda being slapped. Melinda falls silent, bolts without reporting, and alienates everyone. In this way, Melinda is punished and rendered an 'outcast' (Anderson and Carroll 2018, p. 4) and bullied by mostly other girls for the next year. Although no one knows she is raped until late in the text, it is evident that she is sad, fearful, and withdrawn—traumatized—as she attempts to heal. Even her one new friend, Heather, soon dumps her, returning a friendship bracelet because Melinda is 'the most depressed person' and that she 'needs professional help' (p. 184). Even without the knowledge of her sexual assault, Melinda's friendships are fractured by her wrangling with her new survivor identity. As Heather tells Melinda during their breakup, 'You have a reputation' (p. 185), solidifying her unique 'bad' girl status as a snitch. Both Hannah and Melinda shift along the Madonna–whore dichotomy, securing them as social pariahs and different kinds of traitors of compulsory sexuality.

Unlike Hannah and Melinda, Emma from *Asking for It,* Romy from *All the Rage,* and Stacey from *What We Saw* are all understood in their communities as 'bad' girls to some degree from the very beginnings of the stories. Emma, Stacey, and Romy are thus not recast because they are already classed; what unites all three is their lower economic status and so their poverty already informs how they are understood as 'trash' before they get 'trashed' and are attacked. Emma repeatedly laments her girlfriends' wealth before her attack. Romy consistently makes note of her poverty, from her broken down house, worn bras that even the girls at school call 'an embarrassment' (Summers 2015, p. 39), crooked teeth her family cannot afford to fix and, like Emma, Romy pointedly notices the wealth of her peers. Finally, Stacey is a known 'messed up, alcoholic loser who's been a slut since seventh grade' (Hartzler 2015, p. 305), living in a trailer park. The girls' precarious social capital is exacerbated by their rapes, leaving them with either fewer girls to share solidarity with as compared to Hannah and Melinda, or none at all. For example, while Emma has a circle of girlfriends, their relationships are tenuous at best due to competition, jealousy, and slut shaming. When Emma is gang raped, her girlfriends believe this is Emma's 'bad' girl personality being amplified by drinking. Emma has always been smug about her beauty and so they literally see the photographic evidence of her rape as another exhibition of her drinking and sexuality. When two girls visit her, one blurts: 'But are you sure, Em? ... You were pretty wasted ... I was just asking if it was *rape* rape' (O'Neill 2016, p. 229). She never hears from another friend, acquaintances from school tweet cruelties, and her mother drinks heavily, avoiding dealing with her traumatized daughter. Romy and Stacey, however, seem to start without many close female bonds, aside from their mothers. While Romy does connect with an older waitress coworker, she mostly feels bonded to her stepfather and a boy at work, leaving her without female peer confidants; girls at school casually 'mutter about what a whore [she is]' (Summers 2015, p. 17) in the girls' locker room. Even though Stacey is a secondary character, it seems clear that she is without close girlfriends. Some girls then, especially those of lower socio-economic class status, are already understood as 'bad' girls at the beginnings of their stories, cementing their fates as 'whores' by getting drunk at unsupervised parties.

Allyship

Across our corpus of texts, opportunities for allyship are often lost among straight female characters but are alternatively taken up in complex ways among queer characters as the girls navigate the fallout from their trauma. Although the idea of allies can be a highly contested arena (see Indigenous Action Media 2018; Powell and Kelly 2017, for example), for our purposes, we understand allyship as solidarity work wherein an ally holds some degree of social power, recognizes a range of oppression(s), and supports those who suffer because of it, regardless of whether they share those experiences (DeTurk 2011; Gaffney 2016).[9] Gender- and sexually-diverse characters especially step up as allies while the straight girls surrounding the victim survivors largely either drift away or damagingly break bonds.

Straight girls surround the victim survivor characters in *All the Rage*, *Asking for It*, *Speak*, and *What We Saw* and, in many respects, fail on the allyship front. In *All the Rage*, Romy has already long been abandoned by most of her victim-blaming peers after coming forward about her rape, including her former best friend, Penny. She is something of a loner but never left alone, as classmate Tina fulfills the mean girl archetype by continually tormenting Romy and dismissing her trauma. Tina is an example of a straight girl who not only fails to act as an ally, but is actually an accomplice to the violence Romy experiences. Tina relentlessly bullies Romy, gossiping to other girls that she got too drunk at a major party, lied, and cried rape. Tina actively encourages 'vicious whispers' (Summers

2015, p. 135), sabotages possibilities for allyship, and actively supports another boy who endangers and harasses Melinda. Tina protects Brock, friend of Romy's rapist, who wrote the words 'rape me' across Romy's stomach while she was passed out, before abandoning her on the side of the road as a 'practical joke.'

In *Asking for It* and *Speak,* even though the straight girls surrounding Emma and Melinda do not encourage violence against the protagonists, like Tina does with Romy, they all similarly exercise cruelty in particular ways, demonstrating that girls also contribute to maintaining rape cultures. In *Asking for It*, Emma's girlfriends are dysfunctional at best. As we have noted, their bonds are brittle due to competition, envy, and internalized sexism that manifests in behaviours such as criticizing, ignoring texts, flirting with boys the others like, and slut shaming. For example, Emma is shocked when Ali—one of the kinder girls—suggests: 'Well, maybe Emma, you could try to be less of a whore. Just a thought' (O'Neill 2016, p. 120). One male character even laughingly observes: 'You girls are such a bunch of bitches to each other' (p. 61). Unsurprisingly, they are not allies to Emma after her rape; rather, she finds comfort in the communication and care of a boy named Conor.

This negative representation of girls' relationships is particularly clear in the novel *Speak*. Melinda's former friends—like Penny from *All the Rage*—all doubt and eventually abandon her. For example, when Rachel starts dating Andy, Melinda—acting like an ally—tries to warn her, only to be brutally rebuffed when Rachel screams: 'Liar!' (Anderson and Carroll 2018, p. 333). However, a particularly telling moment that showcases Melinda's lack of female solidarity is when Andy attacks Melinda again, in a school closet. After hearing the struggle and screaming, the girls' lacrosse team bang and holler at the door; finally, Melinda has a team of female witnesses. Yet it is anticlimactic; the next panel shows a bewildered and bloodied Melinda having to instruct the largely shadowed, faceless, girls to call for help. In the final pages, although one girl cautiously asks about her wellbeing, a former friend calls her, and we are told she is 'suddenly popular' (p. 367), the novel implies that she discloses to her male teacher rather than seeking out the solidarity of other girls. Unfortunately, the majority of the straight girls (and women) surrounding the victim survivors allow opportunities for allyship to sink as drinking and rape cultures interferes with their judgement.

In contrast, *Exit* and *Girl Made of Stars* are exemplary texts in which gender fluid and/or sexually diverse characters take up allyship. As Moore (2018b) has argued elsewhere, *Exit* is unusual in its representation of solidarity for a victim survivor of rape; Hermione's best friend Polly is a significant newly out, queer ally and friend throughout Hermione's entire ordeal. Examples of Polly's acts of solidarity include threatening Hermione's boyfriend when he speaks rudely about another girl, accompanying Hermione to the hospital immediately following the rape, not allowing Hermione to feel 'damaged' (Johnston 2016, p. 84), ferociously coming to Hermione's defense when a journalist victim-blames her, and engaging in a number of 'behind the scenes' ally behaviours, such as shutting down a straight girl gossiping about Hermione's attack. Polly demonstrates multiple examples of ally behaviour and communication including advocacy, concrete support, political action, providing comforting targets (frequent check-ins, words of affirmation, validating language, and so on), public rhetoric against manifestations of rape culture including the victim blaming, and use of authority (DeTurk 2011). Hermione recognizes, deeply appreciates, and reciprocates Polly's allyship and one of the most powerful illustrations of how much Polly represents comfort and strength is how Hermione repeats Polly's name to herself at the hospital to self-soothe. Polly crawls into the hospital bed with her and they mourn her rape together, Hermione admitting: 'I can't tell you whose tears are whose' (Johnston 2016, p. 59). Through her exemplary ally work, Polly secures and strengthens her intimacy with Hermione after the rape even though their relationship is a strictly platonic friendship. As Hermione asserts: 'What Polly and I have is forever' (Johnston 2016, p. 43). Polly's ally and queer identities emerge at the same time, arguably with each strengthening the other. Polly's capacity to care for all the girls around demonstrate that friendships are places where both allyship and queer praxis can be enacted (Hunt and Holmes 2015), which is an opportunity Polly seizes.

Diverse gender and sexual identities especially emerge in *Girl Made of Stars,* and these characters certainly stand apart from the crowd of straight girls who, for the most part, abandon or admonish the victim survivors in the other texts. Charlie is a gender and sexually diverse young person—queer and nonbinary—who is a former romantic partner to protagonist Mara and close friend to the victim survivor Hannah. As Charlie patiently explains to Mara, Charlie found Hannah on the trail following the attack and 'half carried' her to her car.[10] Like Polly in *Exit*, Charlie accompanied Hannah to the hospital and acted as both ally and witness to her rape examine experience, during which Hannah screamed for hours. When Mara is distracted by jealousy, asking if Charlie was with another girl at the party, Charlie quickly calls attention to Mara's misplaced concern: 'This isn't about you and me … Do you understand what's happening, Mara?' (Blake 2018, p. 44). This moment underscores Charlie's effective and educative allyship. In her advocacy, she teaches Mara to step up in her friendship and feminist identity (Mara runs a feminist group and newspaper at school), calling her to recognize the rape and provide concrete support. Such moments directly inform how Mara eventually comes to successfully author herself as an ally as well. Charlie directly demonstrates ally behaviour with Hannah through small gestures, such as texting Hannah for permission to visit, effectively enacting a consent-based ethic of care, and doing so in front of Mara so as to continue her ally education. Further, Charlie had unknowingly been an ally to Mara when she was dealing with the aftermath of her own sexual abuse. Although Charlie never knew her story, she made Mara 'feel safe', especially in how she respected Mara's sexual boundaries, being 'absolutely fine with whatever [they] did or didn't do physically' (Blake 2018, pp. 67, 71).

Finally, largely due to Charlie's ally teachings, Mara works in solidarity with Hannah rather than with her own brother. However, she is not a complete novice; as briefly mentioned, Mara founded a feminist group at school—'A place to talk about all the shit girls and queer kids deal with everyday'—and subsequently 'quickly became known as Queen Bitch at school' (Blake 2018, p. 68). Charlie and Mara especially felt such a space was necessary because of the homophobia they experienced. Mara had a foundation of ally identity to build on to enact resistance against rape culture. Much like in *Exit,* when Mara and Charlie visit Hannah to witness her testimony, Mara believes her and they hold one another, 'a little knot of friends and tears' (Blake 2018, p. 123). Mara's commitment is especially clear when Hannah returns to school and is verbally harassed by many peers, who jeer sexist slurs at her. While Charlie escorts Hannah away from the mob, an enraged Mara attacks one of the boys: 'I shove his chest. I scream … I keep pushing him. Keep hitting him. Keep screaming' (Blake 2018, pp. 176–177). It takes the principal and a security guard to stop her. Later, Mara does even more difficult ally work when she confronts her family for believing Owen. More particularly, she battles her mother—from whom she initially learned about feminism—for defending her son. Mara's mother 'flinches' when Mara insists, 'I'm not stupid … Hannah. She's not stupid. She's not a liar' (Blake 2018, p. 257). Mara then attacks Owen. Seemingly soaked in shame, Owen collapses, 'eyes bleeding tears' (Blake 2018, p. 258), and finally their parents recognize that their son is a rapist. Fuelled by her queer praxis (Hunt and Holmes 2015), Mara proves her allyship to Hannah as she comes to terms with her own victim survivor identity.

While the straight girls falter as friends after the rapes in these texts, the queer characters serve as the antidote to the violent boys who pursue and produce hetero and toxic masculinities in both drinking and rape cultures. Although the majority of straight female characters in the novels we analyze in this chapter at best disappoint and at worst demonize and endanger the victim survivors, queer characters powerfully demonstrate that female friendship can be a significant site of both allyship and resistance. Characters such as Polly, Charlie, and Mara illuminate how friendship is critical for most adolescent girls. In the wake of their attacks, the victim survivors experience abandonment to varying degrees as their female friendships are compromised, resulting in a diminished potential for them cultivate or participate in feminist solidarity building at a time when they need it the most. With few exceptions, the communities of the victim survivors dry up to varying degrees and leave her responsible for navigating recovery either alone or with few allies. As a result, readers are positioned to witness the tainted testimonies (Gilmore 2017) of these characters and confront the thin veil between these fictions and the realities of rape culture.

Conclusion

We began this chapter with a curiosity about the links between compulsory heterosexuality, rape, and alcohol abuse. On one level these texts are cautionary tales that might best be defined as 'neo-temperance narratives' with roots in nineteenth-century feminist movements to prohibit alcohol use.[11] The current #sobercurious movement echoes the implicit temperance discourses in these YA novels and its ties to male violence and alcohol. In a 2019 article, a reporter from *The New York Times* writes that 'at a politically fraught time, clarity of the mind is a potent weapon, and the #MeToo movement has also helped give abstinence from alcohol an extra kick' (Williams 2019). As such, a kind of distillation ensues as alcohol is neatly and repeatedly represented as a weapon that men can use, but that women should refrain from to protect themselves from sexual violence. What the #sobercurious movement and the YA texts analyzed in this chapter largely sidestep are the deep complexities that inform rape cultures. Combatting sexual violence and those who perpetuate it requires more than a mere abandonment and/or interrogation of drinking culture. Rather, a more robust examination of the blurred intricacies of other issues such as compulsory heterosexuality, toxic masculinities, and patriarchal discourses is also needed. As Michelle Dean argues about Steubenville: 'Whatever these young men did or didn't do … these young men in Steubenville were performing for each other'; as Michael Messner (2005) argues, men use women's bodies during gang rape to bond with one another. Dean also asserts that public discussions of this case 'are proof of the flippancy and indifference' toward sexual assault that remains largely unchanged as we enter a new decade—just two entangled issues that require nuanced analysis.

Within rape culture, alcohol is frequently central. Implicit in these stories are the ways in which white heterosexual male violence is often excused through alcohol consumption just as girls and women are blamed for rape when they get drunk—a phenomenon taken up in much YA fiction. In stories like those under discussion in this chapter, the authors navigate two cultural taboos—underage drinking and sexual violence perpetrated by young men. Even as the authors attempt to make rape visible, they simultaneously reinforce compulsory heterosexuality as the norm through two strategies. The first places blame on alcohol rather than on male violence and the second represents girls' friendships as superficial, competitive, and easily splintered. Across these novels, allyship is often submerged in favor of scripts that reproduce and reinforce myths about alcohol consumption, compulsory heterosexuality, and rape. We note how this script is challenged when gender and sexually diverse characters offer solidarity to the survivors. The idea that girls' friendships are unstable leans on stereotypes and fails to acknowledge how girls themselves are dialoguing, networking, and organizing activism across digital technologies to combat rape culture (Mendes et al. 2018). It also fails to acknowledge the feminist activism that brought Steubenville to light and that Chanel Miller employed through her victim impact statement.[12] Overall, opportunities for allyship between and among girls are infrequently taken up in YA rape novels, making girls in some ways simply victims rather than agents.[13]

The writers of these texts are likely well-intentioned and importantly address the insidiousness of rape culture. With some exceptions, these texts, as well as many other YA rape novels, contain representations of drinking and sexual violence that reinforce familiar and troubling cultural scripts as the norm. The YA texts that we read in this chapter tell stories of assault, drinking, and intoxicated heterosexualities that slice bonds—both potential and in-progress—between girls. However, it is also encouraging to see more representations of gender fluid and sexually diverse young people, as well as portraying their unique (if somewhat romanticized) capacities for allyship and resistances to rape culture. In general, YA texts seem to then be moving toward including more diverse and dynamic characters who hold great potential for pushing back against rape culture in nuanced and necessary fashions. We end this chapter where we began with Brock Allen Turner, who is now the textbook definition for rape (Rennison and Dodge 2018). It is because of allyship and activism on behalf of and by Chanel Miller that led to this designation.[14] It is our hope that YA authors writing about rape will broaden familiar scripts to include feminist alliances between and among girls as a way to challenge compulsory heterosexuality and resist rape culture, especially the myth of alcohol as the cause of sexual violence.

Notes

1 See Miller's 2019 memoir *Know My Name*.
2 In this chapter, we are explicit that the male privilege we discuss is specifically white male privilege. We recognize that Black, Indigenous, and other men of colour do not experience the same kind of male privilege we address and critique here due to their racial identities and the particular racism(s) they encounter.
3 Please note that this 2018 graphic novel is another version of the original 1999 novel by Laurie Halse Anderson.
4 For more on rape scripts see, Marshall (2009; 2018); Gilmore and Marshall (2015; 2019); Moore (2018a; 2018b).
5 See Gilmore and Marshall (2019). Elizabeth Marshall points out how comics artists like Una in her memoir *Becoming Unbecoming* offer up a graphic feminist pedagogy to fight back against gendered violence.
6 #MeToo has been both celebrated and criticized for the ways in which it has been taken up in popular discourse. Since turned into a hashtag, much debate and discussion has emerged, such as how individuals—particularly famous

white women and their pain—are centred or remain a focus rather than on more vulnerable groups such as queer folks, people of color, undocumented people, and so many others lacking access to institutional and systemic justice and support.

7 It is worth noting that, while we acknowledge that queer men can engage in toxic masculinity, we employ the term to signal that we are focused on straight men in this chapter.

8 O'Neill (2016) states that *Asking for It* was 'inspired in part by a few incidents: Todd Akin's comments about 'legitimate rape'; Whoopi Goldberg's 'rape rape' comments about Roman Polanski; the Steubenville case in the US—and the treatment of the so-called 'Slane Girl' in Ireland….'

9 See, for example, Indigenous Action Media (2015) for an excellent critique of allyship.

10 Although Charlie identifies as nonbinary, she explains to Mara that she would prefer to continue using she/her pronouns—'for now' (Blake 2018, p. 52) which is also reflected in this chapter.

11 During the nineteenth century, temperance movements emerged in a range of locations, including the US, Canada, Ireland, and the UK. The British Association for the Promotion of Temperance was established in 1835. In the US, the Women's Christian Temperance Union (WCTU) was founded in 1857. These temperance movements aimed to convince the public to moderate or abstain completely from alcohol and were also often tied to other social reforms, such as women's suffrage as well as less appealing movements like anti-immigration efforts.

12 For more on the politics of Miller's victim impact statement and women's testimony see Gilmore (2019).

13 Jennifer Mathieu's *Moxie* (2017) is an exception.

14 Knowledge of this comes from Amber's work in secondary classrooms. Amber was teaching secondary English at the time and one of her students—a girl who has previously disclosed that she had been sexually harassed—showed Amber the post and asked her to read it. By the end of the school day, most of Amber's female students had read the statement; it was everywhere.

References

Ahmed, S 2017, Living a Feminist Life, Duke University Press, Durham, NC.

Anderson, LH and Carroll, E 2018, *Speak: the Graphic Novel*, Farrar, Straus and Giroux, New York.

Baker, KJM 2016, 'Here's the powerful letter the Stanford victim read to her attacker', *BuzzFeed,* 3 June, accessed 15 December 2019.

Blake, AH 2018, *Girl Made of Stars,* Houghton Mifflin Harcourt, Boston.

Brown, S and Miller, C 2019, 'Chanel Miller describes how Stanford failed her', *Chronicle of Higher Education,* vol. 66, no. 7, unpaginated, www.chronicle.com/article/chanel-miller-describes-how-stanford-failed-her/.

Buchwald E, Fletcher, P and Roth, M 2005, *Transforming a Rape Culture*, Milkweed Editions, Minnesota.

Creighton, G and Oliffe, JL 2010, 'Theorising masculinities and men's health: a brief history with a view to practice', *Health Sociology Review*, vol. 19, no. 4, pp. 409–418, https://doi.org/10.5172/hesr.2010.19.4.409.

Dean, M 2013, 'The lessons of Steubenville', *The New Yorker,* 11 January, accessed 15 December 2019.

DeTurk, S 2011, 'Allies in action: the communicative experiences of people who challenge social injustice on behalf of others', *Communication Quarterly*, vol. 59, no. 5, pp. 569–590, https://doi.org/10.1080/01463373.2011.614209.

Gaffney, C 2016, 'Anatomy of an ally', *The Education Digest,* vol. 82, no. 3, pp. 43–48, www.tolerance.org/magazine/number-53-summer-2016/feature/anatomy-ally.

Gay, R 2018, 'Why the #MeToo movement still has a lot left to do', *Refinery,* vol. 29, 4 October, accessed 21 November 2019.

Gilmore, L 2001, The Limits of Autobiography: Trauma and Testimony, Cornell University Press, Ithaca, NY.

Gilmore, L 2017, *Tainted Witness: Why We Doubt What Women Say About Their Lives*, Columbia University Press, New York.

Gilmore, L 2019, 'Chanel Miller and the new power of women's words', *Cognoscenti*, WBUR, 17 September, accessed 9 December 2019.

Gilmore, L and Marshall, E 2019, *Witnessing Girlhood: Toward an Intersectional Tradition of Life Writing*, Fordham University Press, New York.

Gruber, A 2016, 'Anti-rape culture', *Kansas Law Review*, vol. 64, no. 4, 1027-1053, https://scholar.law.colorado.edu/articles/10

Hall, R 2004, '"It can happen to you": rape prevention in the age of risk management', *Hypatia*, vol. 19, no. 3, pp. 1–19, www.jstor.org/stable/3811091.

Hartzler, A 2015, *What We Saw*, HarperTeen, New York.

Hunt, S and Holmes, C 2015, 'Everyday decolonization: living a decolonizing queer politics', *Journal of Lesbian Studies*, vol. 19, no. 2, pp. 154–172, https://doi.org/10.1080/10894160.2015.970975.

Indigenous Action Media, 2015, 'Accomplices Not Allies', *Taking Sides: Revolutionary Solidarity and the Poverty of Liberalism*, Ed. Milstein C, AK Press, Oakland US.

Johnston, EK 2016, *Exit, Pursued by a Bear*, Dutton Books, New York.

Kahalon, R, Bareket, O, Vial, AC, Sassenhagen, N, Becker, J and Schnabel, N 2019, 'The Madonna–whore dichotomy is associated with patriarchy endorsement: evidence from Israel, the United States, and Germany', *Psychology of Women Quarterly*, vol. 43, no. 3, pp. 348–367. https://doi.org/10.1177/0361684319843298.

Lynch, C 2015 [2005], *Inexcusable (10th anniversary edition),* Simon and Schuster, New York.

Marshall, E 2009, 'Girlhood, sexual violence, and agency in Francesca Lia Block's "Wolf"', *Children's Literature in Education*, vol. 40, no. 3, pp. 217–234, https://doi.org/10.1007/s10583-008-9083-7.

Marshall, E 2018, *Graphic Girlhoods: Visualizing Education and Violence*, Routledge, New York.

Marshall, E and Gilmore, L 2015, 'Girlhood in the gutter: feminist graphic knowledge and the visualization of sexual precarity', *Women's Studies Quarterly*, vol. 43, nos. 1–2, pp. 95–114, 10.1353/wsq.2015.0014.

Mathieu, J 2017, *Moxie*, Roaring Brook Press, New York.

Mendes, K, Ringrose, J and Keller, J 2018, '#MeToo and the promise and pitfalls of challenging rape culture through feminist activism', *European Journal of Women's Studies,* vol. 25, no. 2, pp. 236–246. https://doi.org/10.1177/1350506818765318.

Messner, M 2005, 'The triad of violence in men's sports', Transforming a *Rape Culture*: Revised *Edition*, Eds. Buchwald, E, Fletcher, PR, and Roth, M, Milkweed Editions, Minnesota.

Miller, C 2019, *Know My Name: a Memoir*, Viking, New York.

Moore, A 2018a, 'Traumatic geographies: mapping the violent landscapes driving YA rape survivors indoors in Laurie Halse Anderson's *Speak*, Elizabeth Scott's *Living dead girl*, and E. K. Johnston's *Exit, pursued by a bear*', *Jeunesse: Young People, Texts, Cultures*, vol. 10, no. 1, pp. 58–84, 10.1353/jeu.2018.0003.

Moore, A 2018b, 'We believe her: sexual assault and friend/ally/ship in *Exit, pursued by a bear*', *The ALAN Review,* vol. 44, no. 1, pp. 15–27.

O'Neill, L 2016, *Asking For It*, Quercus, New York.

Pennington, R and Birthisel, J 'When new media make news: framing technology and sexual assault in the Steubenville rape case', *New Media and Society,* vol. 18, no. 11, pp. 2435–2451, https://doi.org/10.1177/1461444815612407.

Powell, J and Kelly, A 2017, 'Accomplices in the academy in the age of Black Lives Matter', Everyday Practices of Social Justice, vol. 6, no. 2, pp. 42–65. http://lib.dr.iastate.edu/jctp/vol6/iss2/

Rennison, CM and Dodge, M 2018, *Introduction to Criminal Justice: Systems, Diversity, and Change*, SAGE, Los Angeles.

Rodier, K, Meagher, M, and Nixon, R 2012, 'Cultivating a critical classroom for viewing gendered violence in music video', Feminist Teacher, vol. 23, no. 1, pp. 63–70, https://doi.org/10.5406/femteacher.23.1.0063.

Summers, C 2015, *All the Rage*, St Martin's Press, London.

Williams, A 2019, 'The new sobriety', *The New York Times*, 15 June, accessed 15 December 2019.

Wunker, E 2016, Notes *From* a *Feminist Killjoy*: Essay on *Everyday Life*, BookThug, Toronto.

11 On the Straight and Narrow

The Homonormalising of Australian Queer YA Literature in the Age of Marriage Equality

Adam Kealley

John Stephens has suggested that Australian literature for young people is 'driven by a schema consisting of a particular bundle of ideological presuppositions' that is peculiarly local (2003, p. viii). The resulting metanarratives 'promote conformity to socially determined and approved patterns of behaviour, which they do by offering positive role models, proscribing undesirable behaviour and affirming [Australian] culture's ideologies, systems and institutions' (2003, p. xiii). In the context of the fierce debate that preceded Australia's most recent – and ultimately successful – bid for marriage equality for same-sex couples, the question arose as to how contemporaneous queer Australian young adult (YA) literature might respond. Would it, through a homonormative discourse, serve to reinforce conservative norms surrounding the institution of marriage and intimate relationships? Or might its readership instead be offered a more radical, queer view of relationships?

The three Australian novels examined here – *The Things We Promise* by JC Burke, Sean Kennedy's *Micah Johnson Goes West* and *The Love Interest* by Cale Dietrich – were all published locally in 2017.[1] It was a year when same-sex marriage featured heavily within our national conversation in the lead up to a plebiscite and subsequent legalisation. Each explores the intimate relationships of queer cis-gendered male characters, the group most privileged by homonormativity[2] – although *The Things We Promise* is focalised through the queer character's heterosexual sister. Roberta Seelinger Trites once posited that queer male YA fiction has 'a well-entrenched tradition of delegitimizing its own agenda' by normalising experiences of overcoming trauma or marginalisation to provide 'a sense of catharsis or validation or acceptance of homosexuality' within its readers (1998, p. 149). This is often evident in the tensions between what Peter Hollindale (1988) terms the 'surface' and 'passive' ideologies operating within children's literature. Close reading of these three Australian novels reveals that, despite their overtly queer-positive surface ideology, they are pervaded by a passive ideology that is distinctly homonormative, limiting the range of legitimised queer male subjectivities to those that mimic traditional heterosexual norms.

This passive homonormativity implies that positive queer subjectivity is contingent upon conformity to a relationship model of long-term monogamy and acceptance by the heterosexual majority, typically represented in the form of the biological family. This delegitimises other, queer, forms of sexual intimacy and kinship, and contributes to the establishment of a hierarchy of queer subjectivities in which some are perceived as lesser or more lacking than others. The idealisation of monogamous coupledom and the centrality of the biological family in conferring legitimacy fails to recognise the reality of many young queers, whose experience of familial and intimate relationships may run counter to these norms. Mollie Blackburn, Caroline Clarke and Emily Nemeth argue that, rather than insisting 'that gay and lesbian people are just like straight people', truly queer YA literature acknowledges 'a variety of genders, sexes and desires, as well as foregrounding the sexual, thereby challenging the notion of what counts as normal among them' (2015, p. 11). With this definition in mind, the repressive passive homonormativity operating within these novels undermines their overt liberatory intent, suggesting that these novels are not queer *enough* for a time in which the question of queer legitimacy is at the forefront of Australia's national conversation.

The Homonormalising of the Marriage Equality Agenda

The passing of Australia's Marriage Amendment (Definition and Religious Freedoms) Act on 7 December 2017 – granting same-sex couples the right to legally marry – might likewise be viewed as a liberatory act that ultimately served to reinforce heterosexual norms rather than queer them. While same-sex couples had been somewhat protected by Australia's laws governing de facto marriage, the legal right to wed was seen by many as a watershed moment in the march towards genuine equality for queer Australians. Within queer communities, however, the focus of contemporary Australian queer politics on same-sex marriage has not been without its critics, largely because of its erasure of queer difference and reinforcement of heterosexist norms. Luke Gahan, for example, suggests Australian marriage quality advocates have embraced a 'conservative family values discourse' that offers:

> images of mainstream, conventional and responsibly centrist gays as a way to win over middle Australia. Within this discourse, same-sex couples and families are positioned as no different to heterosexual couples and families, and the dominant heterosexual nuclear family model is left uncontested.
>
> (2013, np)

This argument seems borne out by the rhetoric of the ultimately successful 'Yes' campaign active during the twelve months preceding the plebiscite that led to the Act.[3] Amy Thomas, Hannah McCann and Geraldine Fela critiqued the strongly homonormative discourse employed by the 'Yes' campaign, concluding that it functioned to 'reify lifelong-coupled monogamy as the normative expectation for everyone, regardless of sexual orientation' while sidelining criticisms of the nuclear family as 'a source of violence, inequality, and sexism' (2019, p. 479). Furthermore, images of a white, heteronormative and gender-conforming nuclear family advocating for same-sex marriage became a common trope employed by the 'Yes' campaign, further promoting assimilation into the mainstream. This idealised family acted as the 'gatekeeper of society', able to 'bestow legitimacy onto "same-sex" couples' (Thomas et al. 2019, p. 486). While inarguably a boon to queer Australians who wish to formalise their relationships, the centrality of marriage and the nuclear family within the queer political discourse ultimately reinforces institutions based on conservative values, limiting the potential for equal recognition of alternate expressions of queer intimacy and kinship.

This introjection of heteronormative ideals within queer identities has been termed 'homonormativity'. Lisa Duggan defines it as a politics 'that does not contest dominant heteronormative assumptions and institutions but upholds and sustains them, while promising the possibility of a demobilized gay constituency and a privatized, depoliticized gay culture anchored in domesticity and consumption' (2002, p. 179). Homonormativity represents anything but genuine queer liberation and is simply the tokenistic acceptance of 'a fixed minority' of queers who reinforce 'state-endorsed heterosexual primacy and prestige' through mimicking the heteronormative and patriarchal institutions of marriage and the nuclear family (Duggan 2002, p. 190). Tanja Dreher further suggests that homonormativity fails to 'recognise the diversity of queer experience' and devalues intimacy 'outside of the "couple" formula' (2016, p. 181), while Judith Butler questions the hierarchy a homonormative marriage equality discourse creates between legitimate and illegitimate queer identities: 'What does this do to the community of the nonmarried, the single, the divorced, the uninterested, the non-monogamous, and how does the sexual field become reduced, its very legibility, once we extend marriage as a norm?' (2002, p. 21). Homonormativity, then, operates to legitimise a limited palette of queer subjectivities, de-emphasising difference in favour of assimilation within the heteronormative mainstream.

Homonormativity has particular implications for queer youth and the cultural media created for them. The discursive limiting of queer subjectivities is particularly concerning, as newly minted and popularly reproduced homonormative stereotypes are typically introjected by young queers before they have the opportunity to participate in queer communities, that is:

long before the opportunity to realise just how diverse and complex most queer people really are. The perception that one is required to perform and, indeed, conform to a set of narrow stereotypes in order to be coherently queer is … an added pressure that increases vulnerability.

(Cover 2012, p. 119)

This argument is extended by Michael Warner, who implies that future generations of queer youth will find it progressively harder 'to aspire to a different kind of sexual maturity besides that of the married couple' (1999, p. 125). Indeed, he suggests that such an alternative would be harder than ever to articulate or legitimate, since marriage 'would have received the imprimatur of the very movement that had come into being to open up different life horizons for them' (Warner 1999, p. 125). Family relationships, too, require diversity, with Lydia Kokkola noting that queer YA 'has the potential to fill that "Oh, I went through that, too" gap for queer teen readers who must seek their "family" outside their birth family' (2013, p. 96).

This bears significant implications for queer Australian YA literature and the range of queer subjectivities that might be represented within it. On one hand, YA literature has the potential to be radically subversive. On the other, it can be inherently conservative, offering pathways to subjecthood that are predicated along normative lines.[4] Interrogating the passive ideologies operating within *The Things We Promise*, *Micah Johnson Goes West* and *The Love Interest* positions them firmly within this latter camp. In privileging monogamous coupledom and the biological family, while delegitimising alternate expressions of queer intimacy and kinship, they serve to reify homonormative identities as vastly preferable, if not ideal.

Micah Johnson Goes West: Shame and the Delegitimisation of the Non-monogamous Queer

In Kennedy's *Micah Johnson Goes West*, the idealisation of monogamous coupledom extends throughout its main narrative arc and is reinforced by the dynamics of shame associated with queer desire outside of its bounds. The novel begins with eighteen-year-old Micah and his boyfriend, Kyle, breaking up when Micah moves across the country after being drafted by a Western Australian football team as they believe a long-distance relationship would fail. Suddenly single, Micah experiences a sense of loss and loneliness:

Recently, he had a taste of what it was like to have a boyfriend and the intimacy that came with it … He missed Kyle. Not just the sex, but the conversations, the cuddles, the light touches. The feeling that he was wanted.

(Kennedy 2017, p. 13)

When he returns to Melbourne for an important game, Micah meets up with Kyle again, revelling in 'this feeling of *normalcy* that happened to be there now they were together again' (Kennedy 2017, p. 74, emphasis added); the language here clearly situating long-term monogamy as both desirable and the norm. Kyle, however, has moved on to a new relationship, leaving Micah bereft. The thematising of Micah's subsequent spiral into depression, and his fruitless attempts to find fulfillment through sexual encounters with strangers, creates a discursive binary in which casual sexual intimacy is posited as meaningless, shameful and ultimately dangerous, in contrast to the fulfillment offered by long-term monogamy.

The non-monogamous are constructed as the illegitimate 'other' of this homonormative binary. On one hand, casual, polyamorous intimacy is depicted as unfulfilling. After breaking up with Kyle, Micah 'turned to apps' despite the fact that 'he knew they weren't giving him what he needed' (Kennedy 2017, p. 13) and which, in fact, left him feeling 'even lonelier' (Kennedy 2017, p. 13). However, such encounters are also inflected with shame and defilement. Micah's first experience is with a young man 'flushed with embarrassment [who] wanted the deed to be over and done with as soon as possible' (Kennedy 2017, p. 13.). Casual intimacy is described as 'grubby' (Kennedy 2017, p. 13), a behaviour after which Micah feels the need to 'scrub himself clean' (Kennedy 2017, p. 141) or go swimming in order to be 'cleansed' (Kennedy 2017, p. 14). Michael Warner argues that such conservative views of sexual intimacy are predicated on 'the homophobic equality of "gay bars, pornography and one-night stands" with immorality – the very equation against which the gay movement came into being' (1999, p. 131). As a mechanism to valorise monogamous coupledom, the novel suggests the only alternative is casual promiscuity, which it discursively constructs as shameful and immoral.

This shame leads Micah to keep his casual encounters secret from those around him: 'He covered his tracks well, though, fitting in quickies just after training and before he arrived back home at Sam's in North Beach – usually encumbered with some shopping to explain his tardiness' (Kennedy 2017, p. 88). Micah's behaviour reflects the dynamics of queer shame as articulated by Eve Kosofsky Sedgwick. She suggests that, for queers, shame 'defines the space in which a sense of self will develop' due to its historical proscription, leading to a subjectivity characterised by the dichotomous movement towards 'painful individuation, uncontrollable relationality' (2003, p. 37). Micah's sexual behaviour fills him with shame, isolating him from his heterosexual peers. Yet, at the same time, he is driven to find companionship with other queers. The anonymity of these encounters, their ritualistic cleansing, as well as their secretive nature reveals their inflection with shame. This tension between his queer sexual desire and the homonormative ideals that proscribe promiscuity or casual polyamory eventually lead Micah into a struggle with depression.

Micah's secretive sexual life and its effects on his mental health coalesce in what is cast as his 'morality play moment' (Kennedy 2017, p. 141), when he decides that his promiscuity has been an attempt to fill the 'void' since ending his long-term relationship with Kyle. After learning of Kyle's new relationship, Micah decompensates. He gets drunk and picks up another casual partner from a bar as a direct response to his feelings of inadequacy, heightened by knowledge of Kyle's participation in normative coupledom. Inebriated and reckless, he engages in unprotected sex. This taboo nature of this encounter establishes a sense of estrangement within Micah, who describes himself as 'Not-Micah', someone with a 'strange, lustful porn actor voice seeming to speak from his dick rather than his mouth' (Kennedy 2017, p. 140). This description clearly exemplifies Warner's observation that normative society correlates pornography and promiscuity with immorality. This persona is contrasted with '[s]ensible Micah, the real Micah' who wakes next day 'in a cold sweat' (Kennedy 2017, p. 140). Whereas other sexual encounters are dealt with in a line or two, this encounter is recounted in some detail, heightening its discursive purpose. Shame results in Micah 'berating himself' and being 'savage as he washed himself' in another instance in which he feels the need to be 'scrubbed clean' (Kennedy 2017, p. 141), this time heightened by the unprotected nature of the encounter.

Despite stating 'there was nothing wrong with one-night stands' (Kennedy 2017, p. 141), any sex-positivity that might be read into this statement is undermined by Micah adding that sex is 'fraught with danger' (Kennedy 2017, p. 141), reflecting Robert McRuer's observation that in children's literature featuring AIDS, 'sex that is not equated with love and commitment is "bad" and "wrong"' (2011, p. 191). Miserable, Micah concludes that 'like some cheesy high school video meant to scare you off sex, he was paying the price' (Kennedy 2017, p. 141); a clearly didactic comment aimed at the implied reader. Additionally, the course of post-exposure drugs Micah takes for the rest of the novel's duration serves as a continuing reminder of Micah's transgression. Melissa Gross, Annette Goldsmith and Debi Carruth (2008) have argued that novels representing HIV/AIDS are more effective if representing 'actual contexts that readers might find themselves navigating' (p. 414), which this novel clearly does. However, Thomas Crisp's criticism of such an approach is that it seems to 'campaign for didactic if not cautionary tales intended to scare young readers into "appropriate" behaviour' (2013, p. 259), in this case to adopt homonormative ideals of long-term monogamy as a safeguard against HIV infection. Furthermore, Micah's history of casual sex is characterised by his doctor as 'self-destructive behaviour' (Kennedy 2017, p. 145) stemming from undiagnosed depression. Thus, not only is non-monogamous sex shameful, immoral and dangerous to one's physical health, it is also correlated with mental illness and depicted as antipathetic to selfhood.

Margaret Morrison has suggested that queer shame such as this can drive homonormativity, leading queer people to appropriate hetero-sexual norms to form a sense of selfhood that seems 'more stable, less deadly, less shameful' (2015, p. 22). This argument clearly plays out in this novel, foreclosing the possibility for alternate modes of queer sexual expression by resolving Micah's shame through the establish-ment of a new monogamous relationship. After his HIV scare, Micah comes to the 'realisation' that his casual sexual encounters are an inad-equate substitute for monogamy: 'All he wanted all along was to recap-ture those feelings he had with Kyle. Where sex was fun, passionate and also kind of gross, weird and messy – but perfect all the same because it was about connection' (Kennedy 2017, p. 141). He decides to give up casual sex, instead contacting one of his previous lovers 'who had actu-ally wanted more from him' (Kennedy, 2017, p. 168). While they ini-tially meet on the hook-up app Grindr, Todd gives Micah his number and suggests they maintain contact 'the more *traditional* way' (Kennedy 2017, p. 185, emphasis added), thus abjuring the Grindr app and the kinds of queer relationships it facilitates. Signalling a shift from the shame that characterised his casual experiences, Micah and Todd end their date with a public kiss in front of some of Micah's fans. Despite the fact that some 'looked a little shocked' (Kennedy 2017, p. 185), the heterosexual affirm-ation of this nascent homonormative relationship is implied when a child asks Micah for his autograph. Thus, the novel clearly uses a discourse of shame to promote homonormativity, not only in terms of the moralistic language used to demonise casual sex, but also in the construction of a clear binary between such a mode of sexual expression and the proud, publicly affirmed notion of monogamous coupledom, as if these are the only two options available for queer relationships.

Further fueling Micah's misery, the novel includes the happily partnered Simon and Declan, who are engaged to be married. As a mentor for young gay and lesbian athletes, Simon's homonormativity is posited as aspirational; his long-term relationship with Declan presents a stark con-trast to Micah's brief encounters: ' "We've survived this long. We're stuck with each other." He didn't need to tell Micah how happy he was with that revelation. It was written all over his face' (Kennedy 2017, p. 40). Rob Cover asserts that homonormativity by its very nature excludes queer youth, who are unlikely or unable to access the privileges of long-term monogamy (2016, p. 127). The relationship between Simon and Declan merely serves to remind Micah of 'how lonely he was' without Kyle (Kennedy 2017, p. 40), exacerbating his unhappiness at failing to meet the homonormative standards established by his adult role model. Adding further pressure is Micah's mentor Sam. This slightly older and heterosexual teammate, who is in a long-term relationship, asserts that '[p]lenty of people get together at eighteen and stay together' (Kennedy 2017, p. 86) after Micah suggests he and Kyle broke up because of their youth. This implies that long-term monogamous coupledom is a realistic goal, or norm, even for the teenaged Micah. Through the protagonist's clear misery, and his juxtaposition against a range of role models firmly engaged in hetero- or homonormative relationships, long-term monogamous coupledom attains an idealised status. Casual intimacy, on the other hand, is abnegated through the discourse of shame, while the possibility of a queer young adult being happily single is overlooked entirely.

The Things We Promise: Resurrecting the Threat of AIDS to Proscribe Queer Sex

The Things We Promise similarly reifies homonormative relationships, instead invoking the spectre of AIDS to proscribe queer sex outside of its bounds. The novel is set during the AIDS crisis of the early 1990s; author JC Burke's stated 'feeble attempt to not let that time be forgotten' (2017, p. 2). The novel is focalised through the character of Gemma, the teenage sister of Billy, who, with his long-term partner Saul, occupies a clearly homonormative relationship in New York. This relationship is torn asunder when Saul succumbs to AIDS and Billy returns to the family home in Melbourne. It transpires that Billy contracted HIV in his earlier, more promiscuous life, transmitting it unknowingly to his partner. Billy, too, passes away and, at his funeral, is memorialised as a kind of tragic queer martyr for monogamy.

The novel offers a representation of queer lives that reflects the problematic ideologies typical of queer YA literature in the 1990s through the choice to focalise the narrative through the eyes of Billy's sister, positioning the reader to view Billy and Saul's relationship through a heteronormative lens. Cart and Jenkins (2006) note that queer YA of that decade typically erased representations of queer communities by focalising narratives through either heterosexual characters or isolated queer characters:

> This was particularly true for novels that included AIDS as a plot element and that typically involved a gay character and his family dealing with the disease. One common scenario—always told from the perspective of a young person—involved an older brother or an uncle who had made his home in a city with a sizeable gay/lesbian community. Before the book opens, however, the character has contracted AIDS and in the course of the story he returns to his family of origin to die.
>
> (Cart and Jenkins 2006, p. 96)

Despite its contemporary publication, *The Things We Promise* follows this pattern entirely: in its choice of a heterosexual focaliser and the virtual absence of queer communities, it applies a conservative, heteronormative view of what constitutes a legitimate relationship to its queer characters.

Although Gemma lives within a non-traditional family structure – in a single parent family with her mother, supported by an elderly migrant couple living in the same building – queer people are held to a higher standard. Billy and Saul are described as 'like a married couple' (Burke 2017, p. 6), a fact that is reiterated multiple times throughout the novel. In fact, Gemma notes that 'an old married couple' is her 'family's favourite line' (Burke 2017, p. 92), as if to mitigate Billy and Saul's transgressive sexuality. Billy tells Gemma that 'when he'd met Saul and fallen so deeply in love he realised that the good sex he thought he'd been having was like thinking oranges were tasty until you discovered mangoes' (Burke 2017, p. 10), further privileging the homonormative ideal. Even while clearly foregrounding the sexual aspect of queer relationships, monogamous coupledom is posited here as sweeter and, perhaps ironically, more exotic. Billy and Gemma's mother also frequently praises the relationship, stating that the two men love each other 'more than any other couple I've ever known' (Burke 2017, p. 14), and in doing so reinforces their contrast to the stereotype of the transgressive, sexually profligate queer.

However, despite the apparent sanctity of this marriage-like relationship, it is not enough to save Billy and Saul from the spectre of AIDS. As in *Micah Johnson Goes West*, non-monogamous sex is problematised with the threat of illness, but in *The Things We Promise* it takes on a much more sinister resonance with virtually every queer character succumbing to AIDS. Much of the novel focuses on Gemma's trauma as she is confronted with the realities of her brother's illness: vomiting, bacterial infection, Kaposi's sarcoma, pneumonia, and lymphoma, his 'ribs jutting out across his shrinking body' (Burke 2017, p. 280). This, combined with the loneliness and terror of the AIDS ward and the prejudice experienced by those who occupy it, serve to offer a stark denunciation of queer sex. The grotesque spectacle of Billy's death and its focalisation through the character of Gemma seems to 'tokenize queer death for heterosexual characters' growth' (Browne 2020, p. 2), as Gemma educates herself and her friends on the tragedy. The historic *Silence = Death* campaign is referenced, and disseminated through Gemma's school when she, along with her friends, decides to print and sell t-shirts with this message. The AIDS memorial quilt project also features, and one of the final scenes of the novel features Gemma and her heterosexual friends sewing panels to honour Billy and Saul, as well as another character Zane, an image that seems to imply the conferral of legitimacy upon the queer characters by their heterosexual counterparts through the act of memorialisation. In seeking to memorialise the tragedy of the AIDS crisis, and bring it to the attention of a contemporary audience largely unfamiliar with its ravages, the passive ideology in operation suggests that queer sex = death, and that even a long-term monogamous relationship is not enough to preserve wellbeing if one has had previous partners.

The idealisation of homonormativity, however, is so overtly reinforced within the depiction of Billy's funeral, however, that it cannot really be regarded as merely passive. Although passing reference is made to Billy's career and swimming prowess, his mother's eulogy foregrounds the homonormative nature of his relationship with Saul:

> 'When Billy told me he was going to stay in New York and move into Saul's apartment, I was worried, like any mother would be', she said. 'Your child, thousands of miles away, changing their life for someone – what if they're not the one and your child gets their heart broken?'
>
> 'This is what Billy said. "Mum, it'd feel like half my limbs had disappeared or that I was suddenly just a shadow and not a whole person. That's how much I love Saul. I can't even bear to think of my life without him because it wouldn't be worth a thing"'.
>
> (Burke 2017, p. 294)

She concludes the eulogy by stating that Billy 'taught me … what real love should and could be' (Burke 2017, p. 294), not only valorising her son's relationship, but also positioning this homonormative ideal as an educative device for both queer and heterosexual readers. In studying the pernicious trope of queer death, Katelyn Browne suggests that 'religious notions of sainthood are frequently attached to either literal death or a symbolic overcoming of the mortal, imperfect self. Whether perfect or dead (or both), the queer characters … are held to troublingly rigid standards' (2020, p. 6). Despite the many reasons for which Billy might be memorialised – as a loving son and brother, a talented hair and makeup artist, a swimmer, a courageous young man who moved to New York to pursue his dreams, someone who rose to the challenges of homophobia and paternal rejection – these are virtually overlooked while Billy's homonormative qualities are represented as redemptive, purifying him of his earlier transgressive sexual identity and rendering him as almost saintly to the funeral attendees and, by extension, the implied reader.

The Love Interest: Pitting the 'Good' Queer Against the 'Bad'

Unlike the previous two novels, *The Love Interest* seems, on the surface, to engage in a deliberate deconstruction of the discursive nature of YA representations of normative relationships. Nonetheless, its passive ideology works to limit queer male subjectivities to the homonormative, with its characters ultimately eschewing alternate models of queer relationships in favour of domestic, monogamous relationship.

Although it is set in a recognisably contemporary world, *The Love Interest* strays from the realist genre, with its central characters acting as the unwilling agents of a nefarious intelligence organisation called the Love Interest Corporation (LIC). Caden and Dylan have been trained as operatives intended to win the affection of their targeted subject, in this case a gifted young woman named Juliet. Removed from their families, they have been brought up within the corporation's secret compound, trained as 'honey-trap' spies and then placed within Juliet's school. Within the LIC compound, the two are reconstructed as archetypal and complementary models of desire – Caden configured as a 'good' guy, while Dylan is a 'bad' guy – and both are tasked with winning Juliet's affection. Whoever succeeds is expected to pair with Juliet for life, in anticipation of using that relationship to mine useful intelligence from Juliet – whose almost preternatural intelligence has meant that she is already an accomplished inventor. The imperative to enter into a long-term monogamous relationship with their mark is given an added dimension in this novel; competition between 'good' and 'bad' agents is heightened by the omnipresent threat of death, as the unsuccessful candidate will be hunted down and executed by the LIC. The LIC's intentions are queered, however, when Caden identifies as gay and enters into a flirtation, and ultimately a relationship, with Dylan.

Through the conceit of LIC training, the artificiality of monogamous relationships is exaggerated to the point of campness. The Love Interests learn how to kiss, seduce and dress appropriately – even undergoing cosmetic surgery – in order to heighten their chance of being picked as the subject's 'soul mate' (Dietrich 2017, p. 64). Once in the field, the Love Interests have handlers who monitor their progress and provide real-time advice on how to manipulate the mark into choosing them as his or her long-term partner. The discursive nature of relationship norms in YA texts is suggested through the novel's moments of ironic self-awareness, such as when Caden asks why the LIC 'is so focused on pairing us in high school'. When he argues that '[n]o one finds the love of their life in high school', his handler replies, '[y]ou haven't read any YA novels recently, have you?' (Dietrich 2017, p. 39), a comment that foreshadows that Caden will, in fact, replicate just such a script. This is reinforced at the novel's climax, when Caden exclaims '"I'm the protagonist, fucker"' (Dietrich 2017, p. 356) as he shoots the head of the LIC, thus freeing himself and Dylan from its corporate clutches. While intended as a marker of agency, this somewhat ironic statement reinforces Caden's subject position as one determined by normative schemata, and by the novel's end he still engages in a normative, monogamous relationship – just with Dylan rather than their mark, Juliet. Even with this subversion of heteronormative scripts, Caden's subjectivity is shaped through discourse. As a queer male character he is simply re-encoded with another stereotyped subject position when Juliet forgives him, saying: '"Anyway, isn't it pretty normal for a straight girl to fall for a gay guy? All the sitcoms treat it like a rite of passage, something that all girls must go through"' (Dietrich 2017, p. 333), a position that Caden resents for its implied lack of agency in being reduced to a narrative trope. Despite its sometime ironic tone, this motif of narrative tropes reinforces the notion that relationships are largely performative, operating according to heteronormative scripts that, in this case, are drawn from an established canon of social texts.

On the surface, it appears that this triangular romance between Caden, Dylan and Juliet may serve to disrupt the heteronormative scripts that direct the individual relationships. However, the novel avoids any radical deconstruction of relationship norms, with the queer dynamics between Caden, Dylan and Juliet ultimately used to reinforce monogamous coupledom as the ideal. Juliet is caught between the two young men, initially desiring both and even going so far as to kiss each. Despite the potential here for an alternative, polyamorous relationship, the novel takes great care to place emphasis on the choice that Juliet must make between the two young men. Indeed, much of the tension in the first half of the novel derives from this conflict: it is literally monogamous coupledom or death. Moreover, the novel carefully articulates that Caden and Dylan technically never stray into territory that might be characterised as infidelity:

> I want to kiss you because I want to kiss someone, just once, because I want to do it. And as soon as one of us starts dating Juliet it'll be cheating and I know neither of us will do that. But we're not hers yet. We're free men.
>
> (Dietrich 2017, p. 169)

Infidelity is further censured in a subplot involving a heterosexual character – Trevor – who, despite having a long-term girlfriend, receives oral sex in a public toilet from another girl, causing a crisis of conscience in which the character refers to himself as 'weak and scummy' and, in a reflection of the sanitary discourse of *Micah Johnson Goes West*, 'dirty' (Dietrich 2017, p. 208). Furthermore, his critique of engaging in casual sexual intimacy in a public toilet, 'where people piss on seats and take shits' (Dietrich 2017, p. 208), clearly alludes to the phenomenon of the beat, a historically queer form of sexual expression, and correlates it with the abject imagery of bodily waste. Although presenting the reader with a queer, triangular depiction of desire, and casual sex outside the bounds of monogamy, *The Love Interest* clearly circumscribes what constitutes acceptable behaviour, proscribing relationships outside of monogamy as immoral or disgusting.

Juliet eventually chooses Caden, unaware of its lethal consequence for Dylan. At this very moment, Caden realises the artificiality of living a life defined by a monogamous relationship with Juliet, crafted, as it has been, by the imperatives of the LIC. He abandons Juliet to save Dylan by going on the run with him. But rather than interrogating the ideological imperative towards monogamous coupledom itself, it is substantiated by the 'transcendent self-evidence of love'; the rhetorical idealisation of true love that Warner suggests has been employed to bolster the marriage equality agenda by legitimising monogamy (1999, p. 134). Caden seemingly breaks free of the heteronormative agenda of the LIC in the realisation that his future happiness – and, incidentally, Juliet's – depends on his pursuit of a relationship with Dylan instead. In doing so, however, he actively reinscribes the idealised notion of true love, a singular 'soul mate' for whom he is prepared to die rather than live without: 'I'm going to sacrifice everything I've worked for to give him a chance to survive. I'm going to put my head next to his on the chopping block' (Dietrich 2017, p. 271). Despite being the unwitting victim of an elaborate plot, Juliet recognises the exalted nature of their love. She puts aside her own hurt to facilitate their escape, stating she is willing to do so '"for all the people out there who deserve to be in love with someone who genuinely loves them back"' (Dietrich 2017, p. 332). Thus, it is the heterosexual Juliet who confers legitimacy upon Caden's relationship with Dylan by suggesting their true love as an aspirational model for others. While the novel does interrogate the discourses of compulsory heterosexuality that act upon queer youth, often consigning them to the closet, it fails to capitalise on its queer potential and radically undermine those discourses. The normative construction of monogamous coupledom and its concomitant mythologising of a singular true love are left intact, if not bolstered.

Homonormative conformity is especially reinforced by the epilogue. After taking down the LIC, the epilogue presents Caden and Dylan waking up together a year later in an idyllic rural home, which they now share as a couple:

> Together, we walk out of the bedroom and through the kitchen. It's simple, with wooden counters and an old-fashioned gas stove, but I like it. The white oven dish Dyl used last night to make lasagna is still on the counter, between a stack of library books and a wooden bowl filled with fruit. I open the glass door and step out onto porch. The sky is clear, and shiny drops of dew have collected on the wooden railing.
>
> The view is of the hills that surround our property. I reach the balustrade and place both hands on the cold, wet wood. He mimics me.
> (Dietrich 2017, p. 380)

This scene presents a sentimental image of domestic bliss in a bucolic pastoral setting for the queer couple, but one that only seems possible far away from the 'small country town' (Dietrich 2017, p. 51) in which the bulk of the narrative is set. It must be noted, however, that the novel avoids the typical trope of having the queer characters 'escape' rurality and find community in the city.[5] Despite the fact that, as Priya Kandaswamy observes, '[o]ne doesn't have to be in a monogamous, long-term, same-sex relationship to love other people' (2008, p. 119), this novel clearly posits just such a relationship as preferred, even while seemingly consigning them to an isolated rural existence in order to conduct that relationship.

The novel also undermines its queer potential in its treatment of the ambiguity surrounding Dylan's sexuality, and the implications of his labelling as a 'bad' Love Interest. While the 'bad boy' is an erotic trope that is clearly exploited for both hetero- and homosexual desire, it clearly carries connotations of subversiveness, transgression and unreliability. Relationships with 'bad boys' are typically depicted as transitory, illicit affairs, before the protagonist 'settles down' with someone more stable or alternately 'tames' the bad boy into relationship norms. Semantically, Dylan's characterisation as 'bad' has the potential to reinforce his identity, and the queer ambiguity he comes to represent, as the dangerous other to Caden's homonormativity. Despite Caden's self-identification as gay, Dylan's sexual identity is never entirely foreclosed. He engages in an undeniably intimate relationship with Caden, establishing an emotional closeness before progressing onto hand-holding, hugging and kissing. When challenged by a suspicious Caden as to whether he likes men, Dylan replies 'I like sex. And I'll take what I can get' (Dietrich 2017, p. 252). Yet Dylan later indicates his queer desire was a ploy to distract Caden and facilitate his own success with Juliet: 'I'm not gay', Dylan tells Caden, 'I like girls' (Dietrich 2017, p. 293). Despite this, Juliet tells Caden, 'That boy is in love with you', a fact that is 'obvious' to everyone else (Dietrich 2017, p. 334). When Caden demurs, Juliet suggests three potential reasons for Dylan's ambiguity: he is lying, he is bisexual – 'don't dismiss that as a possibility' (Dietrich 2017, p. 334) – or he is in denial. While this seems to offer a truly queer subjectivity that resists foreclosure, this queerness is later posited as a threat to homonormative stability when, in the epilogue, Caden reflects:

> I'll never leave [Dylan], and I think he knows this. The cost for us to be together was just too high *for me* to ever give up on us. But that's a problem for another, darker day; *right now* he makes me happier than I've ever been.
>
> (Dietrich 2017, p. 380, emphasis added)

The novel ends with the Dylan turning to Caden, 'smiling that Bad boy smirk of his' and saying '"I love you"' (Dietrich 2017, p. 380). This final scene generates a degree of ambivalence, as the smirk and the oblique reference to a potentially one-sided relationship is juxtaposed with a statement of love, which itself may be undermined by Dylan's history of romantically manipulating Caden.

While the first-person narration leaves the reader with no doubt as to Caden's long-term desires, Dylan's intentions remain unclear, beyond his attempts within the epilogue to initiate sex. Warner has noted that within homonormative discourses,

> The image of the good gay is never invoked without its shadow in mind—the bad queer, the kind who has sex, who talks about it, and who builds with other queers a way of life that ordinary folk do not understand or control.
>
> (1999, p. 131)

The Love Interest articulates this binary literally, in which Caden's desire for stable long-term monogamy is inscribed as 'good' whilst Dylan's more ambiguous, sex-positive queerness – disconcerting for Caden – is associated with his label as a 'bad boy' Love Interest. With the narrative focalised through Caden's clearly homonormative gaze and the negative characterisation of Dylan's queer subversiveness, this scene seems to evoke the shadow of the bad queer, to use Warner's term, in order to promote a homonormative agenda.

Conferring Legitimacy: The Heterosexual, Biological Family as Gatekeeper of Society

These novels also offer a passive homonormative ideology through queer forms of kinship that are forced to give way under a continuing idealisation of the heteronormative, biological, and often nuclear family. In contemporary Australian society this articulation of family remains the convention and continues to exert a strong ideological force within children's and YA literature. The novels studied here privilege heterosexual biological families over the queer expressions of kinship that they also depict, reinforcing its idealisation as the norm to be replicated. Clare Bradford, Kerry Mallan, John Stephens and Robyn McCallum note a 'reluctance' in contemporary children's literature 'to propose or endorse an alternative familial arrangement to those conventionally experienced in society' (2008, p. 153). Furthermore, Ann Alston argues that while texts may 'contrast with the cosy nuclear family', rarely do they 'question the received ideals of family or establish different social models in which children could be socialised and protected' (2008, p. 8). However, as Dennis Altman notes: 'The gay liberation movement developed out of extreme alienation from a model of the family that was predicated on particular gender relations, the pretence of monogamy and the biological link between children and parents' and thus 'we created our own families, so that friends, rather than biological relations, became the central reference point of gay and lesbian lives' (2013, p. 196). In queer literature for young readers, then, a tension can arise between the ideological pull of the nuclear family and the disruption of this norm to establish queer forms of kinship.

The biological family clearly occupies a privileged position in *Micah Johnson Goes West*. Queer kinship forms are, however, established when Declan acts as 'the surrogate parent' (Kennedy 2017, p. 67) to Micah. His partner Simon also refers to Micah as 'our little project, now grown wings and flying' (Kennedy 2017, p. 37), reinforcing their parental figuration. However, this queer kinship model is not enough to prevent Micah's descent into depression over his homesickness and his breakup. Similarly, the Mitchell family – with whom Micah is billeted – may be the very model of the white, middle-class, heteronormative nuclear family, yet even they fail to revive his spirits in the way his biological family are able. Indeed, their ersatz status is revealed through the frequent use of quotation marks in examples such as 'there was his new "family"' (Kennedy 2017, p. 7), 'his "foster" family' (Kennedy 2017, p. 13) and returning '"home"' (Kennedy 2017, p. 14). Despite their repeated attempts to support Micah, his psychological wellbeing is only restored when his biological family move to Perth so they can 'officially be a family again' (Kennedy 2017, p. 188). While the image of a biological family supporting – and indeed relocating itself – to assist their queer child is a welcome message of inclusion, as is its privileged position within Micah's worldview and his internalised resistance to alternate kinships that is problematic. Many young people continue to experience parental rejection upon coming out, yet the novel positions the biological family as fundamental to a healthy queer subjectivity – undermining the potential for queer readers to develop agentic subjectivities and attachments within alternate, queer forms of kinship.

The Things We Promise is perhaps more successful in interrogating the normative primacy of biological families, representing it as a complex source of both love and affirmation for queer people, but also a site of violence and rejection. Billy, Saul and Zane – a young gay man Gemma meets in the AIDS ward – all suffer from family rejection and disapproval. Billy, at least, learns to make peace with his father's rejection, as he explains to Gemma, '[t]hanks to Saul, who had to weather that storm with me' (Burke 2017, p. 268). Yet when Billy recognises that his condition is terminal, he seeks to reconcile with his father, 'to tell him that I love him and that I forgive him' (Burke 2017, p. 268), something Gemma finds difficult to understand. Billy recognises that he, like his father, is 'so, so flawed' (Burke 2017, p. 268), acknowledging the complexities and failures of families. Despite this, Gemma initially tries to reunite Zane with his family on learning of their estrangement, even drafting a letter to them in the hopes she can facilitate a reconciliation, revealing the ideological pull of the concept of the biological family. She eventually realises her naivety and, to assuage Zane's isolation, she develops a friendship with him. When he dies, it is Gemma who sits with him, holding his hand, highlighting Zane's solitude in the absence of his actual family. Biological families are thus depicted as fragile and failing those who are queer. With such family dysfunction represented as tragic, however, its normative value remains uncontested and its loss is overtly mourned. It remains idealised even when, as Alston suggests, the family is fractured.

The Things We Promise destabilises the normative value of biological families to some extent by referencing the existence of queer modes of kinship. This is represented through the circle of New York friends with whom Billy grieves after Saul dies, though the novel, like many other queer YA novels, provides 'few details about the gay community except to locate it Somewhere Else' (Cart and Jenkins 2006, p. 97). Faring a little better is the (minor) character of Aunty Mame, who 'helps guys come out. She shows them around town and introduces them to other guys' particularly those who have come from the country or been rejected by their families, who '"arrive in the big city and it's really scary"' (Burke 2017, p. 51). However, Mame's presence is marginal within the novel, and Gemma is embarrassed trying to tries to explain Mame to others (Burke 2017, p. 51). Thus, while acknowledgement is given to the role aunties play in generating queer kinship, a degree of shame or discomfort is attached to it, of otherness, even from someone whose own family disrupts the nuclear norm.

Zane's isolated death also undermines the role queer kinship groups played in supporting those who suffer with HIV/AIDS. This failure to meaningfully represent models of queer kinship here is ideologically more typical of queer YA novels published in the 1990s, where 'the gay community exists only in the past and is, thus, entirely invisible' (Cart and Jenkins 2006, p. 97). In locating this novel so firmly in the past, its representation of the kinds of communities in which HIV positive (or simply sexually active) teens might find essential education, support and kinship is thus relegated to this status of invisibility. *The Things We Promise* arguably plays into further impulses of homonormativity pervading the era of Australian marriage equality, which de-emphasises the currency of issues such as HIV/AIDS and homophobia, as if these issues are largely overcome. Representation of those affected by HIV/AIDS continues to matter, as does the remembering and validation of queer histories, but representations that are recognisable to contemporary readers are equally important.

Notions of family and queer kinship are seemingly less nuanced within *The Love Interest*, as neither queer character has a biological family. However, the primacy of the biological family is – in general – uncontested by the novel's passive ideology, largely through the simplistic binary opposition of Caden's dysfunctional and non-biological 'family' of adult LIC agents and Juliet's biological family. Not only are Caden's 'broken' pseudo-parents held aloft as a warning of the consequences of failing to find a long-term 'soul mate' (Dietrich 2017, p. 64), their relationship with Caden is equally dysfunctional with Caden's step-father verbally and physically assaulting him. This is contrasted with Juliet's loving family, who fuss over Caden and are introduced amidst the warmth and geniality of a family dinner. Although the idealisation of Juliet's family is mediated somewhat – Juliet reveals that her parents' successful careers meant she was often looked after by her grandparents – their current loving interactions and the inclusion of grandparents suggest that biological families remain tightknit, and that domestic violence and family dysfunction are limited to non-normative families, a problematic implication for those whose families do not or cannot meet the standard of biological kinship.

As with *The Things We Promise*, a queer community, however oblique, provides a support structure for Caden and Dylan. Queer communities have been found to be significantly beneficial for queer young adults. Even virtual communities have proven to 'reduce their experiences of isolation and marginalisation that stem from living as queer young people in a heteronormative world' (Hanckel and Morris 2014, p. 883) and may be even more important for non-conforming teens in the face of the increasing homonormalisation of queer identities. While Caden and Dylan isolate themselves from society at the end of the novel, they have retained friendships with Juliet and Natalie, Juliet's high-school friend who, it transpires, was another Love Interest agent. As such, they can perhaps be read as having established a nascent queer community in the absence of a supportive biological family – but significantly it is one in which other queer characters are notably absent. Furthermore, the value of queer communities and kinship groups lies not only in connecting queer young adults, but also 'by helping them to reframe their understanding of their sexuality as not a problem to do with themselves but as one that is located *within society*' (Hanckel and Morris 2014, p. 883, emphasis added), which may be undermined by this community's apparent divorce from said society.

Conclusion

Micah Johnson Goes West and *The Love Interest* are clearly liberatory in their surface ideology. While *The Things We Promise* is potentially concerning in its strategy of condemning all major queer characters to death (which seems problematic even within the context of the peak AIDS crisis), it too seeks to confer legitimacy on the queer community and those young adults who might identify as queer. However, the passive ideology operating in each novel is clearly homonormative in nature: legitimacy is predicated upon acceptance of, and assimilation within, kinship norms that are heterosexist in origin. A healthy queer subjectivity is associated with monogamous coupledom and the rejection of alternate modes of sexual expression, such as polyamory or promiscuity. Even remaining single seems to be delegitimised as a valid lifestyle choice, with a long-term relationship a driving imperative for many of the characters – queer or otherwise – discussed here. Furthermore, it is typically the heterosexual characters who confer legitimacy on the queer characters, a validation often correlated with their homonormativity.

Queer literature for young adults should account for diverse expressions of sexuality and kinship, and this includes those that are homonormative in nature. As Kokkola notes, normative representations are 'perfectly reasonable' in one novel, but when multiple texts present readers with similar messages, queer YA can seem to be 'continuing the current state of affairs rather than as acting as a source of change' (2013, p. 109). Dreher argues that 'it is vital that queer difference is visible' (2017, p. 189), yet difference in these texts is largely de-emphasised, or even delegitimised. In doing so, these novels seem to replicate the rhetoric of the 'Yes' campaign during the lead up to Australia's marriage equality plebiscite in 2017, affirming Cover's ironic observation that the pressures of homonormativity are amplified more 'through queer political representation than necessarily found today in heteronormative social contexts' (2016, p. 127).

This is not to deny the values of those for whom marriage equality is important, or to downplay the significance of the historic legislative change. But there is a possibility that the prevalence of homonormativity within these novels 'risks excluding those people whose sexual and emotional lives do not fit a primary couple relationship' (Altman, 2013, p. 199), and thus erasing queer difference. It is more productive, Altman argues, 'to offer a range of possible ways of living one's life', recognising that 'there is no one way of acting out human sexuality' (2013, p. 212). As Butler concludes in her discussion of queer kinship and legitimacy, 'a more radical social transformation is precisely at stake when we refuse, for instance, to allow kinship to become reducible to "family," or when we refuse to allow the field of sexuality to become gauged against the marriage form' (2002, p. 40). To participate in such social transformation, queer YA fiction – particularly that which represents those white, cis-gendered males who are most privileged by the cultural dynamics of homonormativity – needs to destabilise historic norms, to challenge the heterosexist and homophobic institutions that have been used to position queerness as an unworthy other. If it fails to do so, it risks simply creating new structures of discrimination and delegitimisation for the very readers the genre arose to represent.

Notes

1 Although *The Love Interest* is set, by dint of a single specific reference, in the United States, its author was born and continues to live in Australia.
2 See, for example, Duggan (2002), Cover (2016), Gilson (2016).
3 The plebiscite was a non-binding, voluntary postal vote initiated by the Liberal–National Coalition government, led by prime minister Malcolm Turnbull, asking Australian voters if they supported a change to the law to allow same-sex couples to marry.
4 See, for example, Lurie (1990).
5 See, for example, Judith Halberstam (2005) on the concept of metronormativity and the trope of the queer migration to the cities.

References

Alston, A 2008, *The Family in English Children's Literature*, Routledge, New York.
Altman, D 2013, *The End of the Homosexual?* University of Queensland Press, Brisbane.
Baumgartner, B 2013, 'It ain't over: marriage (in-)equality and queer assimilation', *The International Journal of Narrative and Community Work,* no. 2, pp. 79–83.
Blackburn, MV, Clark, CT and Nemeth, EA 2015, 'Examining queer elements and ideologies in LGBT-themed literature: what queer literature can offer young adult readers', *Journal of Literacy Research,* vol. 47, no. 1, pp. 11–48.

Bradford, C, Mallan, K, Stephens, J and McCallum, R 2008/2011, *New World Orders in Contemporary Children's Literature: Utopian Transformations*, Palgrave Macmillan, Basingstoke.

Browne, KR 2020, 'Reimagining queer death in young adult fiction', *Research on Diversity in Youth Literature*, vol. 2, no. 2, art. 3, pp. 1–26, retrieved 27 October 2020, https://sophia.stkate.edu/rdyl/vol2/iss2/.

Burke, JC 2017, *The Things We Promise,* Allen and Unwin, Crows Nest. Kobo edition, retrieved 6 August 2019, www.kobo.com/au/en/ebook/the-things-we-promise.

Butler, J 2002, 'Is kinship always already heterosexual?', *differences: A Journal of Feminist Cultural Studies*, vol. 13, no. 1, pp. 14–44.

Cart, M and Jenkins, C 2006, *The Heart Has Its Reasons: Young Adult Literature with Gay/Lesbian/Queer Content, 1969–2004*, Scarecrow Press, Lanham, MD. Ebook edition, retrieved 26 January 2020, http://ebookcentral.proquest.com/lib/curtin/detail.action?docID=1230168.

Cover, R 2012, *Queer Youth Suicide, Culture and Identity: Unliveable Lives?* Ashgate, Burlington, VT.

Crisp, T 2013, 'A review of HIV/AIDS in young adult novels: an annotated bibliography', *Journal of LGBT Youth*, vol. 10, no. 3, pp. 256–261.

Dietrich, C 2017, *The Love Interest,* Feiwel and Friends/Macmillan, New York. Kobo edition, retrieved 6 August 2019, www.kobo.com/au/en/ebook/the-love-interest.

Dreher, T 2016, 'The "uncanny doubles" of queer politics: sexual citizenship in the era of same-sex marriage victories', *Sexualities*, vol. 20, nos. 1–2, pp. 176–195.

Duggan, L 2002, 'The New Homonormativity: The Sexual Politics of Neoliberalism', *Materializing Democracy: Toward a Revitalized Cultural Politics*, Eds. R Castronovo & D Nelson, Duke University Press, Durham, NC, pp. 175–194.

Gahan, L 2013, 'Keep family values out of marriage equality', *New Matilda*, 20 February, retrieved 20 May 2019, https://newmatilda.com/2013/02/20/keep-family-values-out-marriage-equality.

Gilson, D 2016, '"Homonormativity" and its discontents', *The Gay & Lesbian Review Worldwide*, vol. 23, no. 1, pp. 22–24.

Gross, M, Goldsmith, A and Carruth, D 2008, 'What do young adult novels say about HIV/AIDS? A second look', *The Library Quarterly: Information, Community, Policy*, vol. 78, no. 4, pp. 397–418.

Halberstam, J 2005, *In a Queer Time and Place: Transgender Bodies, Subcultural Lives*, New York University Press: New York.

Hanckel, B and Morris, A 2014, 'Finding community and contesting heteronormativity: queer young people's engagement in an Australian online community', *Journal of Youth Studies*, vol. 17, no. 7, pp. 872–886.

Hollindale, P 1988, 'Ideology and the children's book', Signal, no. 55, pp. 3–22.

Kandaswamy, P 2008, 'Is Gay Marriage Racist?' *That's Revolting! Queer Strategies for Resisting Assimilation*, Ed. M Bernstein Sycamore, Soft Skull Press, New York, pp. 113–119.

Kennedy, S 2017, *Micah Johnson Goes West,* Harmony Ink Press, Tallahassee, FL. Kobo edition, retrieved 6 August 2019, www.kobo.com/au/en/ebook/micah-johnson-goes-west.

Kokkola, L 2013, *Fictions of Adolescent Carnality: Sexy Sinners and Delinquent Deviants*, John Benjamins Publishing Co, Amsterdam.

Lurie, A 1990, *Don't Tell the Grown-Ups: The Subversive Power of Children's Literature,* Little, Brown, Boston, MA.

McRuer, R 2011, 'Reading and Writing "Immunity": Children and the Anti-Body', *Over the Rainbow: Queer Children's and Young Adult Literature,* Eds. MA Abate and K Kidd, University of Michigan Press, Ann Arbor.

Morrison, M 2015, '"Some things are better left unsaid": the "dignity of queer shame"', *Mosaic: a Journal for the Interdisciplinary Study of Literature,* vol. 48, no. 1, pp. 17–32.

Sedgwick, EK 2003, *Touching Feeling: Affect, Pedagogy, Performativity,* Duke University Press, Durham, NC, retrieved 1 August 2019, ProQuest Ebook Central, http://ebookcentral.proquest.com/lib/curtin/reader.action?docID=1167951.

Stephens, J 2003, 'Editor's introduction: always facing the issues: preoccupations in Australian children's literature', *The Lion and the Unicorn,* vol. 27, no. 2, pp. v–xvii.

Thomas, A, McCann, H and Fela, G 2019, '"In this house we believe in fairness and kindness": post-liberation politics in Australia's same-sex marriage postal survey', *Sexualities,* vol. 23, no. 4, pp. 475–496.

Trites, RS 1998, 'Queer discourse and the young adult novel: repression and power in gay male adolescent literature', *Children's Literature Association Quarterly,* vol. 23, no. 3, pp. 143–151.

Warner, M 1999, 'Normal and normaller: beyond gay marriage', *GLQ,* vol. 5, no. 2, pp. 119–171.

Index

For Product Safety Concerns and Information please contact our EU
representative GPSR@taylorandfrancis.com
Taylor & Francis Verlag GmbH, Kaufingerstraße 24, 80331 München, Germany